GHETTO LEGEND GRADUATE

CORNELIUS KINCHEN

Ghetto Legend Graduate
Cornelius Kinchen

Copyright © 2009 by Cornelius Kinchen

ISBN# 0615284434   Soft cover

All rights reserved. No part of this book may be reproduced or transmitted in any form or by any means, electronic or mechanical, including photocopying, recording or by any information storage and retrieval system, without permission in writing from the copyright owner.

This book was printed in the United States of America.

To order additional copies of this book, contact:
Cornelius Kinchen
Determination2makeit@yahoo.com

Published by
Legend Graduate Publishing Co. LLC
www.LegendGraduatePublishing.ning.com

Ghetto Legend Graduate
Cornelius Kinchen

Acknowledgements

First and foremost, I would like to praise God and thank Jesus for inspiring me to write and make history with this book.

Special Thanks to: Wife: Roberta Kinchen. Children: Cornelius (Whip) Kinchen, Amaya, and Javar. Cornelius Dixon, Illene Kinchen, Bertha Johnson, Family and Friends President Obama, Langston Hughes., Paterson & Paterson Public Schools and students.Philosopher George Santayana, 1642 Massachusetts Bay Colony, Thomas Jefferson, and Horace Mann. Thank You for love and inspirational support.

Sincerely,
Author Cornelius Javar Kinchen.

Ghetto Legend Graduate
Cornelius Kinchen

The early days 7
Growing up 21
My first experience with death 25
It's a hard knock life 35
Boys in the hood 38
6th grade 47
Easter 1995 59
Seventh grade 85
New beginning 91
New people; new drama 97
End of 7th grade 101
New girlfriend 112
Going to church 128
A new environment 137
Tiana is back 161
End of summer 170
Sasha 175
My new bike is gone 182
Fight with Red 193
Life in the hood 208
Last day of summer 219
Momma on my mind 228
Can't wait to see Tiana 239
First encounter 254
Thanksgiving 262
The big football game 270
Needing love 275
Prom time 277
May 1997, prom day! 302
June 1997. From Sandy Hook to Graduation. 310
Graduation 319
Florida 333
Back to school 345
Ghetto Legend Graduate II 349
First Day of High School 351
Thanksgiving 366

Ghetto Legend Graduate
Cornelius Kinchen

Introduction

It was love at first sight.

Illene Kinchen and Cornelius Dixon were instantly attracted to one other, and somewhere along the line, I was born. Because my mother was stressed out by life during the eighties, she wanted to have an abortion. At least that's what I learned from my Aunt Doris. Maybe the influences of life pressure and drugs in my neighborhood had something to do with her wanting to terminate her pregnancy. But I'm glad she didn't, because if she had, I wouldn't be able to tell my victorious story. She already had another child, and wasn't ready to have another baby, but Aunt Doris convinced Mom to birth me.

So, here I am! Cornelius Javar Kinchen.

Born February 2, 1983, in Paterson, New Jersey, premature: just two pounds and five ounces, and was not expected to live. At the time, my parents were living at 111 Straight Street, on the second floor. There were five of us in that apartment, my parents, my two older sisters, and me. We were somewhat happy as a family. My father spoiled me at times, which let me know that I was "Daddy's little boy." He gave me the best birthdays and

Ghetto Legend Graduate
Cornelius Kinchen

Christmases up until third grade, which was when things began to get rough.

My mother decided to pursue her American happiness, causing a breakup in an otherwise happy home. At times, I wish she would have loved and pursued me the way she pursued her American happiness...At the present, it's extremely hard for me to talk about her American life, liberty and happiness at this stage in my life.

Ghetto Legend Graduate
Cornelius Kinchen

The early days

    Even as a five year old, I never understood Illene's addiction, and was clueless as to why she made the decisions she made. But as a free moral agent, God respected her deception-American life choice of death. My mind and heart were as a *tabula rasa,* a clean slate that was easy to write on. Even if it was a lesson to be learned, I was able to take it in and accept it. My first day of school was a good example.

    In my mind, the decision my mother made to walk me to Public School Number 6 was a beautiful one. At that moment, Motherly love and concern was deeply felt. It was September 1988, it was drizzling and the sky was gray. I was dressed in a green and black Bill Cosby sweater over a white turtleneck, khaki pants, and a pair of black shoes. While waiting in line for my kindergarten teacher, Mrs. Turner, to take us inside, I introduced myself to By'ron Johnston; he was born in New York City and just moved to Paterson.

    I could not believe what happened next. After I introduced myself, this ignorant bastard quickly put his left leg behind my legs, stretched his left arm across my chest, and clipped me! I fell back into a puddle of dirty water. Slashhh!! My pants were all wet and dirty all over the back. Understandably, I was upset. I looked up at By'ron in disbelief. *I'm going to get in trouble when I get home,* race through my mind. I quickly got up out the

Ghetto Legend Graduate
Cornelius Kinchen

puddle gazing at my muddy looking khaki pants wondering how can I clean them before I got home.

Right after that happened, My fifty year little old kindergarten teacher, Mrs. Turner came out to get her assigned class. She introduced herself and began calling each name on her class list, "John Haye, By'ron Johnston , Cornelius Kinchen." While waiting on line listening to my classmates answer in a zone-fading echoe,, "Present..". I thought about starting a fight with By'ron. That was how upset I was. The rest of the day, I thought about how I was going to tell my parents and get my revenge on By'ron. I was so worried and scared of my parents' reaction to my no longer new; but muddy khaki pants. I decided not to tell them and just wait for them to notice.

At three o'clock, school dismissed for the day and I walked home with my two older sisters: Meaka, eight years older than I was, she was light-brown skin with long black hair, hip-hop style and knew how to dance in that way; and Esha, four years older than I was, she was dark skin with short black hair, pearly-white teeth and wild acting. We had just moved to Grandma's house at 156 Straight Street, having to move from our apartment because Mom had spent the rent money on her American-Ghetto happiness. At this point, my father could no longer trust my mother with the rent money, or any of the bill money. Long story short, when I walked into the

Ghetto Legend Graduate
Cornelius Kinchen

kitchen, my father and mother noticed the stain on my pants. They were livid.

"Neal, what happen to your pants?"

At first, I didn't want to tell them, because I was embarrassed by the whole situation. Then the question was repeated.

"Neal, what happen to your pants?!"

I mustered up the courage to give them a response. "This boy clipped me and I fell on the ground in the water," I explained.

My father had hands that reminded me of cement. He slapped me in the head with one of them.

"You don't let *nobody* put they hands on you! Ever! Do you hear me?!"

My mother was very angry. So I did what I knew how to do, what I was taught to do.

I simply answered, "Yes, Ma."

From then on, I followed my mother's advice. That was a valuable ghetto-lesson written on my *tabula rasa*. What a ghetto-lesson for a five-year-old to learn on the first day of public school in Paterson.

Later on that evening, I did my homework and ate dinner, after which my mother gave me a bath. We went down to the basement where we lived for the time being, and my mother put me in the bed and said, "Go to sleep." After she did that, she went behind the wall near the back door of the basement, and the source of her American life, liberty and happiness began to find its way into her

Ghetto Legend Graduate
Cornelius Kinchen

lungs and into her bloodstream. I saw and smelled the sinful death smoke in the air ; moreover, horror. So I covered my head with the bed sheets and tried to sleep. I strongly, wished my father was here, he was at work, and my sisters were upstairs talking and playing around with their friends. Eventually, I fell asleep.

Week after week, my mother's addiction worsened and Grandma had to kick her out of the house. The worse controlled dangerous substance of the eighties had a pretty good hold on Mom leading her to a physical-spiritual death if she don't find Christ.. Being addicted to physical defilement (crack) was no joke.

Therefore, In order to have some positivity in this life, I began to express myself by getting good grades while I was in kindergarten. The A's and B's on my report card made me look good in Mrs. Turner's eyes, who I felt wanted to see her students progress academically, and I respected that. Not only that, academic successful achievement in the class hid my ghetto-home circumstance. Mrs. Turner couldn't identify my ghetto-home life based on my academic performance in the class.

In September 1989, I was promoted to Ms. Hilton's gifted and talented first grade class. She was younger than Mrs. Turner. Ms. Hilton had just graduated college, intelligently-fair, very-light skinned (red bone), looked like a model height and weight, too. I was honored to be in her class. She taught me basic Spelling,

Ghetto Legend Graduate
Cornelius Kinchen

English, Writing and Math; and the class and I worked on these four subjects daily. Everyday, classroom participation was a regular occurrence in her class; For example, on the board, each student that participated in classroom activities would choose their favorite color marker and fill in the blanks on the poster-like paper in front of the class. To show what we did in class that started the mourning. Later that day, around 3pm who ever was chosen to complete the academic poster were allowed to bring it home as a reward and sense of accomplishment. When I came home with my academic poster, my father and grandmother expressed how proud they were of my accomplishment as a first grader. My dad hung my work on the wall near his important items and clothing in the basement. When he did that, I felt lovely support. My work inspired him to continue working hard and to continue taking care of my sisters and me during hard times while Illene was in the ghetto-streets of America.

 Seeing him smile with-in his spirit gave him healing strength made me happier. It motivated me to continue getting good grades in public school. Each day, I consistently worked hard to make my dad and myself proud. At, the same time, hiding the pain was practice in an academic setting was naturally done.

 Week in and week out, in the classroom the pain I hid was from the love I craved from Illene; moreover, it eluded me. The results from my mother's sin,left me in

Ghetto Legend Graduate
Cornelius Kinchen

the rain all wet and cold feeling neglected, abandoned, even ultimately unloved. The feelings of loss and unwanted separation were taking their toll on me. I found myself wondering, "Where is my Mother? Why isn't she here with us?" Here I was, really learning and getting good grades in school, but she in hell-ghetto missing her death results upon me to be inspired to turn to Christ for eternal life. I was proud and excited about my accomplishments, and I wanted her to witness. However, it seemed she did she continued to sin and burn carelessly beyond her control. She was living her life, enslaved by a sinful addiction to defilement (crack), and happy getting high on hell-ghetto drugs.

    One weekday, my mother took me with her to visit her friends on Hamilton Avenue, between Summer and Auburn Streets. The house was a disgusting place for any sane individual to live, and was no environment to bring or raise a child in. The house was like that house on *Nightmare on Elm Street*. I never saw so many Freddy Kruger-looking crack abusers in my life. It was extremely foggy and I couldn't breathe, nor see too well. It also smelled like dead, burning corpses. I wanted to leave but couldn't, so I awaits in the hallway, near the door to get some fresh air. I guess about twenty minutes had passed during which Illene got the high that she sought. We left that defiled (crack) place; I was relieved to finally be away from there. I made up my mind at that point that I never wanted to go with her there ever again as long as I

Ghetto Legend Graduate
Cornelius Kinchen

lived. Somehow, I noticed she put a straw and juice carton in her coat pocket, too; not sure why she did that. I continued to hope for childhood.

That Saturday, my mother came to pick me up. It was warm outside, so we went to my Aunt Darlene's house on Governor Street. I was introduced to my cousin Q for the first time. We were exactly the same age, and shared the same birthday. He was tougher than I was. I guess he had to be, because he lived in the roughest area.

He knew karate, and decided to show me some kicks and moves to defend myself in case I got into a fight. He demonstrated moves on me, which I really didn't like because I was the victim. Next, I was in a choking headlock that moment, I began to turn ice blue in the face: he had me so tight; I couldn't get out of the choke.. I thought I was going to die. Then seconds later, he finally let go. My face returned back to normal red. Afterwards, we played upstairs in his room where bunk-beds were while my mother and Aunt Darlene hung out downstairs in the kitchen. He played dangerously, and I was welcomed to be a daredevil, too. I never liked going to his house to play with him. He was dangerously weird.

In September 1990, I was promoted to another gifted and talented class, this time with Ms. Patt. she was white, intelligently-strict, at least early forties, skinny, looked like a vegetarian with orange-red hair color. Around that time, I started watching *The Simpsons* every day. I was highly influenced by and felt that Bart

Ghetto Legend Graduate
Cornelius Kinchen

Simpson personified character was ghetto-cool. Eventually, I thought and acted like a nonchalant Bart Simpson kid. When I got to school, I would put Bart Simpson on my paper in the blank next to 'Name.'

One day, Ms. Patt gave a test in class. After the test, I wrote Bart Simpson on my test as my name. She corrected test papers and asked aloud, "Who wrote Bart Simpson on their paper? There is no one in my class named Bart Simpson." She couldn't figure the mystery out; and my behavior was good up to that point.

She was Caucasian-white, and her face turned Red from angry frustration. And, since my test paper was the only paper without a proper name, after minutes passed with no confession Ms. Patt figured out that the Bart test paper belong to me. I didn't want to confess to such a silly act, especially after I argued with her about it.

She said, "Cornelius, your name is *not* Bart Simpson."

"Yes, it is," I responded, being argumentative.

She called Grandma's house and notified my mother of my inappropriate behavior in class. When I got home from school, nobody chastised me. Therefore, I thought I was off the hook, since my mother was gone by the time I came home.

The next day at ten o'clock in the morning, Illene, a.k.a Fat Momma, showed up at school for my inappropriate behavior. At first, I didn't recognize her. Then I took a second look, and acted like I was busy

Ghetto Legend Graduate
Cornelius Kinchen

being a good student. Everybody in the class was quiet as if they were scared, too. They were probably scared of the fact that their parent could show up at any time to check on their behavior, too. Illene showed up unexpectedly as if she just received the message, and then had the nerve to look like she just crawled out of bed. She looked extremely ghetto-ghetto.

    According to the smile on Ms. Patt's face, my mom and Ms. Patt seemed to be real close friends in the *"best interest of the child's education,"* such as myself. They walked into the hallway to discuss my behavior. They talked as if they were business partners who were in a conference meeting. Five minutes passed, I was on my best behavior, along with the whole class. At this point, the whole class was wondering and giggling, "Who's mother is at the door looking ghetto?" It seemed like an hour passed before she called me out into the hallway. I walked into the hallway and saw that my mother had a girlfriend with her that looked just as ghetto if not worse .

    Mom looked at me and said, "Let's go." She walked to the basement bathroom as I followed. "Pants down." I wanted to doodle on my self I was so scared. Mom commenced to whooping my behind with a belt. The whooping was so long and bad, that her friend felt the need to intervene. I was crying, my but was on fire; and all from my inappropiate behavior in class.

    "Fat Mamma, stop beatin' that boy like that! He had enough!"

Ghetto Legend Graduate
Cornelius Kinchen

By God's grace she stopped. She said to me, "Don't let me hear another bad report. Do you hear me?"

"Yes, Ma," I said, in a humbly crying voice. My mother left the building as a champion, and I went to class in tears and embarrassment.

After the episode of drama and rear-end abuse, I still did not learn my lesson. I felt snitched on by the teacher, so I continued to give her a hard time for snitching. That same day, Ms. Patt would not allow me to go to the bathroom until I *"got my act together."* I had to make-up and sing a song called, "I got to go to the bathroom" these were the entire lyrics in the song. I had to piss on myself numerous times in order for Mrs. Patt to get the point. She got so Red, angry, and frustrated with me, that she put her blue ink pen in my back as if she was in jail getting revenge on an enemy with a shank. This went on throughout second grade. Until I stopped misbehaving, she continued to get *her* revenge on me.

Another time, she called my mother about my misbehavior and bad attitude toward her. Fat Mamma came to school again, in the same way as the first time. This time, I was called out into the hall. Fat Momma words nor questions asked, "SLAPPP!!!" The security/attendance officer took notice and shouted, "Don't slap that boy like that! He is only in second grade!"

Ghetto Legend Graduate
Cornelius Kinchen

Fat Mamma responded in a loud voice, "Mind your business, this is my son. I will do what I want to do to him!"

From the loud tone of her voice, I thought she was going to beat the security/attendance officer up. My mom was light-brown skinned, short hair, a little over three hundred pounds, 6'2 and very heavy-handed. I would have bet my money on my Mom. Finally, she eased up and said, "Straighten up your act. I am tired of coming up here for your sh*t every other week."

I learned my lesson. I got tired of getting my but whooped and face slapped off in public by the heavy weight champion in and out of my life. I had no desire to endure such embarrassment through the rest of the school year. My grades were good and my behavior eventually improved.

One day after school late evening, my Mom sent Meaka and me to the supermarket to buy groceries. I thought I was tough. After Meaka and I came out the supermarket, I stared this white kid up and down like I wanted to fight him.

The kid smiled "What are you looking at?" he asked.

I responded, "Why? Do you wanna fight?"

"Yeah," he said, with a foreign accent.

So we squared off in the parking lot of the supermarket. He kicked my butt some kind of bad. I had no idea he knew karate. He had me on the ground

Ghetto Legend Graduate
Cornelius Kinchen

punching me in the face, and it didn't help that he was stronger than me. Meaka tried to help me by grabbing my fist and trying to get me to fight back. I wouldn't, because I couldn't see to hit. He was too fast, and his karate skills gave him an advantage.

Meaka stopped the fight and said, "I'm telling Mommy when we get home." My eyes were black and my face was swollen from the severe beaten. When we got home, my mother was in the basement doing my sister Esha hair. My mother noticed my face was beaten and bruised up.

"Mommy, Neal let another boy beat him up, and he didn't fight back," Meaka told her, effectively getting me in trouble. Well, actually, it's not like my face wouldn't have told her something happened to me.

"Neal, what happen to your face?" my mother said, looking at me. "Why didn't you fight back? Are you a punk? I should make you go back and fight until you win."

I remained quiet in defeat. Esha hair was almost done, so my mother said to her, "Beat him up until he gets tough and learns to fight back, until I say stop."

So she did. Esha beat on me in an effort to teach me how to fight, for at least an hour until my mother finished doing Meaka's hair. And Meaka had long hair, too. I was tortured and humiliated until my mother thought I had enough.

Ghetto Legend Graduate
Cornelius Kinchen

While in second grade, I was in another gifted and talented class, and managed to pass to the third grade. I thought to myself: a new year of school, a new attitude and most of all, a new teacher. Each day, I went to school with this positive mind and attitude toward a teacher trying to help me better my education. I even worked to become Student of the Month during that first month of school, meaning that I achieved my full potential for academic standards for September.

Mrs. Taylor and I took a picture together, and the picture was placed in an 'October Student of the Month' frame for hallway display. This magnified my accomplishment and motivated my classmates and me to work harder in class. Seeing that photo each day, and knowing it was being recognized by everyone in the School 6 building, represented something good for me. A month later, I was able to take the picture home to my dad. Just like before, he was proud of me, which inspired me to work even harder daily.

When November came, in spite of my mother's drug addiction, I felt good about what I could do as far as my behavior improvement and education as concerned. Things started flowing easily for me in that regard and I kept on striving and working hard in school.

A glimpse in to my spiritual life, God worked a miracle through me for my cousin Travis that same year. According to Doctors, Travis was disabled, and unable to walk or talk. Also, he suffered from seizures.

Ghetto Legend Graduate
Cornelius Kinchen

So when God led/used me to help him walk and talk, his mother and father cried tears of joy to witness such miracle with their baby boy. I couldn't understand it at the time. Now that I think about it, God performed *through* me. This confirmed that God is real to me to this day, because I have proof and witnesses to testify to it. The spiritual blessing was a reward in itself.

Ghetto Legend Graduate
Cornelius Kinchen

Growing up

After about three years, By'ron and I became friends. We started hanging together more. We were in Mrs. Taylor class together. Although I never forgot what he did to me in kindergarten, I plotted to get my revenge on him while we were in third grade, and I did. I would ask Mrs. Taylor if I could sit at the back table with By'ron and help him with his class assignment, and she allowed me to. I would sit with my back facing the chalkboard. When I talked, joked around, or disturb the class lesson; However, By'ron were blamed. The scheme worked well, and the fact that I was 'Student of the Month' worked on my behalf. By'ron had not made it to 'Student of the Month' for the entire year, due to his behavior, which was provoked by me. Each day in class, By'ron reaction to me provoking his disruptive behavior agitated him. No matter how hard he tried to ignore me, I made it impossible for him to behave well in Mrs. Taylor class.

In September 1992-1993, a boy named Rob: Dark skin, 100 pounds, 4'7 with a tough-ladies man attitude just transferred to Mrs. Cole class. By'ron and I wanted to test Rob. We wanted to see if he could fight to hang with us. First, By'ron slapped-boxed him and I followed. We slapped-boxed for weeks straight to test Rob's toughness. He was tough. He could slap box well.

Ghetto Legend Graduate
Cornelius Kinchen

Eventually, By'ron and I approved and welcomed Rob to the class gang. Now we were a gang of three.

We began to bully and run the fourth grade classes. Meanwhile I still did all my work. It wasn't long before my academic influence rubbed off on Rob and By'ron to do their work, too. Actually, I made class an academic performance competition that consists of who would make the higher and better grade on class assignments, tests and homework. The three of us agreed to the academic competition.

Around lunchtime, we would play fight against the other fourth grade classes, roughing them up for fun. Nothing serious, all fun n' games .For example, 4.2, 4.3, and 4.4 would be challenged to a class war almost every day during lunch period. It was fun. Sometimes we would play wall ball or football with the other fourth grade classes, too. By'ron, Rob, and I were the leaders of the class and were running things. At least, that what we thought base our respect from the other classes.

It wasn't long before Black History Month. During Black History Month in 1993, we rehearsed for a historic play about slavery and freedom called "Let My People Go." As we rehearsed day in and day out; Suddenly, I became the pretty boy of the class. The girls thought I was cute. This came about because we rehearsed the play so many hours together as a class: however, the girls in 4.1 began to have crushes on me and

Ghetto Legend Graduate
Cornelius Kinchen

my performance during and after the play. I wasn't thinking about a girlfriend up to this point in my life.

I was the worst dressed kid in the class. I just had confidence in my rehearsing performance; and I did all my work in class. Most of all, I paid little attention to them. I couldn't afford to think about a girlfriend. Also, I played rough with the other class boys as the girls noticed. All the pretty girls in my class were writing me notes.

First, there was Neria, who stood 5'1, 90 pounds with light brown skin,and brown eyes. She looked liked Regina King from *Thin Line Between Love and Hate*. At the time she was the second tallest girl I the class. After Black History rehearsal and lunch, while I sat in the back of the class sitting at a group table: she walked up to me with a note and slid it to me on the table with a cool-aid smile in her face with hearts in her eyes. I took the note, opened it and read it to myself. Her name was on the note, 'Do you want to go with me? Circle yes or no.'

Second, there was Tanisha, 4'7, 81 pounds brown skin, and brown eyes; she favored Roxy from 106 and Park. I nick named her 'E.T. fingers': she had long fingers and would always bite her nails to the nubs. Her note was passed to the back to me. It read the same as Nerias'.

Lastly, there was Shannon, 4'6, 82 pounds with her brown skin, and brown eyes; she favored the girl from *Baby Boy,* who was Jody's girlfriend; however, in

Ghetto Legend Graduate
Cornelius Kinchen

the fourth grade. These were the top three beautiful girls in the class, and I definitely took notice of them.

After, I received the date notes,,, "Do you want to go with me, yes or no?" I responded "Yes" to all three notes, with a flattered smile feeling cheesy inside. I passed each note back to each girl feeling like the man.

After the success of the slavery-freedom play, all three girls were my girlfriends after my circled response. I felt weird to have three girlfriends for the first time. It wasn't long before we ignored each other as girlfriend and boyfriend. Before, I knew it the school years ending and headed into a new summer.

The summer of 1993, I didn't think much about those three girls, and could have cared less about having a girlfriend. God worked another miracle through me in the month of July. It was my cousin Kent's birthday, and in spite of the fact that his doctors said that he was never going to be able to talk or walk, God had me work with him diligently until he was able to walk and talk. That had to be an awesome birthday present for him! Strange as it may seem, I didn't learn how to talk until I was three years old.

Ghetto Legend Graduate
Cornelius Kinchen

My first experience with death

After, such a miracle performed from heaven through Lord Jesus, the following month on a dark and thunderstorm rainy night in Paterson, Lord returned to heaven. As I remained on earth where evil activities in the ghetto' take place were all children witness. I on the first floor in the hallway I sat with Grandma, my older cousin Roger, light skin, 5'7, about 219 pounds; wearing army fatigue pants, a black rain jacket with a hoodie on, and Tim boots: walked outside to get his hustle on selling ghetto-c-rock.

After he left, I got up off the hallway stairs to go outside to watch the rain. I didn't care nor think much of Roger and what he was doing.

I looked at the peach-colored street lights while the rain fell. Each rain drop catching color from the street light; and making them sparkle like gemstones. I looked across the street only to see Roger hanging out across the street from Grandma's house, leaning against the brick wall of a burned down house. I watched him wait and work in the rain for some bucks.

Suddenly I noticed, a black car with tinted windows slowly making a right on Fair Street where Roger hung out in the dark. It was pitch black on that side of the burnt house. While the driver in the black car waited, a 'thug' with a black hoodie got out of the car and slammed the car door. The he walked up and asked loud,

Ghetto Legend Graduate
Cornelius Kinchen

"Yo, you got change for a hundred dollar bill?!" Roger turned his back to count the change for the 'thug'. As Roger turned around to give him the change, Pop!!Pop!!Pop!!! the 'thug' shot Roger while I watched from the front porch. BOOOM!!!! A loud thunder noise sounded and light the sky.

At first, it was so dark I thought it was a firecracker. But when I saw the 'thug' get in the car and speed off, I knew something was wrong. I ran across the street to Roger, laying on the wet ground, being soaked by the rain. He was hurt bad, and the t-shirt under his raincoat was turning burgundy from the blood that seeped from the gunshot wound. Our Hispanic neighbors, also heard shots, cautiously came outside to find out what was going on. They noticed Roger was bleeding, they ran to get towels and called 911. We kept talking to Roger, trying to keep him from slipping into unconsciousness. He blacked out many times. Whrrr!!!!Whrrrr!!!Whrrrr!!!Whrrr!!! The ambulance showed up and took him to the hospital.

After seeing what happened to my cousin, the possibility of being shot caused me to be very fearful of my life in the ghetto. And at the time, I couldn't understand why that happened to him. But as I got older, reality set in, and I realized that people can be dangerous and will kill you for drug money. The summer ended on that ghetto tragic experience. Rogers' release from the

Ghetto Legend Graduate
Cornelius Kinchen

hospital by the end of August and quick recovery was a miracle in disguise.

September of 1993 saw the beginning of another school year. A new kid named Cantrell, 4'11, 83 pounds, brown skin, curly hair, who need glasses but never wore them: he always squitted his eyes to see, talk, and hear transferred to our class from another school. By'ron, Rob, and I plotted on him, wanting to pick a fight with him. The three of us wanted to fight him first, 'Yo I want to fight him.' By'ron, 'Let me lump him up.' "No, I got him. Let me say something to him to bate him to talk slick. Then I will beat him up", Rob said. Since Rob was the new edition to the crew, he was granted the opportunity to prove he had heart.

The next day, Rob walked up to Cantrell asked, "What school are you from?" 'School 4, why you want to know? You have a problem?' "Why you got to get smart? I asked you nice." Right then, Rob fought Cantrell and defeated him by a knock down in the first round. After the fight, Rob was suspended for ten days because he started and finished the fight. Cantrell was suspended for five days because he lost.

When Rob returned from suspension, while class was taking a test quitly; however, By'ron and Cantrell broke out into a fight students moved from their desk, left their test to watch. When looked up By'ron and Cantrell were walking up to each other with their fist up toward each other beginning to swing at each other face hitting

Ghetto Legend Graduate
Cornelius Kinchen

each other. Cantrell and punched him in the face. After hitting the class floor, Cantrell got up and started getting the best of By'ron. Then By'ron grabbed and body-slammed him and started beating him up. By'ron was suspended for ten days and Cantrell five days. They did their time and returned to school.

Another kid in our class, Frank, 4'8, light skinned, 81 pounds, always acted like a slick hustler chased home every day for acting like a queer at times. Frank wanted to feature in a fight with Cantrell. He figured this would prove he had heart and could gain our respect. So, Frank called him out, "Yo I want to Cantrell!" Cantrell got up from his seat quick fast to fight. They put up their hands and fought like boxers. When they finished fighting, it was a tie. Both fighters had blood in their mouth. Frank was light skinned, so the donut around his eye stood out. Cantrell ended up with a swollen eye and lip. Afterwards, they were suspended for ten days each. I continued to chill in class while the fights were going on.

During all this time, and the months that had passed, I hadn't seen my mother. Life on the streets and carrying that monkey on her back had her caught up and addicted. Everything she was going through was traumatizing to me, breaking my spirit and my heart, which also had a negative physical effect on me.

One afternoon in February 1994, I was walking with By'ron and Rob down Hamilton Ave toward Summer Street. I flashback in my mind, 'this where

Ghetto Legend Graduate
Cornelius Kinchen

Illene bought me to 'Elm Street'.hosue right there next to the corner store. This ghetto area was well-known for high drug trafficking, and crack was the drug of choice. They were quiet, because they knew that what was going on, was not a happy sight for me to see. They noticed Ilene before I did.

They pointed over to the left. "Look in the field.. Your mother?"

And sure enough, it was her. There she was, buying her version of American-happiness in a plastic vial. I just stopped and watched in disbelief, pain, anger, neglect, embarrassment while spiritually being taken to hell.

She bought in need.

I watched in sorrow.

By'ron and Rob felt my pain and hopelessness. "Come on, man," they said to me as I continued to stare at my mother. We continued to walk down Hamilton Avenue to Grandma's house. We walked in silence, and all three of us were in shock. From that experience, we grew to be brothers in the hood for life.

We sat in Grandma's kitchen trying to cope with the enlightened nightmare we all just experienced. Our hearts were all busted up, as we sat there waiting for the dull ache in our chests to pass. Ten minutes later, we started doing our homework. After we were done, we went to the basement to play with my toy action figures for a while.

Ghetto Legend Graduate
Cornelius Kinchen

About quarter to five, they went home before their parents got worried. Before they left, they told me not to worry about anything, and that everything would be all-good. We shared an experience and a secret nightmare together on that day, which was how we became brothers.

The next day, we went to school acting as if nothing happened. They made me stronger each day. Also, school helped to distract me from reliving the horrible experience, and from having feelings of hopelessness. We created so much fun, laughter, and competition in class, that I became distracted from my family world. It was great. Also, I did very well in school, making the honor roll each marking period. I channeled my negative feelings into positive results without even noticing.

My boys weren't around to have fun with me all the time to cope with the loneliness and pain. Therefore, I had to adapt and cope to the best of my ability. I was all alone, neglected, hurt, and angry, and couldn't do anything about Illene's addiction. So I started to listen to rap music to entertain myself. I became interested in ONYX's lyrics. Every day, I would come home, do my homework, then cope with my problems by listening to hardcore lyrics. I wrote them and recited them with the pain I felt inside to release that negative energy. This was a form of therapy and release of tension through loud lyrical expression. I even started dressing like ONYX rappers.

Ghetto Legend Graduate
Cornelius Kinchen

    I considered them my role models at that time, from whom I derived negative-mental strength and hope. In doing so, it help distract my mind to get through some of the stress of wondering why this and that was going on in my life. Once the music got boring to me, I played with my toy character action figures, and had my own fun using my imagination. Once the action figures became boring, I watched basketball. Every role model of mine seem to wear a bald-head: Michael Jordan and ONYX. I eventually cut my hair bald, too.
    The next day in school, my boys plotted on slapping the dog-dookie out my head. I did the same, and planned to slap their bald-heads, too. They would do it in a sneaky way, especially By'ron and Rob. If anyone else tried to slap my head, I took it personally and wanted to fight. My other classmates knew not to try me. I had a quick temper and was ready to fight at any time. Right before class started By'ron, Frank, and Rob all slapped my head until it sting real bad.
    May 1994 came, and I felt like speeding up time so summer would come faster. I was in a pugilistic mood, and guess who I wanted to fight?
    Good old punching bag Cantrell.
    Yeah.
    It was a peaceful day in Mrs. Knight's class. No one expected this fight to happen. I decided to surprise my boys with the fighting talent I had. So I called Cantrell out to fight.

Ghetto Legend Graduate
Cornelius Kinchen

"I want to fight," I said.

"Who me?" he said, and put his hands up.

We squared off and he started throwing punches in my direction. Mrs. Knight politely asked, "Class clear out into the hall quickly and quietly. They want to act stupid hurting themselves: we will not be apart of that nonsense." As the class left, we continued to fight., Cantrell landed one punch; I was too fast for him. I landed punch after punch, then I grabbed him and we ended up wrestling, which was when he started landing more punches on me. Then I picked him up and slammed him to the floor.

I came from behind him and started punching him in both his jaws while he sat on the floor. Mrs. Knight walked into the class showing mercy on the poor boy by putting a stop to the fight. After the fight, the asked to enter the class and take a seat quietly. After writing her report, She gave me ten days suspension and him five days suspension sending us to the vice-principal office. The fight was fun while it lasted, but the suspension didn't make me feel like a responsible student.

When I returned from suspension, I felt my student-pride and confidence come back to me from being back in class learning from Mrs. Knights. I didn't get a beating from anybody during the ten days of suspension, because my mother didn't know about it. Illene hadn't come around for a while.

Ghetto Legend Graduate
Cornelius Kinchen

    I could feel the momentum as I sat in class at my desk. My boys had headlined the surprise fight. Meanwhile, the girls felt my student-swag and crushed me for my battle efforts. I felt like a Don-fighter. My fight was the talk for the rest of fifth grade year.

    The talk continued each day, Mom didn't find out about the fight until the last minute. When she brought me back to school, she spoke to both Mrs. Knight and me together out in the hallway. "A mind is a terrible thing to waste," Mom stated sincerely. I took that into consideration. Mrs. Knight agreed very strongly, "Your mother is right Cornelius. I'm sure we will never have this problem again will we Cornelius?," said Mrs. Knight. 'No, we will never have this problem again'..

    From that point on, I didn't do anything stupid to get myself into trouble, nor jeopardize my education by missing school for fighting. I appreciated that strong influential statement coming from the most important person in my life.

    Rob and my cousin Red, 4'7, 100 pounds, light-skin, both transferred from Edward Kilpatrick Public School. Red was in and out of School 6 because of his behavior. The school only went up to fourth grade, leaving them the only option to transfer to another school.

    Red was a tough kid. He was placed in 5.3, which was next door to my class. He was extremely disruptive, throwing tables and chairs around the class, and at the teacher. His behavior got him kicked out of School 6, which was starting to earn a reputation as one of the worst schools in the Fourth Ward school district.

    My Uncle Lawson, Aunt Barbara, and Red moved from Grandma's house to an area near Martin Luther King School 30. MLK was a new and great school, but it was near the Alabama Projects. The projects were terrible, and most children from the projects attended 'ghetto' School #20, right down the street from 'rural' school # 30.

    Red was doing well in school. He visited Grandma's house on weekends. He would tell me about MLK every weekend. He said, "Yo, the school is new, the teachers are great and the kids are cool there. We have a basketball league inside the school, too. It's really fun there."

    I believed him. He looked happy throughout the conversation.

    I thought of my Mom toward the end of our conversation. Illene was out running the streets and still hadn't come around or straightened up her act. I had no choice but to keep on living and to stay hopeful that she would come around.

Ghetto Legend Graduate
Cornelius Kinchen

It's a hard knock life

If it wasn't for my sister Esha and cousin Red bullying me, beating up on me to make me tougher, I wouldn't have won that fight I had in School 6. Whenever my mother was around, she would still have Esha beat me up, which forced me to defend myself and fight her back. Red and I didn't always get along, and what made things worse for me was that Grandma favored him at times, and my other two cousins, Bobby and Fanny, too. I was treated like an outcast. I also felt like alone, but where else could we go? My grandfather L. D. was the one who convinced her to take custody of us, meaning my sisters, my brother, and me.

Taking us in was not her first choice, but when she did decide to do so, she stuck us in the basement. On weekends and during the summer in three-day increments, she treated us like slaves. We scrubbed walls, swept and mopped floors, washed dishes, cleaned bathrooms and her bedroom, and took out trash, as well as did the grounds outside of the house. She also had us washing the front porch, of all places! All this was done to the amusement of our cousins, who laughed at us. If we refused to do chores or talk back to her: we would get whooped with a branch, a belt, or get slapped by her rough hands.

At times, Red helped us clean. This drew Red and I closer. The more he volunteered to help, the happier I

Ghetto Legend Graduate
Cornelius Kinchen

was with his efforts to cut the workload down. From that we developed brotherly love.

Grandma showed no sympathy for our situation. I guess that if it weren't for Mom addiction, we would not have been in this situation. On top of all of that, being treated like second-class citizens didn't help strengthen my self-esteem. Having to deal with favoritism really hurt my siblings and me. I no longer wanted to live, and many times wished that I could starve to death to escape the tragedy of this life that I lived in my grandma's home.

Red got any and everything he wanted and needed from his mother, father and Grandma. Bobby and Frances were even more spoiled than Red. Their mother and father were loveable, responsible for their children, educated attending college;, and more importantly, had no kind of addiction to drugs, and held down jobs.

Red's parents had common sense and good paying jobs. They worked. My Uncle Lawson worked at a liquor store. His wife Barbara worked at an overnight daycare residence. My Uncle Lawson had an alcohol addiction, which drained some of their money. My Aunt Barbara would drink occasionally, but they managed to take care of Red and his sisters. He was well dressed and had every pair of sneakers that came out. He had all color Etonics sneakers.

I had to constantly ask for what I wanted at times. My father always said he had no money. Plus, he had to take care of my two older sisters' needs and the bills; so,

Ghetto Legend Graduate
Cornelius Kinchen

I believed him. However, before school, the begging and crying worked a little bit. He would buy me a nice jacket and a pair of sneakers I wanted. But this was only before the school year started. He would buy me two pair jeans and two shirts for the entire school year. I tried mixing and matching my clothes, but it didn't always work. Eventually, I started wearing some of my sisters' hand me down jeans that were too small for them and way too big for me. At the time, I was grateful for the hand me downs from my sisters and Red. I was tired of wearing the same jeans to school every day.

Ghetto Legend Graduate
Cornelius Kinchen

Boys in the hood

The summer of 1994 rolled around, and all of the cousins (of whom I was the leader) played together and did chores together. There were nine of us: *Crystahl was a daddy's girl from E.19, 4'6, 77 pounds, short hair, sassy-classy, brown skin, with a colgate-smile, *Red (the little bully), **Fanny, brown skin, 4'5, 76 pounds, sassy-classy like Crystahl, shorter hair,,**Bobby Fanny's twin, 4'7, 95 pounds, brown skin, wore glasses, *Kevin, dark skin, 4'6, 76 pounds, E.19 wild, *Pooka, 4'5, brown skin, 71 pounds, fat belly button, with glow bug eyes, *Mick, 4'3, 66 pounds, dark skin, big head and no teeth in the front, my little brother Torrie, 4'3, 65 pounds, brown skin, quiet looked like a little me and me. Crystahl was tough in a girly kind of way, and would try anything I would do, and still act like a little girl. Fanny was a little tough and looked up to Crystahl. Anything Crystahl did, Fanny tried.

Red played all sports with us. He was the best 'ghetto' homerun hitter out of the boy cousins. Kevin could play baseball well, too. Bobby joked around playing any sport. You had to push him to get him mad or take his video game for him to take something serious. He loved to play video games with Red. Bobby and Red mastered Mario Brothers for Nintendo. Pooka cried and boo-hooed at times he wasn't suppose to. He cried so

Ghetto Legend Graduate
Cornelius Kinchen

much, he was worse than a one-month-old baby with colic. I never could understand.

Mick was a cool dark-skinned kid. He admired me for sport and intellectual reason; and was the only mental challenge I had at that time. He would get on my nerves, like a little brother would. Every sarcastic remark I made, he would repeat it. It irritated the hell out of me. Whenever we argued, it was like two warriors fighting to the bitter, bloody end. But when I played basketball, I did get a kick out of him watching me with his mouth hanging open in amazement.

I had two Hispanic friends as a kid. I met Ali, 4'6, 79 pounds, long-black hair, always thought he was a pretty boy; however by fighting him we became friends. After, we became best friends we hung out everyday on the block. We would fight every week after that, and then play video games like nothing ever happened. Goya, the tallest of my cousins and friends, 5'2, he was like inspector-gadget.

Most of the time, we challenged Red and Goya in basketball, football and baseball. When it rained or snowed, we went outside to play two-on-two football. Ali and I were like Montana and Rice from the 49ers versus Red and Goya. You would think they had an advantage, considering the fact that Red was fat and round, and Goya was tall. They should have been able to score a touchdown at will.

Ghetto Legend Graduate
Cornelius Kinchen

Whenever they won, they used our mistakes to defeat us. But when we won, our advantages were our skills, speed, and smarts. Our win-loss records were 25-11, with theirs being the reverse of ours.

Through out the summer, Goya considered himself a movie director, and after we finished playing football, he pretend he had a camera, and would pull some crazy script from his head. The imaginary movie set was the field near the train tracks on Fair Street. We filmed jungle scenes in the tree that stood in the field. There was a wood-ladder we built for us to climb up the tree. The climb in the tree caused itching and scratching from playing around among the branches, but we didn't care. As long as we were having fun, it didn't matter.

But Goya had the nerve to get upset when we didn't say our parts right, and Ali and I would use this to our advantage. Three to four days out of a week, we were filming that hot-sweaty jungle scene. Goya took directing seriously; we could care less.

At night, all eleven of us (the cousins, Goya, Ali, and I) played tag up and down Fair Street and in the churchyard on Broadway and Fair Street until midnight, and then we would all head to our homes, tired from exercise and happy looking forward to awaking the next day to Grandma's breakfast. Next day and everyday throughout the summer vacation, Grandma cooked a big breakfast for the family. There was always a nice breakfast spread, all my cousins and I were in the kitchen

Ghetto Legend Graduate
Cornelius Kinchen

eating bacon, cereal and milk, grits, pancakes, eggs, biscuits, and sausages. Then we were out the door to play. We all had our own bike, and would fix our flats, broken chains, raise seats higher, and then off we went on another adventure in the neighborhood. After a long hood adventure, we at Wendy's drinking free water. Summers in Paterson were always hot and humid, we did our best to keep cool.

After drinking from the yellow and red cup full of ice, we rode bikes back home for lunch, and back out to play basketball on our homemade court. Our basketball court was made out of a milk crate, and used piece of wood six feet long to nail the crate to it, then stood it up wrapped tied to a gate with three hangers; and we shot baskets. We had a rule, if you didn't help build the hoop, you couldn't play. Red knew this rule backwards and forwards, but never helped us build the hoop, but always wanted to play. When we told him "no," he got angry and imitated Shaquille O'Neal dunking in the homemade hoop: breaking it to the ground. That would be the source of many arguments throughout the rest of the summer.

Later on, we walked to the field near the railroad tracks to play baseball. It was always the same crews versus each other. Ali, Kevin, and I played against Red, Goya, and Bobby, and since I was "da man of our team always batted first. We usually got spanked, similar to the way we beat them in football. They were hitting home runs like it was no big deal, scoring over us every time.

Ghetto Legend Graduate
Cornelius Kinchen

After a full day of playing and having run, it was time to go home for dinner, then back outside for a game of tag, then home for bed.

That next evening, my cousins drove down to my house with my Aunt and Uncle. It was about ninety degrees outside. It was so hot and humid, I felt like I was baking in the oven. My cousins felt the same way. We decided to go to the supermarket and steal water guns.

Anyway, we walked together to the supermarket and separated when we got there. We walked up and down the aisle until we found water guns in the third aisle. We took turns going into that aisle stealing water guns that were small enough to fit under our shirts. Then we left out the supermarket unnoticed. We raced to Grandma's house to put water in them, taking turns in the kitchen filling the guns with cold water and squirting each other.

The next day, I was stupid enough to go to the same supermarket alone to steal another water gun. This time I was caught before I could even put one under my shirt. Before I could get out the door, an undercover store detective grabbed me hard by the arm, and took me to the back of the store. It smelled of raw meat and wet cardboard, I will never forget that smell for as long as I live.

He put my hands behind my back, and put handcuffs on me. I thought it was a scare tactic. I wasn't

Ghetto Legend Graduate
Cornelius Kinchen

so much scared as I was angry for getting caught. I was so mad, tears formed in my eyes.

"I should take you to jail for coming in here trying to steal," detective said. I had some defiance, but I didn't say anything. "The next time you come in here, you better be with a parent."

I was pissed off that I was in the hands of the law, but he cut me a break, for which I was grateful. He warned that the next time I came in there alone, I would go to jail. He took the cuffs off my wrists and let me go.

"Get out of here before I change my mind," he said. So I left, still angry. The first time I stole from that place, it was fun, or at least I thought it was fun. But it's never fun when you get caught. As I walked to Grandma's house, I felt bad about stealing like a true criminal from the 'ghetto'. I felt humiliated for stealing. I didn't understand why I was stealing. I did what I saw unconsciously. I didn't think about the consequences of stealing. I sat on the porch for a little while. Minutes later, I walked to Ali's house to get my mind off that.

My Mom decided to stop by Grandma's house during the last week of summer. My Aunt Doris, 5'5, dark skin, 310 pounds, wore glasses was moving into her own apartment, so that left her old room available for Grandma and Illene to talk in private.

"Illene, come in and close the door," Grandma said to her, so she did. While I sat on the hallway steps, I could hear the conversation between the three of them clearly.

"Why are you doing this to your children? Hanging in the streets, hurting your self and your children. It's not right nor fair to your children." Grandma asked and talked in agreement with Aunt Doris. My mother started crying. She was blinded of what she was doing, but the addiction was a hard thing for her to kick naturally. She needed Christ to help her through the grace of God. Not only was it hurting her physical health, it was taking an emotional-spiritual torment on her. The ones who loved her knew that she wanted to stop, but she couldn't do it on her own. She really needed Jesus help.

"You're hurting your children, Illene. And they love you, girl. You need to get some help."

"I am, Mama," she sobbed. "I am."

Grandma and Aunt Doris prayed with her, for her, and loved her. I appreciated Grandma for the love that she showed Illene, and the concern for her health. The prayer was heartfelt and genuine, and very touching. Grandma offered her to stay to get her self together.

Illene left the house after Grandma finished prayers. God is good, because Grandma gave her another chance to live with us again. So she stayed with us in the basement. I slept on the extra pullout bed, my sisters slept on the sofas, and my parents slept in a layout bed, with only room for one person. I was excited to have my mother back home, and thanked God for it.

Ghetto Legend Graduate
Cornelius Kinchen

That Friday, my mother and my sisters left me home with Dad and went clothes shopping for the upcoming school year. While they were out, they picked up a few things for me. When they came home later on that evening around seven, my mother made me try on my new clothes. She pulled the clothes out the shopping bag "Here try your pants and shirts on to see if it fits."

I hated it when she did that. But after I did try them on, she observed and straightened my clothes appropriately; and I wanted to wear them. It was a tease, to try them on, and then take them right off again. I went to bed dreaming about wearing my new clothes, knowing how good I would look in them for school.

Well, the girls had their day in the sun with Mom, so the next day, Dad and I got up early and went to McDonald's for breakfast. We both had the Big Breakfast, which came with a sausage patty, scrambled eggs, and a buttermilk biscuit. On Sunday, we went to Jimmie's; a diner that Dad knew had good food. We were able to get a fresh homemade breakfast, and on some days, he would bring the girls and Torrie along, and we would have breakfast together as a family.

Our weekends excursions to Pennington Park were pretty much routine. Dad drove a royal blue Pontiac coupe with brand new black leather interior, and we would pile into it for our trip to the park. He read his newspaper and drank coffee, and we would sit and listen to old school 70's music on the radio. That Sunday before

Ghetto Legend Graduate
Cornelius Kinchen

school started, there were some guys in the park playing basketball that needed an extra man to play, so Dad played. I watched in awe as he exhibited his skills on the court. It was like watching a pro, he was that good. Watching him dribble, pass, shoot, run, rebound, and play defense almost made me want to try out for the New Jersey Nets or the New York Knicks.

On the way to the car, I said, "Dad, I didn't know you could play basketball."

All he said was, "Yeah." Not in a bragging way, just humble. I wondered what other sport he could master at his age. Also, I tried to imagine when he was younger how much of star-all American he probably was in sports.

I'd listen to my uncles boast about my father's sports talent. "He was an all-American in sports in his younger days", said Uncle T.D. Witnessing my father play basketball was evidence to just one of his athletic talents. I was honored to be able to watch him play. I wanted to see more from him, but he was getting older.

Ghetto Legend Graduate
Cornelius Kinchen

6th grade

Summer was officially over; and here it was 8 a.m., my first day in the sixth grade. My new Penny Hardaways were too tight. I wore a size seven and a half, and these damn sneakers were two sizes too small. From 8 o'clock, to when my new teacher, *Mrs. Avery, 5'3, dark skinned, 120 pounds, old school, with a strict attitude and funny clown voice, came to get us, until the end of the school day, my tight sneakers were murdering my feet. My toes were curled up inside them, trying to find some kind of comfort from somewhere. I even took them off while we were waiting for Mrs. Avery to take us inside that morning. They burned and ached from having my toes balled up inside the sneakers. During that entire day, I never let on that I was not happy with the sneakers. I dealt with the discomfort because the sneakers were the "in" latest sports sneakers, and I wanted to keep them, so all day long like they didn't bother me. At least that what I tried to fool myself into believing.

Months passed, and I got used to the sneakers' discomfort. I continued to play. Eventually, my feet bust through the Penny Hardaway sneakers and became torn. I wore those bad-boys down so much, when the time came to get rid of them, my feet had corns and bunions on them. I never did such a thing again.

Dad was forced to buy new sneakers for me, and bought some off-brand kicks called Street-Lights. They

Ghetto Legend Graduate
Cornelius Kinchen

looked like Japps that had little lights in the back of them. I used them to play in real city basketball games. I gained exposure while playing on the First Zion AME Church basketball team. My average was twelve points a game, with four assists, 4 rebounds, and two steals. My friend Quisee would come and watch my games, impressed with my basketball skills. Sometimes he would start in games, other times he would just watch and wait his turn to shine on the court.

    I played the whole game like a star. My other teammates, Trav and J'mal, were cousins from across the bridge in the Paterson Towers Projects. Dave, who was the coach's son, was another team member. So, the official starting lineup was the tower boys, Dave Marquise, and I. The cousins were jealous at times of my talent, and did very little to hide it. Coach had me putting in the winning shot in tied games, and games that were down to the last few seconds. After making the final basket in many games, Trav wanted to fight, and tried to provoke me by calling me a punk jock. I started ignoring him, as this would always happen in the locker room. But the more I ignored him, the angrier he became. He wasn't hurting me with his behavior; however, I knew what my skills and abilities were. It wasn't my fault if he wasn't as talented as I was.

    So whenever Trav would be feeling guilt and jealous of my game, J'mal would get him to back off. "We won the game, right?" he would remind Trav.

Ghetto Legend Graduate
Cornelius Kinchen

J'mal had a point. We did win, and that was what really mattered the most.

What I didn't realize at the time was that my performances during each basketball game caught the interest and attention of each team league's coach one of the best teams in the Paterson league was coached by Dennis, one of my older cousins. He wanted me on his team 'Positive Impact' the following basketball season, and would come to Grandma's house everyday until he got me on his team.

Eventually, my grades and performance in games would affect by each other. For the most part, I still earned good grades in Mrs. Avery's class. She was an excellent teacher that believed in giving a lot of homework. When my grades suffered, the team suffered: because I wasn't able to come to some games. The rule in my home was that my education always came first. The consequence of failing grades was being whipped with an extension cord.

Ghetto Legend Graduate
Cornelius Kinchen

Months after basketball season was over, I wanted Rob to hook me up with a girl named Manae. She was pretty, smart, and straight ghetto.

"Rob, hook me up with Manae," I said to him one day. He looked at me.

"A'ight, I got you," he said.

During lunch, he went to her and put in a word for me. She sent one back through him.

"Manae said, "you have a mouth, come ask yourself.'"

I was surprised. "Word?"

"Stop being scared and go ask."

"I'm not scared. What are you talkin' about?"

"Then go ask her!"

So I went up to her later on while she was jumping rope, and just asked her straight out. "Manae, do you want to go with me?"

It took her four full seconds to come up with an answer.

"Yes."

From that point on, she was my girlfriend. A week later, a kid named Nas, 4'6, light skin, 83 pounds, with a cocked eye with a little 'ghetto-gangster attitude' transferred to School 6 and was placed in Mrs. Dudley class. Rob told me one day that Nas tried to kick it to Manae in the hallway.

"All right, I will handle it," I said.

Ghetto Legend Graduate
Cornelius Kinchen

    I saw this new kid in the hallway during bathroom break. He was knocking his fists together, trying to scare me. I knew how to fight, so his threat meant nothing to me. My reputation in that school was established and solid. He was unaware of the consequences of his actions.

    I played the punk and ignored his threats. After bathroom calls, I said to Rob, "Ask him if he wants to fight at three o'clock in the park across from the school." I was sure the new kid wasn't expecting a request to fight. He was acting tough and tried to take my girl. I didn't appreciate that in *my* school. My pride wouldn't allow me have mercy on him.

    So at three o'clock, it was time for the ultimate challenge. Nas got to the park ahead of me. By'ron, Rob, Manae, and I walked to the park together. Rob and By'ron were smiling because they were confident of my fighting skills. Manae said, "You better f*ck him up!" I smiled at the crowd of ghetto students wanting to see a fight. No one could mess with my extraordinary swag.

    Nas had his shirt off already to fight me. I took off my windbreaker and dropped my book bag. I put my dukes up, squaring off with Nas toe to toe. I threw a quick one-two combo and hit him in the face. Nas had no time to react. I followed up with a clip and two more punches to his face. The crowd was on my side. Nas left his things in the park and ran home.

    The fight was over, and once again, I stood tall among the School 6 community.

Ghetto Legend Graduate
Cornelius Kinchen

Meanwhile, Cantrell and Andre from Hamilton Avenue were fighting. I stayed and watched that fight, which ended in a tie. Both were bleeding from the mouth and lumped up. They fought for at least six minutes. My fight was over in 60 seconds.

The next day after the fight, that punk Nas was stupid enough to bring an unloaded nine-millimeter gun to school in his book bag to shoot me, or rather, to make me think he was going to shoot me. I didn't take it serious, because we were young. It was 8:27 a.m. and time to go to class from the playground. It was raining and the teachers didn't come out to pick us up. Marv, who was Nas's cousin, had spread the word to my boys about the gun.

"Yo," he said, "my cousin has a black gun in his book bag for Cornelius." My boys quickly ran up to me telling me about the gun. I still didn't care. I started walking toward the blue school doors and up the stairs, and Nas was nowhere in sight.

The school day passed. Things were going smoothly. There was no approach from my former opponent. It was three o'clock and school was out. It was still raining. I had no umbrella to hide my face. Since I didn't see Nas, By'ron and I went to the public library to do homework and to have some fun.

We made it to the library a little after three, and went to the basement where the girls from Auburn Street hung out to do their homework. We left our books on the

Ghetto Legend Graduate
Cornelius Kinchen

table just in case the security came to warn us. We would act like we were still doing homework. We did our homework first and all of us clowned around for a while, making a great deal of noise.

We got our kicks by bullying four of the class nerds. Clark long feet, skinny, Joaquin, big ears with a cock-eye, Joe-sef light skin with fish lips with glasses, and Allen tallest boy in the class, wearing glasses were honor roll students that always got better grades than we did. One time, Joe-sef was so upset over getting a C on his report card, the punk started crying. I felt he was so soft to be crying over a C. So that made bullying him and his friends even more fun for us. We would hit on them, making them cry, and then we would stop. The whole time this was going on, the girls were watching us, thinking we were tough. They would smile and act like they had crushes on us.

Unfortunately, we were too loud, and the librarian came to warn us about the noise. We quieted down some, but went back to being loud again. She decided it was enough, and called the security guard, who looked like buck-toothed Otis on the sitcom *Martin*. He came to the basement where we were clowning around, and laid down the law.

"The librarian," he said in a Southern accent, "had to tell you too many times to keep the noise down."

He was right. She did. We couldn't deny that fact.

Ghetto Legend Graduate
Cornelius Kinchen

"Y'all two," he said, indicating By'ron and me, "has to go, because I know y'all is startin' all the trouble." So, while he stood there watching us, we grabbed our things and left the library.

We walked out slow just to annoy the security guard.

As soon as we walked up the stairs and out the library on the Auburn Street side, the girls were on their way out, too. We were talking and laughing about how we were put out the library. The girls had really enjoyed that moment. Slowly we all began to walk in the same direction toward Broadway and Fair Street. We all went our separate ways home. Fair Street was in the direction of Grandma's house. By'ron lived on Hamilton Avenue and Auburn Street, and the girls lived on Auburn Street and Fair Street. I branched off and Joaquin and his boys went to his house in the village to play video games.

I went home, ate dinner, then I listened to the radio. I couldn't afford the actual hip-hop songs played on the radio, so what I did was record over my sisters' slow jam tapes. They had so many slow jam tapes; I figured they wouldn't notice one missing. I would always try to record the whole song. I hated how when the song was ending, the station would say their name, messing up the recording. To me, that was embarrassing. Still, I would record and memorize the lyrics of different songs for hours until it was time for me to get ready for the next day.

Ghetto Legend Graduate
Cornelius Kinchen

By time my sisters came in the house at approximately 8:45p.m., I was in the bed almost asleep. My father worked the night shift from 11at night to 7 in the morning, so they would do pretty much what they wanted to do. That night, they were with their friends Angela and Tiffany. Before they went to sleep, they would usually listen to slow music from the time my father left for work up until three in the morning. While I was trying to sleep, they would be playing, pausing and writing the words to the slow songs half the night. This was a nightmare for me because all I could do was ask them to turn the music down. They would turn it down, but I still could hear it. It seem like they would never turn off the radio.

That night, I slept for four hours. I dreamed of being a rich and successful R&B artist. The dream seemed so real, I hated when I awakened to the harsh reality of living in a basement with my father and sisters.

When Dad finally came home from work, he had many goodies from his job, such as Oreos, Lorna Doone and chocolate chip cookies, juices and sandwiches for all the kids in the house. Those were the days that I loved being a kid. After all, what kid doesn't like cookies and juice?

Dad would get me ready for school. I had a short 'fro, and since my hair was extremely nappy, he had to spray Jheri Curl juice in my hair just to get through it with the comb. By the time he finished, my scalp was in pain. But it was well worth it, because before I walked

Ghetto Legend Graduate
Cornelius Kinchen

out the door in my casual school clothes, he let me put on some of his brut cologne to smell good for the girls. And believe me, there was no lack of confidence on my part, because I knew I was the BMOC. For the ones who don't know what that means, that's short for *big man on campus*.

Once everyone was ready to walk out the door, we all left together. The girls and I would walk with Angel and Tiffany, who met us at our house. I decided to stop at the corner store and rack up on Now-n-Laters before we got to school. Once we got there, we all seperated. I went with my boys to play a game of gourmen. Ten to fifteen boys would line up against the gate and one person would say "gourmen" and try to catch someone to help him catch someone else, until everyone is caught trying to make it from one gate to another gate. We played until it was time to go inside for class.

I couldn't escape school. Education was therapeutic for me. By the time the teacher came out to get us at 8:23 a.m., I was the ninth person to get caught and the last to get caught was the winner, and that was Li'l Mikee; short and fast. The game was over. When my school mother Mrs. Avery came out to pick up my brothers and sisters of my class, I was reminded of how much I was missing my Mom. I appreciated my sixth grade teacher for teaching me some morals and providing me with an education to get me to the next level.

Ghetto Legend Graduate
Cornelius Kinchen

After school, Nas and I walked to his house. We had squashed the beef between us and become somewhat cool with each other. I wanted to see if the rumor about him having a 9mm gun to shoot me was true. Nas lived in the middle section of the Village next door to Kim, a girl Kevin had a crush on. There wasn't much to talk about on the way to his house; I just wanted to see the gun I had heard about. We made it to his house just before it started drizzling. When we got to the room, he confirmed the rumor.

"I wanted to shoot you after the fight," he said. "Marv and Rob told me to chill."

I said, "That's your word? Let me see the gun."

He went over to his bed and pulled out a black semi-automatic nine-millimeter handgun. I was amazed he had a gun at his age. He put in my hand, and still in awe, I held it, turning it over and looking at it. It was heavy. I felt like a true tough person, and the gun made me feel powerful. At the same time, I thought to myself, *This boy really bought a gun to school for little old me!* I stayed for thirty minutes after I held the gun and left. I never talked to him again after that. On my way to Grandma's house I hoped the rain would slow down. It didn't. It started to speed up and rained harder: it got darker outside. I began to run home to get out the rain hoping my homework isn't wet.

When I got home, I took my coat off and took my homework out to complete it. It was wet at all. Minutes

Ghetto Legend Graduate
Cornelius Kinchen

later I was done with my homework, I began listening to and recording new songs from off the radio. I didn't worry about eating dinner. I ate some potato chips that I had in my book bag.

Ghetto Legend Graduate
Cornelius Kinchen

Easter 1995

    I rehearsed with the Highway Church choir all week. On Easter Sunday 1995, I had to lead a rap gospel song in front of the whole church on this day. I practiced at home until it was perfect. But on that Sunday morning, I was nervous. This was the first time I had ever been on the spot. I was from the streets. The choir director thought the song fit me perfect.

    It was time to go to church. After Sunday school, I went to the store and bought a snack. After I finished my snack, I went to rehearse my rap verse. The entire choir was in the basement during prayer and scripture reading. Salina, 5'4, brown skin, light brown eyes, brown hair, beautiful the choir director, came up to me,

    "Neal, are you ready?" she asked.

    "Yes, but I'm nervous," I admitted.

    "Don't worry," she reassured me. 'You'll be fine. Just relax." After prayer and reading of the scripture, it was time for the choir to open up on Easter Sunday with the song I was leading. The musicians began to play the music. The choir was very large full of young people. We began marching up front near the pull-pit from the basement. I felt confident with my light brown hand-me-down suit from Bobby and a fresh haircut to go along with it. I was feeling what was about to happen. As we marched to the front, I looked around and saw so many saints standing and clapping. The church was packed.

Ghetto Legend Graduate
Cornelius Kinchen

The choir sung and I rapped my verse with a gospel edge. While I rapped, the whole church full of saints continued standing; and cheered the choir and me to glorify God through song of praise. The director was doing a great job, too.

    After the song, we took our seats. Grandma and her friends were very proud of my courage to give God the praise through singing. I was happy she was happy. From that moment, I wanted to continue going to church. I became involved with things going on in the church and reaching out to young people through the music ministry. At the time, I really didn't fully understand what was going on in my life. I just knew the attention I was receiving felt good and that people were happy. But as I got older, I received wisdom, knowledge and understanding from the book of Proverbs. I learned about the Bible on a consistent basis throughout the school year and the summer, too. Grandma wanted me to read the bible, read the bible, and live accordingly to the will of God.

    The summer of 1995 arrived again like a water-blue Lamborghini drop-top in traffic. This summer was fun. I was promoted to the seventh grade. I was proud of myself. I survived the sixth grade with Manae on my side. I called her every day during the summer. She was still my girlfriend. I felt like a gangster and pimp, but I didn't know how to kiss. She was the right one to practice on.

Ghetto Legend Graduate
Cornelius Kinchen

So one day we made plans to go to her sister's house on Godwin Ave and Summer Street. When I got there, Rob and his girlfriend were there, too. I watched Manae wait for me to get courage to walk up to her and kiss her. Rob said, "This is how it's done." He walked up to his girl and tongued her down. I stared at their lips and tongues slither like two snails in each other's mouths. Then they stopped. They kissed like they were having fun.

I was nervous. I didn't want to seem like a punk, so I walked up to Manae and froze like a snowman. Then she backed off and said, "You're scared and you're not ready." I backed off and got some coach kissing tips from Rob. Then I built up enough courage. I walked up to her again and tongue kissed her. The kiss felt brand new, good and fresh. I had butterflies in my stomach. I really didn't understand what I was feeling at the time. I wanted to try again.

The sun was going down and it was time for me to go home. I told Manae to call me later. As soon as I walked through the door, she called. My cousin Fanny answered the phone.

"Neal, a girl name Manae wants you on the phone."

Hastily, I went to Grandma's room to talk on the phone in private. I picked up the phone.

"Hello," I began. "Did you like our kiss?"

"Yeah," she breathed. "What are you doing?"

Ghetto Legend Graduate
Cornelius Kinchen

"Sitting in Grandma's room, looking out the window, thinking about our kiss."

I could hear and visualize her smile. We talked for a little while. Then we agreed to call each other later. Then we hung up phone.

I went downstairs to eat dinner. I could smell the steak, gravy, rice and corn. I had two plates of food, and then went back upstairs to watch Red and Bobby play Sega Genesis. We took turns playing Mortal Kombat and Sonic. I watched them play the game for hours until it was time for Bobby to go home.

My Aunt Branda was busy at work in the daytime, and at night, she attended college. She would stay late at Grandma's house, talking to her sisters and friends on the porch. My cousins would always come over to Grandma's house to play. The next day, Grandma took her time cooking breakfast to allow my aunts and cousins time to arrive to eat with us.

After breakfast, the boys went upstairs to play the game again, and the girls went down into the basement to play. Sometimes I watched my sisters play "Walking Down the Street," with one girl holding the books in her arms, while the other girl had to bump her and knock the books out of her arms. Then they would argue about it. Eventually, they ended in a play fight. Once they were tired of playing that, they practiced dancing.

My oldest sister, Meaka, was a very talented dancer. She watched hip-hop music videos and taught

Ghetto Legend Graduate
Cornelius Kinchen

herself how to dance. Then she taught my female cousins how to dance as a group. Then they would show off the dances to the neighborhood. This was fun to watch. The dances looked like real hip-hop choreography from a music video. I was surprised.

The boys played the game for a little while, and then we went outside on the porch to play Royal Rumble. We wrestled for a long time. To win the Royal Rumble, one of us had to throw each contestant off the porch, so I did just that and won the royal rumble.

I convinced Pooka to wrestle me one on one. We started wrestling. I took it easy on him to make it seem like he was a good young wrestler on the rise. He threw me against the rail (wrestling ropes). I hung from the rail like I had no energy left to fight. He ran toward me with his head down. I moved quickly to avoid being hit, and he hit his head over his right eye and deeply cut his skin. He cried and was immediately rushed to the hospital to get stitches. I didn't mean for that to happen to him. I was just in the hype of the moment, needing to win.

We had stopped playing wrestling until Pooka was all right. Three hours later, he returned from the hospital with stitches and a Band-Aid over his right eye. Until he healed well enough to play with us, he stayed in the house.

While he was in the house healing, cousins and friends were playing tag in the 'ghetto-jungle until it was time for dinner. Even after we ate dinner we went back

Ghetto Legend Graduate
Cornelius Kinchen

outside to play tag in the 'ghetto-jungle, in the parking lot and church-yard on the side facing Wendy's. Everyone got caught and was tired and thirsty, so we went across the highway to get ice-water from Wendy's. It was at least fifteen of us getting served several cups of water. We were always lucky to go to Wendy's while it was empty. If it was crowded, we would have to share five cups of water. We drank our water. It was growing darker outside. We walked up the street to play tag around the house, where our parents could watch us.

    The next day, Manae called me and told me that she wanted to visit me. She planned to come over to Grandma's house at two o'clock, and showed up promptly with her cousin Rob. I wasn't expecting her to have anyone else with her. It almost messed up my groove.

    Rob saw Crystahl and was enraptured by her. "Yo, who is that? Hook me up!"

    "Don't you have a girl?" I asked.

    "Yeah, I will break up with her." Just like that, he would dump one girl to be with another girl. Typical hood-male behavior.

    "I will talk to her for you." I wasn't much better, going along with this crazy scheme.

    "Please do that."

    I promised to introduce him to Crystahl, but the problem was that she liked Ali.

Ghetto Legend Graduate
Cornelius Kinchen

    I introduced them to each other anyway. After the introduction, I said, "Crystahl, Rob wants to go with you."
    "Let me think about it," she said.
    I told Rob what Crystahl said. Two days later, they were boyfriend and girlfriend. They were calling each other on the phone and holding long conversations.

Soon after the four of us hooked up as couples, Fanny wanted a boyfriend, Red wanted a girlfriend, and Pooka wanted a girlfriend.
    Manae and Rob had more cousins who were single. I became acquainted with some of them. The three available and age-appropriate singles were Hasan, Queena, and Cannaya. Manae and I hooked Hasan and Fanny up together, Queena (also known as Shaq) and Red became a couple, and Pooka and Naya ended up together. We had an elementary love connection thing going on.
    Once every one got to know their partner, we took it to a dare level. It was the Fourth of July, and we thought we were independent because we had our girlfriends and boyfriends. We all met at Grandma's house to chill and spend time with each other. The ones who were without someone to chill with had to find something else to do. We all met up together and went down the street under the train tracks for a whole lot of kissing and experiencing puppy love with our respective girlfriends or boyfriends.

Ghetto Legend Graduate
Cornelius Kinchen

Manae and I would start the kiss-kiss thing. Crystahl didn't want to kiss Rob. She said, "Neal, I don't want to kiss him, because his lips look like monkey lips." He had to talk game for a good thirty minutes to get a tongue kiss.

While Crystahl was being dramatic, Fanny and Hasan showed Crystahl and Rob how it was done. They would kiss like they were on a soap opera. While Fanny and Hasan were showing off, Pooka and Naya kissed like kids; not adults. Red and Shaq kissed wildly, as if they were on the Spice Channel.

Every time Red and Queena kissed, we all took lessons from them. They were slobbing and rubbing tongues like they were born to kiss. It was an adventure to watch them make out.

After the make-out sessions, we would sit and chill under the train tracks. We laughed and joked at Red and Shaq's wild kissing show. We couldn't believe Hassan and Fanny kissed. Naya and Pooka were young, and always tried to follow us. We sat on the church steps, the guys sitting between the girls' legs while they wrapped their arms around our necks in puppy love mode.

All too soon, it was quarter after eight, which meant it was time for us to head home. We all started walking up the street, showing off the fact that we were couples. I had my arm around my girl, but Red and Shaq were walking separate, acting shy toward one another.

Ghetto Legend Graduate
Cornelius Kinchen

"Y'all always act like you ain't just slob on each other," I said. "What is the problem?"

Manae, Rob, and Hassan laughed. Naya, Pooka and Red smiled shyly and didn't respond. We continued to walk up the street. By time we finished laughing and joking, we were at the corner by Grandma's house about to cross Straight Street to continue up Fair Street. We split up and went to our respective homes.

Crystahl, Red, Fanny, Pooka, and I walked down Fair Street happy. We went and sat on the corner down the street from Grandma's house. Esha, Meaka, Angel, Tiff, and my cousins played jump rope on the side of the house for a little while, until somebody didn't turn the rope right and they started arguing. Then they'd stop arguing long enough to dance.

The boys watched until we got bored, then we decided to go down the street in the dark parking lot to play duck-duck goose with Ali and his cousins and Goya and his sister. We sat in a circle and Goya was it. The only light we had was from the streetlights near the church where we sat earlier. They were quite dim, but we could still see well enough to play. We goosed and chase around the parking lot for at least forty-five minutes.

After we got tired of playing that game, we decided to play freeze tag, and then played that game for another twenty-five minutes. After playing, we caught a breather on the church steps, and then we went up the street to play tag around the house. This meant it was

Ghetto Legend Graduate
Cornelius Kinchen

almost time to go home and get ready for the next day. While we played tag, Grandma, my aunts and my uncles were on the porch talking about church service, church folks, family business, and friends. They never had enough to say. Some nights the adults would sit on the porch until the early hours of the morning, just talking.

    We heard the ice cream truck from Broadway and Straight Street. The ice cream truck came to the hood late nights in the summer. They knew we made them many dollars. My Uncle Chubby bought all the kids ice cream. Approximately twenty-one dollars bought ice cream for us. Including the adults, another twenty dollars bought strawberry sundaes.

    That was like pennies to my kingpin uncle. He was a corporate drug dealer from the eighties up until this year. He and my Uncle T.D. had a big team of dealers on the streets of Paterson. They were known for the weight they dealt. They were in and out of the state. Two other kingpins, who went by the names Rich and Poe, traveled from Harlem to Grandma's house to do business with my uncles and their boys.

    Uncle Chubby introduced to the drug game by his little brother T. They sold at a street-city level. Chubby became an entrepreneur in the drug game, selling from state to state. He rode from upstate New York to the Carolinas and Miami. He sold the bigger portions, such as key loads, making over a million dollars a year.

Ghetto Legend Graduate
Cornelius Kinchen

Every time the ice cream truck came around, my Uncle Chubby bought ice cream for every child. He gave kindly to us. But by the end of that summer, he had to do a stretch in federal prison for ten years. His actions finally caught up with him.

After eating the ice cream and wrapping up the family gossip, my aunts and uncles were saying good night to each other.

"Neal take the chairs off the porch, and put them in the kitchen and in the dining room," Grandma said to me.

"All right, Grandma," I said, obediently, and I put all five chairs back where they belonged.

Dad was preparing to leave for work at eleven, so I went downstairs to the basement. I was sleepy and tired from all that running around.

When I took off my sneakers, my feet smelled so bad, I had to wash my feet first before I lay down. There was a black pail that Dad and I used to wash our feet and bodies, so I used it.

The bathroom on the second floor was always in use. By the time everyone on the second floor finished bathing and showering, the water was ice cold. It was no fun trying to wash up in cold water; I wanted the funk washed off me quick, fast, and in a hurry. But, I did what I had to do.

After I washed and dressed, my sisters, Angel and Tiff, were walking down the basement steps. They were

Ghetto Legend Graduate
Cornelius Kinchen

laughing at me and saying, "It smells like soap." I felt that was a stupid thing to say, because after a person takes a bath or a shower, what else were they suppose to smell like? I got into Dad's fold-up bed and under the covers. Angel and Tiff were allowed to stay over for the night to keep my sisters company; so all the girls came downstairs and went straight to listening to slow jam tapes. I just wanted to sleep, not listen to those songs that I grew to hate listening to.

Surprisingly, they listened to only two slow songs and got ready for bed. Tiff, Meaka, and Esha each slept on the couches that surrounded the bed. I slept at the foot of the bed in my spot with Angel, 5'1, brown skin, long black hair, pretty brown eyes and beautiful lips. I was happy to sleep with her. I had a huge crush on Angel, but I'm not sure if she knew it or not. I was nervous and excited to have her sleeping in my bed. The lights were out and I couldn't sleep. *Wow, my favorite girl is sleeping in the same bed with me!* I thought to myself.

The next morning as usual, Dad came home with goodies. He saved some for the girls, and passed them around to his nephews. I ate my cookies, drank my juice, and then went to wash my face while it was still early. Then all the boys went outside to work on our bikes, which we built from scratch. There were always bike parts under the steps for us to use. Bobby's crazy behind didn't have on any socks or sneakers, like he was at a

Ghetto Legend Graduate
Cornelius Kinchen

pool or something. So while Grandma was fixing breakfast, he sat on the porch watching us fix our bikes.

    After we fixed the bikes, we worked on the basketball court. We had a real basketball rim this time, and it was much better than that milk crate we had before. We added a backboard to it and placed it on Miss Joesefina's, old Hispanic, no teeth, a strong Spanish accent tree. Our tree blocked by her gate. She stole half of Grandma's backyard. At one time, our backyard was full and complete. When she moved to the block and put a fence up to divide the backyard in half, all of that changed. Now she had her own backyard with her barking four dogs to keep us out of her yard. They wandered freely around her entire property behind the fence.

    The basketball court was in our half of the backyard, but we put the basketball hoop on her tree, which was against the fence. After we finished building it, we played. I was the best basketball player in my family and on my team. I felt I had no competition. I had beaten everybody in my family and on my block. But I heard about one kid that was related to Manae. His name was Haus. He was taller and two years older than me. I didn't care. He wanted to play me and I wanted to play him.

    It was a coincidence that two hours later, Rob, Haus, and his boys from the Fourth Ward came to

Ghetto Legend Graduate
Cornelius Kinchen

Grandma's house for the basketball competition. My backyard was narrow, half cement, half dirt-dust and uneven in places. The backyard was crowded with people who wanted to see this competition.

I gave him the possession first to welcome him to lose. This was how confident and humble I was going into this hood game. The first player to score twelve points was the winner. I checked him the ball and put my hands up. He drove to the basket and made the first shot.

Score: one zip. He checked the ball again, drove to the basket, and shot again. Swish!

Two zip.

No big deal.

He was tall and it was hard for me to defend his shot as he drove to the basket and shot the ball. All I could do is put my hands in the air.

"Check," he said aggressively. After he checked the ball, he shot a two pointer to make the lead four to zero. After he made the shot, I decided to speak up.

"That's what's up," I said, "your little competition. But you won't win."

He said, "Yo, the score. Pay attention to the score." He checked the ball again.

"Don't miss the shot, or the game is over for you, boy." I must have thrown him off, because he shot the ball and missed. I quickly rebounded. I took the ball back to clear the ball.

Ghetto Legend Graduate
Cornelius Kinchen

"Time out. Mick, get my Street Lights from downstairs."

Whenever I played basketball in my "Street Lights" in the backyard and on special opponents, I was extremely confident in tough game situations. Mick went to get my Street Lights with the quickness, just to see me play like Jordan.

He brought the sneakers up to me and I put them on, and then checked the ball to Haus. The first shot was a two pointer, swish! I cleared the ball by checking the ball. I shot the second two pointer shot, and swish! I was confident; I shot the remaining four shots from behind the two-point line, and made them. The game was over. I won the battle and left my competition at four points. I had capitalized from his one missed shot. In my mind, the game meant I'd proven that I was the best in the 'hood at my age.

After the game, he wanted a rematch. I said, "Maybe tomorrow, I have to get back to my cousins." He walked out of the backyard, embarrassed. His cousins and boys left with him.

I was elated. My cousins and I was represented to the best of my ability. I never gave up hope for a second. I played hard to the very end and believed in myself. And to top things off, I won. I was feeling like a champion for the rest of the day.

After the game, my cousins and I sat on the back porch. I dwelled on how he had no respect for my game.

Ghetto Legend Graduate
Cornelius Kinchen

When he walked out my backyard, however, he had no choice but to respect it.

Half an hour later, we went down the street to hang out in the field next to Goya's house between the train tracks. We saw Ali, who said, "Yo, there are some mattresses my Aunt China threw away."

"Let's get them and bring them to the field to flip on," I said. We went over and carried three mattresses over to the field. We placed them next to the steps where we chilled. We were able to jump off the top of the side of the steps onto the mattresses. We took turns doing front semis, and I tried to do a back flip. I jumped off the step backwards and fell off the mattresses onto the dirty field. I hurt my knees doing that crazy flip. Nevertheless, I kept on trying until I back-flipped right.

Ali tried and fell, too. While Ali and I rested from our falls, we sat watching Red, Bobby, Chacho, Mick, and Pooka jump up and down on the mattress until we built up enough confidence to try the back flip again.

Goya and his parents pulled up in a car. After he helped his mother carry the grocery bags up to their third floor apartment, he came downstairs to flip on the mattress with us. We laughed because he didn't know how to flip. Besides, he was too tall. When he jumped up and down on the mattress, we thought he was going to ruin it. When he came down on the mattress, his weight, feet, and legs would sink deep into the mattress.

Ghetto Legend Graduate
Cornelius Kinchen

We watched and laughed at Goya. When he did a front flip, his legs hung off the mattress. Chacho, who was short and fat, did a front flip and fell on the ground. After we all cracked up laughing so hard, we all took a break on the steps.

I came up with a crazy idea. I said, "Listen, let's put rocks on the train track rails." I ran up the hill in the field to get to the train tracks and put rocks on it. Ali and Red were crazy enough to follow me and go along with it. Then we ran down the hill back to the steps to wait for a train to come.

While we waited, Ali said, "Y'all want to play baseball under the tracks?" We all agreed. He went to his house to get the ball, bat and glove. We took turns hitting and striking each other out, and whoever struck out at bat had to pitch.

We spray-painted a strike-out box to throw the hardball at. Any pitch thrown outside the box was a ball. Four balls ended the series of pitches in an extra set of pitches. The pitcher had to start the count from the beginning.

We played baseball for at least an hour before a train arrived. I listened carefully for a train and heard the screeching of the wheels against the tracks. I said, "Yo, listen a train is coming." So we ran to the field, watched, and listened to the train run over the rocks we placed on the tracks. It sound like shots were being fire from a gun and then sparks flew. Since we didn't get the desired

Ghetto Legend Graduate
Cornelius Kinchen

effect, we threw rocks at the train windows, trying to break them. We threw the rocks like hard-fast balls in a strike zone.

We didn't care if the train tipped over or blew up. There was a myth about a train exploding and burning down the house that use to be in the field, we wanted to spice up the summer with that type of excitement.

The train passed and we stopped throwing rocks. We went back to the field's steps and sat there. My boys from the village walked up Fair Street and entered the field. They were ten deep. They walked in the field and began to chill with us.

"What's good, Birdie?" I said. "Can you flip?"

Birdy was the oldest, but he was little and skinny. "Yeah," he said, then got up, jumped off the steps and did four back flips with no hands. I was in shock. After flipping, he walked backed up the steps, took a knot out of his pocket, and counted his money.

I thought he was my age, but I found out that he was three years older than me. As he counted, I asked, "Yo, where did you get all that money Birdie?"

He smiled and said, "I hustle."

I was impressed. "How can I make that kind of money?"

"Hustle."

I didn't understand what exactly to do. I had to see an example of what he was talking about.

Ghetto Legend Graduate
Cornelius Kinchen

He got up and challenged his boys to a flip contest. They all knew how to do different flips. We watched the entertainment given by my boys from the village. They flipped like they were in the Olympics competition, and were all the same age.

When they left, I practiced a back flip numerous times until I got it. This flip took me two days to get perfect. Then I did a back flip off the mattress to the ground. Ali learned the flip, too. My cousins continued to watch.

Two days later, my boys from the village came to play with us. Every other day they came to the field to see what we were playing. One day Shaun wanted me to hook him up with Crystahl. It was obvious that they liked each other. When Crystahl saw Shaun, she pulled me to the side.

"Neal, is that your friend?"

I said, "Yeah."

She said, "Do he have a girlfriend?"

"I don't know," I said. "But I'll ask for you."

"Yeah, ask him."

So I asked him. He didn't have a girlfriend.

"Shaun, my cousin wants to be your girlfriend," I said.

"Word?" he said, surprised. "A'ight."

I couldn't tell they were together from that day forward. They acted shy toward each other every time he would come around, speaking to each other and blushing.

Ghetto Legend Graduate
Cornelius Kinchen

Bad thing was, Fanny wanted to be with Shaun, too. Crystahl wrote their names in a heart on the gate pole in the parking lot where we played duck-duck goose and freeze tag. When Fanny noticed, she was very upset with Crystahl and held a grudge against Crystahl for the remaining of August. Eventually Shaun stopped coming around to keep any conflict from happening.

The second weekend in August, I wanted to stay over at Bobby's house on Lily Street. Rob's uncle stayed down the street on the corner, but I found that out when I stayed over Bobby's house on that Sunday night. Grandma and my Aunt Branda gave me permission to stay over. We had a blast.

We hung out in the basement of the house, which was better and cleaner than where I lived. It was huge, with a washer, dryer, and a storage room. The floor was waxed, and there was a big television with a living room set. The floor was the most exciting because it was slippery. Bobby, Fanny, Pooka, Mick and I played ice-skating in our socks.

After skating for an hour and a half, the basement started smelling like feet. We didn't care because we were having fun chasing each other around playing tag.

After we finished playing tag, we played hide and seek throughout the whole house. The house had two floors plus the basement. The shower, kitchen, living room, dining room and my aunt's bedroom was located on the first floor. The shower had a Jacuzzi in it with

Ghetto Legend Graduate
Cornelius Kinchen

sliding doors. The children's bedrooms were on the second floor. I was amazed at their house. I wanted to live there for the rest of the summer.

We played until we were sleepy. The next day we took our showers, and my aunt cooked breakfast. The last person in the shower had to mop up the water off the bathroom floor. I was second to shower, so that wasn't my responsibility. Besides, I was the guest.

My aunt left us to watch the house while she went to work. We ate and went outside to play. We rode bikes for two hours. Then we went to Rob's house. While we were headed over there, Bobby said, "Your boy live over here."

"Oh, yeah,' I said. "Show me. Let's go there."
We rode our bikes to Rob's place, which was like a small private housing complex. It was very peaceful and clean.

We all went over and knocked on the door. Rob came to the door.

"Yo, you moved here for the summer?" I asked.

He smiled and said, "Yeah, come in. I'm about to call my cousins over here." We went inside and waited while he made his phone call. He hung up the phone.

"They are on their way over here now," he announced.

Manae and Tanisha arrived fifteen minutes later. I was surprised to see Tanisha because I had not seen her since the school year. They walked in the house and got

Ghetto Legend Graduate
Cornelius Kinchen

comfortable, like they either lived there or had been there before. They went straight to the living room.

I said, "Yo, I'll be back. I'm going to check on the house and take the bike back in the house."

"Yeah, do that," Rob said.

We rode our bikes back and checked on the house. My cousins were about to play Nintendo, so I left my cousins and went back to Rob's house to chill with my girl. Rob opened the door and said, "They are still in the room waiting."

"For what?" I asked. I looked at the television in the living room and he was watching a Spice video. He pointed to the TV.

"Manae wants you to break her virginity."

"What??? Are you serious?"

"Go in the room and look, she's sitting on the bed talking to Tanisha." So
I went to the bedroom.

Lo and behold, there she was waiting to have sex.
Just waiting for *me*.
And ready to get it on.

I was nervous and really didn't have any sexual experience. The first kiss didn't count. I went in the room and closed the door. I was too nervous to do anything sexual with Manae. I didn't know where to start. We just sat on the bed looking into space. An hour later, we still hadn't accomplished anything. We never did

Ghetto Legend Graduate
Cornelius Kinchen

have sex. I ended up leaving and going back to my Aunt's house.

It was the third week in August and it was almost time to go back to school. As usual, I was playing and having fun with my cousins. It was about two thirty in the afternoon, and my mother came to visit. I hadn't seen her in a while. She went to the front porch to talk to Grandma to see how we were doing without her.

Meanwhile, Manae, her cousins and By'ron were on their way down the street to visit. I was nervous. This was the first time my mother and Manae would meet. I was shy, embarrassed, and scared to introduce Manae to my mother because of her drug addiction.

Manae and the girls went on the side of the house jumping rope. I was talking to By'ron, Rob and my cousins on the side of the house near the corner. Grandma mentioned me having a girlfriend to my mother.

I thought everything was fine. My mother sent Red to get me. I heard my mother say, "Tell Neal to come here." I didn't want to go. I ignored my mother and Red. I stayed on the side of the house talking to my boys.

Suddenly, my mother walked around the corner to my surprise. She said, "Neal, do you have a girlfriend?" I hesitated to answer. I said, "Yeah, her name is Manae." Mom smack me so hard, I became dizzy. The smack was so loud, it echoed down the block. I started crying. My boys, Manae and the girls stopped jumping rope and ran down the street screaming like the world was coming to

Ghetto Legend Graduate
Cornelius Kinchen

an end. The girls and boys were racing like they were at an Olympic track meet. They were terrified for their lives.

After the smack, my mother said, "You are not to have a girlfriend!" I went inside the house and went to the kitchen. I cried in embarrassment. When my mother went toward the front porch, five minutes later Rob and By'ron came through the backyard to the kitchen to see if I was all right. They were laughing asking me was the coast clear.

Rob said laughing, "I don't ever want to get slapped like that."

Apparently, By'ron thought it was funny, too. "I felt that smack and I didn't even get hit."

I said crying with my head down, "It's not funny. It's embarrassing to get smacked in front of my girlfriend."

They heard the front screen door open. They jumped off the back porch running out of the backyard for safety. Five minutes later they returned to the kitchen convincing me to cheer up. After laughing at them for running like punks out the backyard, I cheered up a little. After that experience, I could care less about Manae. That was the end of our relationship.

A week later, it was time to go school shopping. I had hoped to get new clothing, a pair fresh sneakers and a winter coat. I really liked army pants. I wanted all colors army fatigue, black, green, khaki, navy blue and black at

Ghetto Legend Graduate
Cornelius Kinchen

twenty-five dollars apiece. I knew I wasn't able to afford all colors based on the money situation with my father. That Sunday afternoon, he had to stretch the money for all four of us.

Esha and I went walking downtown together to buy school clothes with the hundred and fifty dollars apiece. We walked up and down Main Street for two hours, looking for the clothes we wanted before the stores closed. Esha was responsible for the money. We shopped and shopped to stretch the money buying school clothing and school necessities.

We finished shopping and headed home. It was getting a little cool outside. While we were walking up Fair Street, I got in a playful mood, and started this dangerous game called "dance-dance and celebrate." I started this game at School 6 with my classmates. The object of the game was to walk behind a person and clip their feet by stepping on the backs of them or clipping them from the side, and the celebration was that person falling to their knees and me laughing. It was fun while it lasted.

Esha walked fast to keep me from making her celebrate. When we got near the church, I walked behind her and she had no idea I plotted to make her dance. She was heavier than me, and twice the weight. As she walked fast, I walked behind her and said, "Dance-dance." As she fell to her knees in disbelief, I said, "Celebrate." She was on her knees laughing and crying at

Ghetto Legend Graduate
Cornelius Kinchen

the same time saying, "I'm going to get you. Why you do that." I ran in the street to get away from her before she got up. I laughed so hard my stomach began to hurt and tears came out my eyes.

When she got up, she tried to catch me to beat my back up. I was too fast for her. Every time she got close enough to catch me I would juke-move her and run. She still had tears in her eyes saying, "Come here." Then half way up the street, I ran in the house and left her on the side of the house.

I went downstairs in the basement where my father was. I went near his bed and near his important items in the corner. Esha was on her way downstairs. As soon as she got downstairs, she said, "Dad, Neal clipped me down the street." She chased me around his bed for at least four minutes. Her face was ashy from the tears on her cheeks.

"Stop, bullsh*ting, now!" Dad said. "Stop before I whoop y'all, you need to stop playing so much. It ain't no fun when you get hurt, now is it?" So we stopped. Esha put the bags down and cleaned her face. She showed my father the school stuff. He approved of what we bought, and then we got ready for school.

Ghetto Legend Graduate
Cornelius Kinchen

Seventh grade

September 1995, I was promoted to Mrs. Rollins, 5'5, light skin, hazel-brown eyes, golden-brown hair, strictly-intelligent, a no nonsense tolerance lady taught 7.1 gifted and talented class. I was on my best behavior. I didn't want to get on Mrs. Rollins bad side because she would suspend a kid for any little thing. You could make a comment in her class without permission and she would suspend you. That's how strict she was and I didn't like that.

I wanted to live with Red and my Aunt Barbara that semester. I let her know how I felt, and she made a deal with me.

"Neal, be good for two marking periods, and I'll ask your grandmother to transfer you to School 30 for a new setting and you could live with us. How does that sound?"

I agreed.

I did all my work and got C's on my report card the first marking period. This was passing, but I had a problem with the students trying to provoke me. I wanted to get A's and B's. I felt I was going to get in to trouble, so I wanted and asked for change. Besides, I didn't like living at home.

While living in the basement, my uncle was having church and Bible class in the house periodically to see if it would work out. I know it was getting too cold to

Ghetto Legend Graduate
Cornelius Kinchen

be in Mrs. Joe-sefina's garage churching. Also, my Uncle Gilly had my cousins and me helping on Redwood Avenue with remodeling the garage to a church building. I became tired of helping to build the church for free, and moving the sound equipment to and from the Masonic Temple to worship over a night club every Sunday morning. I couldn't take working long hours during the weekdays and weekends anymore. I longed for the day we moved in our new church permanently. I became miserable living in the basement of my Grandma's house and working so hard. I was sure my cousins felt the same way.

    We finally finished remodeling the church building and moved in toward the end of 1995, just after the beginning of winter. Different churches were invited to the grand opening. Many different churches form Paterson supported Judah Deliverance Temple during its first year. Our church was small compared to other churches in Paterson, however, it was a beautiful edifice, and a nice-sized church that couldn't hold over one hundred and twenty-five people. Some churches were invited at different times during the year to support the church. Time went on and we went in the New Year praising God for our new building.

    Almost two months after we moved in, the church was doing great. It was also close to the end of the second marking period. My cousin Quentin transferred to School 6, unbeknown to me.

Ghetto Legend Graduate
Cornelius Kinchen

On a spring-like day, I went to lunch and ate, then I went to the playground to chill with my boyz. Quentin came up to me.

He caught me off guard. I said, "What up? You go here now?"

"Yeah," he said. "I heard you had beef with some boys up here."

"Yeah. You're my cousin because you can sense beef with me."

"Show them to me."

Mind you, the eighth-grade all-boyz class tried to bully me and my boyz. We never allowed it. But when they caught us alone at the bathroom, they really tried to jump us, and we did the same to their class.

By'ron, Rob, Frank, Quentin and I walked over to the all-boys class on the opposite side of the playground. They were against the gate watching us come over to them. We approached them like little gangsters.

"Cousin, which one tried to chump you?" Quentin asked.

"This boy, Randon," I said, pointing him out. He was the ringleader of their class gang. Randon didn't like the fact that I had heart to talk tough and disrespect him. Every chance he had alone with me, he would threaten me. I just continued disrespecting him until he gave me respect.

Quentin said, "Air him out." I immediately punched Randon with a three piece: one to the chin and

Ghetto Legend Graduate
Cornelius Kinchen

two to the chest. I didn't know he had asthma. He went down grabbing his chest. His boys watched and did nothing. We walked away and he went to the nurse for treatment. From that point, Randon and his boys didn't bother my crew for the rest of the school year. This was my way of taking respect and it felt good.

I didn't get into trouble; he never snitched. I lucked up. If he had snitched, I would have been suspended and he would have been obligated to press charges against me. This would have ruined my chance to transfer to School 30.

After school, Rob said, "Let's go to my house."

I said, "Where at, on Lily Street?"

"No, I moved up the street from School 6 to my aunt's house." So By'ron, Rob, and I walked up the street. When we got there, we went into his back yard. We put our book bags down, and then went inside. Rob introduced By'ron and me to his aunt. Then we went back out to the yard. Rob and By'ron began to slap-box and wrestle in the dirt. I watched for at least two three-minute rounds. They slapped-boxed and got dirty. While By'ron caught his breath, Rob and I slapped boxed for two three-minute rounds. We rotated for at least one to two hours. Then I went home, ate, and did homework. When I was done, I got ready for school.

The next day, we went to school. By'ron and Allen had beef. Allen was the tallest geek in the class that hung out with Clark, Joaquin and Joe-sef. By'ron

Ghetto Legend Graduate
Cornelius Kinchen

knocked his glasses off his face. Obviously, Allen didn't like that.

Therefore, they fought twice that day, once in the playground before class started, and again at lunchtime. I couldn't believe it; Allen had heart to fight By'ron. Allen was upset and said, "I will not fight you in class because I don't want to get suspended." He decided to fight By'ron during lunchtime, again. He whooped By'ron's ass both times. I was in disbelief. By'ron disappointed all of his crew. We respected Allen for his heart, and became neutrally cool with him. Rob and I picked on By'ron for getting his ass whooped by a tall nerd.

Throughout the school day, By'ron's ass being kicked was the talk of the class. The girls teased him, too. At the end of the school day, the three of us went to Rob's house for more slap boxing in the backyard and boxed until we were tired. Finally, we took a break. Rob brought us some ice-cold water. After we drank the water, it was time to walk home. By'ron and I always walked home together.

When I got home, it was time to do homework again. I had no one to help me with my homework. My father dropped out of elementary school and worked all his life. My mother completed high school in Georgia, but she wasn't around to help. My sisters were always out hanging with their friends.

Ghetto Legend Graduate
Cornelius Kinchen

I decided to work on my assignment alone. I read the directions and followed whatever example was available. What I didn't understand, I brought to my teacher's attention in class. Once she explained it in detail, I was able to understand the material.

Ghetto Legend Graduate
Cornelius Kinchen

New beginning

It was the beginning of the third marking period, time for a change of scenery. Together, Aunt Barbara and I asked Grandma if I could come and live with her and transfer to School 30.

"This is a great opportunity for him to prove himself academically and behavior wise." Barbara said. "Plus he will share a room with Red."

Grandma looked thoughtful. "Well, can you handle an extra child financial, B?" she asked.

"With me and Lawson working, yeah, we could handle it. Neal is a good and smart boy. He needs this change because he could start fresh at a new school."

Grandma sighed heavily. "If you can handle it, go for it. Neal, listen right now," she said to me, "one bad report, and you are coming right back here to One Fifty-six Straight Street. One bad report, do you hear me?"

I smiled and said, "Yes, Grandma, I won't let you down. I promise. I'll earn good grades in school." I was excited! This was a chance for me to do something new.

I walked out of Grandma's room with a big smile on my face, went downstairs and packed the little bit of clothes I did have. Dad was okay with the decision. My mother appreciated the decision made. It was beneficial to my life and my education.

Red and I were excited. It was like we were going to be brothers. They welcomed me with open arms. I

Ghetto Legend Graduate
Cornelius Kinchen

stayed my last night at Grandma's house. The next day, Aunt Barbara took me to School 6 to begin the process of transferring me to School 30. We went to the main office and got all my paper work and medical records. Immediately after, Uncle Lawson drove us to School 30.

When I got there, I looked around the building, anticipating a warm welcome from staff and students. The walls had Martin Luther King, Jr.'s picture on them, along with colorful animals and jungle paintings in the hallways. It was brand new and clean. I really liked it.

In the main office, the administrative staff finished my transfer. The secretary looked at me and smiled.

"Welcome to your new school," she said, giving me my class schedule.

"Thank you," I said, grinning broadly.

My first class was English. Finding my way around this school would take some getting used to. I happened to see Red while I was looking for my class. "What's up, Red?" I said. "Can you show me where these rooms are?" I handed him my schedule.

He looked at it. "All right, come on." He led me down the hall, and as we were walking, he introduced me to his boys, who welcomed me like family. When we reached the door of my first class, the bell rang.

"Yo, I gotta go to class, I'm late," Red said. "If you get lost, just follow the numbers." He handed my schedule back to me.

Ghetto Legend Graduate
Cornelius Kinchen

I nodded my head. "All right, Red." He walked down the hall back in the direction we had just come.

I got through my first class with no problem. The next class was math. When I entered the class, I saw a young, pretty teacher giving instruction to over thirty students. I had to find somewhere to sit. All the students watched me like I was a star, especially the girls. There were more girls than boys in the class. They melted when they saw me. Before I knew it, I was the talk of the school for the whole year.

I ignored the talk and crushes from the girls. I focused on my academic goal and the promises I made to Grandma. I knew if I allowed myself to be distracted by the girls, I would not accomplish my academic goals, and I would have been on my way back home. My studies became my number one priority.

During recess, I hung out with Red and his boys. We played basketball on the playground. The boys were amazed at my basketball talent. They argued over having me on their team. The girls came over and watched. They have never seen this side of me before. Come to think of it, before I came to this school, they had never seen *me* before.

No doubt, I loved the attention, but I couldn't feed in to the nonsense. I had too much at stake. The attention I received from the girls was like therapy on the inside, but there was no way I would let them distract me from reaching my goals.

Ghetto Legend Graduate
Cornelius Kinchen

It was time to go home. Red and I picked up the twins (our sisters) from the lower grades. We all walked home together. When we got home, we had to do our homework before we could play. If Red or the twins had trouble with their assignment, I helped them.

Aunt Barbara cooked a healthy meal for us. After we ate, we drove to Grandma's house to visit. We made a grand entrance after piling out of that black Oldsmobile. I was the first one out.

"Hi, Grandma," I said.

"How do you like your change?" she asked.

I said, "I like it a lot."

"Are you happy?"

"Yes, Grandma, I really like everything about the school." While my cousins, my aunt and uncle spoke to her, I went in the house to see my father and sisters. Dad was in the basement, listening to oldies and writing in his Pick-It book. I said, "What up, Dad?"

"Hey," he said, with a Gumby smile. He had no teeth.

"Dad, do you have a dollar?" He took his wallet out and picked through his wallet in search of a dollar: and gave me two dollars.

"Thanks," I said, and went back upstairs.

I went out the front and to the store. When I got to the store, my grandfather was there bagging and carrying grocery for the customers. He was surprised to see me.

Ghetto Legend Graduate
Cornelius Kinchen

"Muhammad Ali, Mike Tyson," he said. For some reason, he always said that to me whenever he saw me. He would also put his dukes up and say "right-left" for me to punch them. I never could understand it at the time. While he worked, he would constantly say the two names. He explained to me that they were the best fighters in the history of boxing.

"If a man don't work, a man don't eat." I read this phrase in the Bible on numerous occasions, heard it at church in Sunday school, and Grandma instilled this idea in my mentality. To hear this from my grandfather, a man that didn't go to church, got drunk, and smoked cigars, was amazing. Considering the fact that he was a war hero that had helped to build much of what Paterson is today, next to Dad, he was a great male mentor.

He taught me how to hustle money legally at the supermarket. We had a tip cup and he told me to bag the groceries. He said, "Work from the time the store opens until the store closes." By the end of the night, I had lots of change that I cashed into dollars. I was excited to be making money. Now, I could save money and buy things I wanted.

"You have to come every day and be reliable," Grandpa said.

Learning how to make money legitimately instilled a sense of dignity and pride in me. My grandfather even began to share war stories with me, which kept me interested. My father didn't ever talk to

Ghetto Legend Graduate
Cornelius Kinchen

me about things, but he always disciplined me when I got out of line. Hearing the war stories from Grandpa made me feel that he cared for me in the same way a real father would. Not that my dad didn't care about me, I was sure he did, but with Grandpa it was different.

    I stayed at the supermarket for at least an hour, making some money for school the next day. Then it was time for me to leave, my new family was more than likely waiting for me so we could go home together. When I got back to Grandma's house, they were saying their good-byes to her, so I said mine as well, and said that I would see her tomorrow.

    "All right, Neal," she said. Then we got into the Olds and headed home.

    We started getting ready for bed soon after we got there. While the twins and Travis ate noodles at the kitchen table, Red and I took our showers, and then ate the rest of the chocolate chip cookies. Then we watched TV for a little while, and went to bed afterwards.

Ghetto Legend Graduate
Cornelius Kinchen

New people; new drama

Ahhh, my second day of school was here! I was excited. I woke up with a smile on my face. I was happy to be in a new environment surrounded by love. Red and I got up and got dressed, ate breakfast, then headed out. We went to meet our boys near the store by the projects. When we met, there were about twenty-five boys. At first, I was nervous because I didn't know Red boys were that deep. Red introduced me all around.

"Yo, this cousin Neal from School 6." They all gave me dap and said their names.

We walked to school. It was comfortable and secure. At least, I felt safe and sure; everybody else did, too. When I got to school that day, the girls were jumping rope. We watched for a little while, and then went inside when the bell rang.

We went to our lockers on the second floor to get prepared for first period. In between periods, I was able to get books for my next class. I enjoyed the freedom. After I got my books, I went to homeroom for attendance. The girls all tried to talk to me. It was like a news conference interview. The girls treated me like a celebrity. They were my fans and they wanted my autograph. I answered some of their questions in a shy and polite manner with a smile. I basked in the attention, which kept my mind off my mother's addiction.

Ghetto Legend Graduate
Cornelius Kinchen

My self-esteem was high. This was spiritual healing. Being around my boys also helped, but they respected me off the strength of Red. But there were two haters who didn't like me, their names were Rich and John, and were the two ugliest boys in the school. They were jealous of me for being intelligent, focused and new to the school. They would sit back, watch, and plot in hate of ways to embarrass me in public.

One day, Rich, dark-blue, pink lips, from the projects couldn't take my publicity anymore. The bell had just rung, and it was time to travel to third period math class. Rich stopped me in the hallway. He grabbed my shirt with both hands and threw me against the lockers. I wondered where this hostility came from and who motivated him to do such a thing. I had an idea (John).

When he grabbed me and threw me against the locker, I immediately thought, *don't retaliate, you're a new student. But if he hits you in the face, defend yourself.*

Holding me against the lockers, he said, "You think you're tough, don't you?"

I just looked at him and said, "What are you doing? What's your problem, Rich?" He had no explanation, so he let me go and I was late for class.

When I got to math class, almost all the seats were taken. Ms. Jackson pointed to an empty seat next to one of the most popular girls in school. Her name was

Ghetto Legend Graduate
Cornelius Kinchen

Lisa. She was popular because she was bi-racial, and because she had every pair of Jordan sneakers that came out. I took my book bag off and sat down. I enjoyed Ms. Jackson's class because she was eye candy. All the boys in the class enjoyed the lesson and paid close attention to her.

Lisa and Schoharie competed on the Jordan sneaker level. They purchased their sneakers before anybody else in the entire school could. I couldn't understand how their parents afford one-hundred and fifty dollar sneakers. Toward the end of the school year, I figured out that they were spoiled only child. They were well dressed. From my parents, and my aunt and uncle, I understood that bills were paid first. Whatever was left, we shared as allowances amongst the five of us.

I never hated on their financial situation. I remained cool and friendly with them. I enjoyed their company. I thought to myself, one day I will be able to afford Jordan sneakers. As I talked and hung with them, I got to know them, and they were humble like me. They never acted like they were better than any student. They were just fresh to death every day.

The next day, during lunch Atiya and I hooked up on a music level. I loved doing beats and she enjoyed rapping. While I did beats on the lunch table, she put her lyrics down, entertaining the rest of the seventh grade classes. We sat in the corner drawing attention from the eighth graders and some of the sixth graders. We could have charged them admission, if I was thinking on an entrepreneurial level. They would have paid, too.

Ghetto Legend Graduate
Cornelius Kinchen

End of 7th grade

Months passed, and before I knew it, the end of the school year was near. I could smell a great summer with my new family. I did well in the third marking period, passing all my classes. I was proud of myself, and my aunt, my uncle, and my grandmother were also proud. I felt motivated and rewarded for my efforts. I wanted to do more and accomplish more to continue feeling that way.

I was addicted to learning. It was hard to understand or even explain. It was a high that I could never get enough of. I had to believe in my abilities to achieve the goals that I had set for myself. Besides, if I didn't, who would?

There was talk in my new home about planning a two-week trip to the Southern states. Aunt Barbara's sisters lived down south, and she hadn't seen them in over ten years. I was excited about the plan. I wanted to go, and my cousins wanted me to go, but I had to ask Grandma. I felt this would be the perfect time to travel and get out of New Jersey. Plus, I wanted to experience a different environment. I wanted to experience the African American history of the southern states.

Ghetto Legend Graduate
Cornelius Kinchen

The last day of school, it rained outside. During lunch recess, everybody came together and hung out in the lunchroom for more entertainment. Atiya and I had set it off. I gave her a hot beat and she capitalized with more than sixteen bars. When we stopped, everybody was excited and surprised at the skills we had. I felt like we were partners. I needed her rhymes and she needed my beats.

By the time we left school, the rain had stopped, and the sun began to dry the streets. After dinner, Red and I walked at least eight or nine miles to Grandma's house. We didn't feel like taking the bus, which ran every hour. We were ready to go, and walking was not a big deal since it was warm out outside. I wanted to show Grandma my report card, proving that I passed to the eighth grade and ask her could I travel south.

Auntie had given us some money, so we stopped by the store and bought some juice for the long walk. We walked so long and so far, it felt like we were already on our way to South Carolina.

When we got to Grandma's house, she was cooking dinner. "Hey, Grandma" I said.

"Do you see any horses in here?" she said. "It's either 'hi' or 'hello.' Now, try it again."

I took a deep breath, and was careful not to let it out as an exasperated sigh. "Hello Grandma, how are you?"

She smiled, "Fine, thank you."

Ghetto Legend Graduate
Cornelius Kinchen

Without preamble, I said, "I got promoted and my grades are good."

"I am proud of you," she said, still smiling, "and I know you're smart. You have a lot of common sense."

I showed her my report card. She looked it over carefully, taking her time to notice my good grades. "Keep up the good work."

It was like an encouraging word and a threat all at the same time.

All my cousins came over to hang out. They all walked in and out the kitchen to say hello to Grandma. I was asked to go to the store to get a ginger ale for Grandma, a cola, and two devil dog cakes for my Aunt Doris. Red and I walked to the grocery store. I was allowed to keep the change from the five-dollar bill, after I got the soda and snacks. The change was two dollars: Red and I split the change a dollar apiece.

We were still thirsty from the walk we took, so we bought juice and some chips to go with it. We went back to Grandma's house and dropped off the snacks and soda. Then we went down the street to visit Ali.

There is a tree that we always run from a distance to jump and dunk on. As I got closer to his house, I ran and dunked on the tree. Ali got up from his porch and came up the street to do the same thing.

Game on! This meant competition. So I attempted a three-sixty dunk on the tree about six times a day. I started to get dizzy after the fifth time and I took a juice

Ghetto Legend Graduate
Cornelius Kinchen

break to get some energy. The sixth time I did it, it was perfect! After I dunked, I hung on the tree. Ali was still trying. I was determined to get a perfect three-sixty, and I did it. Ali continued to practice the three-sixty. I believed he would eventually learn how to do it.

While I was taking my break, I came up with an idea.

"Ali, let's play the game in front of your house."

Red agreed. "Yeah, let's play some real basketball. Ali, get your basketball court."

"Okay," said Ali. "Come and help me carry it from the backyard."

We went through Ali's house to get to his backyard to open the gate. When we went in, his little dog started barking and wouldn't stop. Paying no attention to the dog, we went into the backyard, got the court, and went back to the front of his Aunt China's house.

We played a warm-up game to twenty-one points (the first player to score twenty-one points was the winner). We played at least two games. Then I played one-on-one with Red and Ali, until I got tired of winning.

Kevin, Bobby, Pooka, and Mick came down the street to play basketball, too. I won the last twenty-one, and the winner usually started a new game. I started a new 21 once we had more players. The challenge was greater and more fun. After I won, we played again. Then we played two on two tournaments, and then took a water

Ghetto Legend Graduate
Cornelius Kinchen

break. Ali went inside, bought out a jug of water and cups for everyone. We sat in front of China's house, and drank ice-cold water. We talked and bragged about the game we played and how nice we were. Ali and I were always on teams. We were a great team together; moreover, we always won against opponents.

After we cooled off and the sun went down, we went up the street. We hung out on the corner of Grandma's house. My sisters brought the radio outside to dance on the corner. The adults in the family were bringing chairs on the porch to enjoy the weather and talk for a while.

My sisters and cousins created and choreographed dances while the family and neighbors watched. Then when they had gotten it down packed, they performed the new dances for the public to see. It was interesting how they memorized the dances and performed on an almost-professional level.

After they were finished, we all went down the street to hang out. We sat under the train tracks. We tried to smoke, using brown paper and dry leaves. We stuffed the dry leaves in the brown paper and rolled it. Then we lit up and tried to smoke it. The paper was burning fast and we didn't know what we were doing. We were just copying what the adults did. I don't know what the hell we were thinking to do something so stupid. All I know, my cousins and I almost coughed up a lung. Every since that experience, I didn't try that crap again. After that, everyone had a headache that day.

It was getting dark, and everyone was about to go home. I went home with my Aunt, Uncle, and Red.

The next day I brought my clothes to Grandma's house to stay for the summer. I put my stuff in the basement, and saw that Dad had bought another foldout bed. It was like I wasn't missed at all, or like I had never left. After I settled in, I went down the street to Ali's house. As we sat on his porch, a pretty girl he knew from school walked past.

"Hi, Adali," she said, (his real name) and walked over to his porch to talk to him. While they talked, I stared at her.

Ali introduced us. "Zamia," he said, "this is Neal. Neal, this is Zamia."

"What's up?" I was still staring.

"Hi," she said, smiling. She really liked Ali. I wanted to go with her, but Ali was my best friend on the block. I had to give him respect and let him get his flirt on. After a while, it was time for her to leave, so I walked with them up the street to the corner. Ali walked with her past Grandma's house and to the chicken store.

By the time Ali came back, a light rain had started. Red met up with us as we walked down the street.

"Yo, let's get Goya to play two-on-two football," he suggested.

Ghetto Legend Graduate
Cornelius Kinchen

Ali and I agreed, so we went to Goya's house. This was my first time going inside. The house was big and the hallways were clean. We had to climb to the third floor. Ali knocked on the apartment door and Goya's mother answered it. She said something in Spanish to Ali, and he responded. Goya came out smiling.

I spoke up. "Yo, were going to play two-on-two in football. Me and Ali on teams and you and Red."

He said, "Yeah." So we went outside and played football up and down the street in the rain. The first to score seven touchdown points was the winner.

Here's how it played out.

It was tied at six to six, Goya and Red had fourth down. Ali and I played defense very well. Red was at quarterback and Goya played wide receiver. Red said, "Go!" Goya ran as fast as he could, and Red threw the ball. While I counted, we doubled teamed Goya so he wouldn't score the winning touchdown. It worked. I intercepted, and Ali blocked while I ran the ball to our touchdown for the winning score. We won seven to six.

After the game, we went to Ali's house and Goya went home. We played video games for hours. We took turns until the rain stopped and the sun came out, and then went back outside. Then we went under the train tracks and played baseball for a while. Goya came back outside to play. Then we decided to go in the parking lot to play baseball.

Ghetto Legend Graduate
Cornelius Kinchen

    My cousins walked down the street, and we took all of the baseball equipment to the parking lot. Before we played baseball, we wrestled in two dumpsters full of cardboard. We jumped back and forth between the dumpsters. After we were tired of that, we played baseball. We had a contest to see who could hit a ball onto the roof of the Telephone Company building. Goya was the first to hit the ball on the roof of the building. He hit a fastball from Ali, and we were all flabbergasted. I didn't hit the ball on the roof until the third or fourth game played that summer. Red and Ali never hit the ball in a live game on the roof of the phone company.

    After that great homerun, the game was over. We sat and talked about it in the parking lot for at least a half-hour. Then we went into the field to the jungle. We played tag for at least an hour and a half. Then once we got tired of playing tag, we messed with Goya neighbor's dogs in his backyard. We didn't care: his neighbors were at work. They were in a caged gate barking while we played. We gave them something to bark about.

    After we did that, we all threw rocks at the windows of a passing train. Then, we went in the house for a dinner of stewed chicken and rice. The kids sat at the kitchen table and ate, while the adults sat in the dining room.

    After dinner, we all went back outside to catch lightning bugs. There wasn't any in the field next to Grandma's house, so we went back in the front of the

Ghetto Legend Graduate
Cornelius Kinchen

house. Grandma and aunts were sitting on the porch. We played around the house and in the backyard.

Suddenly, Red said, "Yo, it's a party up the street, let's go up there!" Deanna's sister, Erica, was having a party. Red and I walked up the street to see if the party was popping. We walked in and Deanna was standing at the door.

"What's up, Deanna?"

"What's up, Neal?" She let us in. There were green lights and balloons on the wall and in the air. There were girls dancing, and this one girl in particular that I noticed was pretty. I wanted her as my girlfriend.

I followed Deanna into the kitchen. "Deanna, who is that light-skinned girl?" I asked.

"That's my aunt," she replied.

"Let me holler at you in the hall." We walked out the door and into the hallway.

"That's your Aunt and y'all is the same age?"

"Yeah, why?"

"Yo, can you hook me up with her?" I just had to get to know her.

"All right…when I go back inside I will talk to her."

We went back inside and Deanna pulled her to the kitchen and talked to her for me. Then they walked back into the living room. The music was going and I was feeling the vibe. The girl's name was Tiana. She started dancing, and I watched her for little while until I built up

Ghetto Legend Graduate
Cornelius Kinchen

enough courage to dance with her. After the dance, I got her phone number.

After the party, we hung out on the porch all hugged up until her sister came to pick her up. Red and Deanna were between talking in the hallway and the porch, then back again.

Tiana and I hooked up fast because it was love at first sight. We spent time on the porch the first night like we were in love. Her sister arrived forty minutes later. Her sister was cool with us being hugged up. Tiana definitely gave her older sister respect. Tiana immediately moved away from me.

"That's my sister," she said. "You have my number, so call me."

"All right, I will call you later," I said.

Red and Deanna came outside to the porch and hugged. Red walked down the steps. Then we walked down the street laughing.

"Yo, I got her number!"

"Whose number?"

"Tiana, Deanna's aunt, fool!"

"Oh, yeah? Well, I got Deanna's number."

"We have new girls, bruh." We grinned like a couple of idiots.

When we got back to Grandma's house, it was time for Red to leave, so I went inside. I helped bring the chairs inside. After I was done with that, I went to use the phone. The area code was 201. I didn't care about the phone bill. I made the call to talk to my new girl.

Ghetto Legend Graduate
Cornelius Kinchen

New girlfriend

Her mother answered the phone.
I said, "Hello, may I speak to Tiana?"
She asked me to hold on.

I was excited when Tiana came to the phone. We talked and talked getting to know each other. I learned that we liked the same colors, we loved to party, liked the same foods, and not to mention, each other. The phone conversation went smooth. By 3:43 in the morning, we were boyfriend and girlfriend. We even made plans to see each other on weekends. She said, "I'm going to stay over Deanna's on Friday and Saturday night. I became excited. I couldn't wait to spend more time with her.

All week we talked on the phone to the early morning hours. Sometimes we even we fell asleep on the phone. I opened up to her like no other female. She listened and loved me for me. I became more vulnerable and sincere to love her. I fell deeply in love with her personality and her open heart. This was my first real girlfriend.

The weekend arrived. I had gotten twenty dollars from my father. I bought a Bulls practice jersey to play basketball in. I also put my name on the back with the number forty-four on it. I wanted to impress Tiana with my new jersey.

Tiana came over after she went to Friday night seven o'clock church service. Tiana and Deanna went to

Ghetto Legend Graduate
Cornelius Kinchen

church faithfully on Fridays and Sunday. I really loved that about her. She had a wonderful spirit, and she got to know me and to help me deal with the pain I went through in my life. I was all out in love.

After church, we met them up the street at Deanna's house. They left church before dismissal to be with us. We hung out on the porch. So when church dismissed, her parents would drop off Tiana's sister, and Red and I would walk next door to Bianca's house to chill and talk to her. By that time, her parents were on their way home.

Bianca was five years older than us and was dating Deanna's older brother, Chris. She waited for Chris to come from church, too. They were wild. They got drunk and high, and partied until they were tired. We hung out with them, but never did what they did. We just hung out all hugged up, and listened to slow jams in their basement.

Tiana and I enjoyed each other's company. It was 3:21 in the morning and time for me to go down the street, before I got locked out of the house. I didn't want to leave, but it was what it was.

"Red, I'm out," I said. "I'm going down the street." He hugged Deanna and we left. We walked down the street, and when we got to the porch, the door was locked.

We banged on the door and kicked the door. After five minutes, Uncle Gilly opened the door.

Ghetto Legend Graduate
Cornelius Kinchen

"It's late! Where are y'all coming from?" He glared at us.

"From up the street, Chris' house."

He stepped back to let us in. "Y'all know better than to hang out this late. Y'all probably was with some girls." We smiled and went upstairs to the third floor.

When we got upstairs it smelled like feet in the hallway. We turned on the lights and woke up Bobby, Pooka and Mick.

I said, "Yo, who have the channel on Spice?" We talked and joked for a little while about the television being on the nasty channel. Then Red turned the lights off, turned the channel and took his socks off.

"Yo, I will see y'all tomorrow," I said, then went downstairs to the basement. The light was on in the basement hallway, but the basement was dark with only two dim night-lights on. My father was at work and my sisters were asleep. I just took my clothes off and went to sleep.

The next day, my father came in from work and woke my brother and me up for breakfast. He brought us each a buttered roll with jelly. We ate and watched cartoons for a little while until wrestling came on. Then I watched Soul Train to see the girls and who was performing.

After Soul Train went off, I went upstairs to take a shower. Usually, there would be a waiting line to take a shower because there were so many people living in the

Ghetto Legend Graduate
Cornelius Kinchen

house. The first person to go in the shower enjoyed a hot shower. The last person tortured by the cold shower water.

I didn't race my family to the shower. Nor, did I get tortured by cold shower water. I waited until everybody took their shower that morning and waited for the hot water to come back. Nobody rushed me out the bathroom once I got in there.

After I showered, I got dressed and went outside to chill. Kevin and my cousins had come over to hang out. He had some fresh new cross trainers on his feet.

"What's up?" I said. "When did you buy those sneakers? They are dope."

He said, "I got them from downtown. My mother bought them for me." Changing the subject, he said, "Yo, I met this girl, and she's from Hackensack."

"Word? A'ight, let's play ball." We went up the street by Mighty's house where the basketball court was. Mighty was a tall thug with a missing tooth, who was the same age as my sisters. We went up the street to ball on the basketball court he built on the tree. The entire crew from Auburn Street came to ball on Fair Street.

I put my Bulls jersey on to show off. The jersey was reversible too, and my name was on the Red side. My cousins and I played a couple of games of twenty-one. Then before I knew, the crew from Auburn Street called Wood-Chuck. He was two years older than me. He

Ghetto Legend Graduate
Cornelius Kinchen

thought he was going to intimidate me on the court. Little did he know that I had an A-game for people like him.

We started a game of five on five. They shot for first possession and missed. From the beginning, I felt the game was going to go in our favor. I shot the first ball and made it from far. It counted for two. Wood-Chuck was trying to play defense on me throughout the game, however I scored more points than he did to help my team win.

After the game, he was talking slick and wanted to fight me. He wanted a rematch. I just shot the ball around while my cousins walked down the street to get some water. The crew from Auburn Street walked up the street, while Wood-Chuck hated on my game.

"You are a punk and you can't fight," he taunted, trying to provoke me.

"You are too old for me," I said. "I got somebody for you."

"Who? Go get them," "I will..."

Before he could finish his sentence, I cut him off and said, "My cousin, Quinton." He froze for a moment.

"Go get himmmm."

"You don't want to fight him." Then he started walking up the street slowly talking junk to me. I continued to shoot.

I was tired of shooting the ball, so I walked down the street to get something to drink. I thought I'd go to Ali's house. When I got there, I bought a coconut icee

Ghetto Legend Graduate
Cornelius Kinchen

and hung out in front of his house talking to him for a little while. He noticed my Bulls jersey and thought it was fresh. He couldn't talk too long, because he was on his way to a baseball game. He was the starting pitcher. Red played baseball, too. I wondered if they played each other.

I bit into my ice with my front teeth. He said, "How do you do that? That doesn't hurt or make your teeth cold?"

"It feels good to bite ice with my teeth." It seem like every time I bit the ice it annoyed and interest some of my friends. It was something they couldn't do.

Ali left for his game, and I walked up the street. I went in my backyard to chill with my cousins. The little cousins were climbing the pear tree to get that hard fruit to eat. I let them figure that out on their own. After they bit into the pears, they threw them away.

After I finished my icee, I went on the side of the house to play whiffle ball with my cousins. We played for a little while until the ball was smacked over Mrs. Joe-sefine's gate.

Oh, God, I thought.

My cousins hated to get a ball from over her gate, because she had four dogs to keep people from entering her yard. Ali and I were the brave ones and we usually got the balls that got thrown or knocked over. Everybody wanted to play, but no one else attempted to go over the gate. If Ali and I didn't go over the gate we wouldn't

Ghetto Legend Graduate
Cornelius Kinchen

have had a ball to play with. This time Ali was at his game. I didn't feel like climbing over the gate, so I just left the ball over there. I wasn't the one who hit the ball over the gate anyway.

Red and I left the backyard, and walked up the street to see our girlfriends. Being around Tiana was exciting for me. She noticed my jersey and smiled, so I smiled back. Red hugged his girl. While we stood there, Deanna's mother came up the street with groceries in her hands. She smiled at us.

"What's with the love connection?" she said, and the girls laughed aloud.

Red and I offered to help with the bags, for which she was grateful. She gave us the bags and we carried them into the house.

"You guys are gentlemen," she said. "Thank you."

We continued to hang out on the porch and enjoy each other's company. I noticed my cousins were down the street on the corner hanging out. It was crowded on Grandma's corner.

Deanna's little brother came outside, I always bothered him to make him tougher. We wrestled until he cried. Then I stopped. He came outside and ran off the porch. He thought I was going to play wrestle and make him tough. One time, I punched him in the chicken wing and made him cry. I was just playing around. Years later,

Ghetto Legend Graduate
Cornelius Kinchen

he told me about how much it bothered him, and I apologized. I felt bad that it bothered him all that time. When he ran off the porch, I started laughing.

"Yo, I'm chilling,'" I said. "I'm not going to bother you."

"You be bothering my little brother?" Deanna said. "Don't be bothering him, Neal." Tiana punched me on my arm. "Don't be bothering my nephew."

"All right," I said. He then went next door to his uncle's house with a message from his mother. When he came back, he was nervous.

Tiana and Deanna said, "Come on, Jamal, he's not going to bother you anymore."

Jamal looked at me, doubtful.

"Come on, I promise, I won't bother you anymore," I said.

The promise seemed to make him feel better. He walked up the steps into the house.

I hugged up with Tiana, and Red hugged up with Deanna. Tiana loved my Bulls jersey and she wanted to borrow it. I was so happy being with her, I was willing to give her anything.

"I'll let you hold it by the end of the summer. That okay?"

"Okay, Neal, that's cool."

Chris and his boyz pulled up in front of the house. I became cool with his boyz after a few tough-man battles in play-fighting and wrestling. We would test each

Ghetto Legend Graduate
Cornelius Kinchen

other's strength in an effort to get tougher. It was all fun and games to us as boyz to play rough. At the end of the battles, we sat on the curb to relax and talk and laugh about it.

After the battle, I chilled with Tiana in front of the house. She admired my toughness. I hugged her with sweat dripping from my forehead. She enjoyed it. Then she went and bought me a cold glass of water and a napkin for my sweat.

Later that night, By'ron and Rob came by to pay me a visit. I came outside, and to my surprise they tried to initiate me. They wanted to see if I was the same tough kid from School 6. They began jumping and punching on my knees. This was our thing to do. I didn't just allow them to beat my knees up. I fought hard, since I was already warmed up from earlier. I fought back extremely hard. I beat their knees up just as bad.

After five minutes or so, we were done play fighting. I didn't expect them to violate our loyal code. They really teamed up on me. It was fun.

Tiana and Deanna came outside. Tiana looked at me strangely. "Neal, are you all right?"

"Yeah, I'm straight," I replied.

"I'm going to the chicken shack, do you want something?"

"Yeah, a soda."

"Are you going to be here when I get back? We will be back in five minutes."

Ghetto Legend Graduate
Cornelius Kinchen

"All right, hurry back."

She frowned. "Who are you rushing? Don't rush me."

"Nobody! I just want to be with you, that's all."

"All right, Neal."

Deanna pretended to look at a watch on her wrist. "The store is closing any minute now," she said, trying not to laugh. They walked up the street.

Red came outside from Deanna's house with a grin. "Where did the girls go?" he asked.

"They went to the chicken shack to get something to eat." So we hung out on the porch, waiting for them to come back. Then Jamal and Rob, Tiana's nephew, came outside. They were dressed like old men. Red and I smiled at them.

"What's up, y'all?" Jamal said. They looked like they just came from church. A minute later, they began to hum a church song. It was a song I was familiar with. At my surprise, I enjoyed their humming and wanted to hear more.

I asked, "Y'all could sing?"

They both laughed. "Yeah."

"Let me hear something."

With a knowing look, Rob said, "Jamal, hit him with something." Right on the spot, Jamal launched into an R&B song. He had a good voice, capable of making the females swoon. I was extremely blown away by his performance. In the middle of the song, Chris walked outside. Jamal stopped singing.

"You didn't know Jamal could sing?" he asked.

"Yo, I didn't know until now," I admitted. I wanted the whole world to know, even Grandma. Jamal knew every church hymn, including the historic hymns.

I looked up the street and Deanna and Tiana was walking down the street with their bags. Chris let me in on a secret.

"Tiana and Deanna can sing, too."

"Word?"

"Ask them."

As soon as they walked on the porch, I asked them. "Can y'all sing?"

They were shy about it. Then Deanna responded with slight sarcasm.

"Of course, and you didn't know that did you?"

Tiana handed me my cold soda.

"Thank you," I said.

"You and Red should visit our church one day," Deanna said. "We are in the choir, and Chris knows how to play the keyboard."

I couldn't believe they were involved in the church.

"My father is the bishop," Tiana said. I really couldn't believe my ears.

"Maybe we will come visit your church."

Ghetto Legend Graduate
Cornelius Kinchen

The idea sounded good to all of us. It was getting late and the street-lights came on. The girls were eating their food on the porch. While we were sitting there, Terrence pulled up in his old, beat-up car.

He got out and said, "What's up y'all?" He sounded like he was from the Deep South. "Are y'all ready to go down south?"

Tiana said, "I have all my clothes packed." Deanna, Jamal, and Chris said the same.

I looked at Terrance and asked, "Where are y'all going?"

"The church is going down to South Carolina to fellowship with another church. We go every month, the third week."

Wow, that's what's up, I thought. "How much do it cost?"

"Adults are a hundred and ten, and children are seventy-five. Everything included, such as your hotel room and your food."

"That's not a bad price," I said.

"You can go if you want to."

I thought this over quickly. "I'll see if I can get some money up for it."

Terrence walked in the house to talk to Chris, his drinking buddy. Jamal said, "We have weights in the basement."

"Show me," I said.

Ghetto Legend Graduate
Cornelius Kinchen

We all went downstairs to the basement. It was scary. I felt like we were walking into a nineteenth-century basement.

I didn't like this feeling. "Jamal, where are the lights?" After I asked him, he pulled on a string and the light came on, and there was the weight set. He put a clean shirt on the bench. I got on the bench and he put thirty-five pounds on each side. I lifted about ten times, and my arms and chest began to feel tired. I got up and he took some weights off. He lifted four times and got up.

Then Terrence came and put all the weights Chris had on the bar and lifted like a mad man. He was a beast. I watched in amazement. After he was done lifting, I went further down the hall. Tiana, Deanna and Beonnca were talking and listening to the music. There were two mattresses and a chair where they sat. The mattresses had sheets and blankets on them and were on the floor. Chris and Terrence came into the room, and we all hung out there for hours.

Everybody was drinking except me. Jamal went back upstairs after he was done lifting. I watched them party. It looked like they were having fun and feeling good. The time was getting away from me, so, Tiana asked me to walk with her to Netta's house, which was where she stayed.

"All right," I said. Then we left.

We held hands on the way to Netta's house. When we went inside, it was quiet. I was introduced to Netta

Ghetto Legend Graduate
Cornelius Kinchen

and her friends. They were drinking, too. I did my best to be polite. At first, I didn't want to go into someone's house at this time of night. But Tiana convinced me that Netta was cool with it.

"Fine," I said.

I stayed for a little while, and then I left. Tiana walked me outside. We kissed for the first time. It felt like puppy love. After the kiss, she gave me Netta's number so I could call her.

"Call me when you get in the house."

"Be by the phone." I said.

"I will," she promised.

I'm sure some of the neighbors heard us talking while I walked down the street, because it was late and very quiet outside. I left Red in the house having fun.

I was walking down the street, hoping Mr. George's dog didn't come out the gate. I walked fast and quietly. His dog was crazy as hell. When Mr. George would drive off in his car, the dog would chase the car at full speed and then turn around and go back inside the gate. I think the dog was on drugs or something.

I made it to my house with my heart threatening to jump out of my chest. I still had no key to get in the house, so I had to knock on the door at 2 a.m. waking my Uncle Gilly. After a few knocks at the door, he finally came downstairs complaining about the time.

I don't give a damn, I thought. I just kissed my girl, and I felt like I was the man. It was a good night for me. I went to Grandma's room to get the phone. When I opened her bedroom door, it was dark.

"Who is that?" I heard her say in a sleepy voice.

I said, "It's me, Grandma, Neal. I'm getting the phone and when I'm done I'll bring it back."

"All right," she said, and went back to sleep.

First, I had to unplug the phone and untangle the twenty-five foot phone cord, and then I took it downstairs to call Tiana. She picked up on the first ring.

"What took you so long?"

"Nobody wanted to open the door for me, because they were asleep."

"Ohhhhh. Are you all right?"

"Yeah, I'm good. Did you like the kiss?"

"Yes, I liked it. Did you?"

The conversation got deeper after that. I found out that she was wealthy, and was going through some minor issues. Her family looked out for her. They cared for her a great deal, and so did I.

"Would you believe me if I told you that you were my missing link, Neal?"

"Oh, really, now?" I felt like I was falling deeper in love with her. My emotions were about to get the best of me, and I felt things for her that I had never felt for anyone else. I mean, I was young, but I knew what I was feeling was real to me. After hearing that, I felt like I could fly.

Ghetto Legend Graduate
Cornelius Kinchen

I dreamed about our conversation after I fell asleep. Then I received a rude awakening. It was Grandma and Gilly yelling at the top of their lungs.

Ghetto Legend Graduate
Cornelius Kinchen

Going to church

"Neal! Get up for church!"

I stayed in bed ignoring them. I was tired from last night, and this morning's phone conversation. I didn't have any church clothing, except that suit from Easter Sunday. I did anything to rebel. Gilly walked upstairs, waking everyone for church. I couldn't understand his motivation. He was a church person, not me.

Eventually I got up, still sleepy and tired. I freshened up and got dressed. I got tired of hearing the complaining about, "I am the head of the household, I will have this family in order, this demon this and that, rebuking Satan, the devil is a liar this and that..." I didn't want to hear that nonsense in my condition.

Now that I was dressed and ready, the complaining and fussing was directed at Bobby, Red and Pooka. They were moving slow and making everyone late. The van came for Sunday school and said they would come back. Both doors to the house were open, allowing air and sunshine into the dwelling. But near the kitchen, it was always much shade and cooler.

I was the first one downstairs to eat breakfast. When Grandma saw me, she complimented me on how I looked for church.

"You look really handsome," she said with a smile.

Ghetto Legend Graduate
Cornelius Kinchen

I was grateful for the compliment. "Thank you, Grandma."

"The Deacon McClaim and Nate will be here with the church van to pick y'all up for Sunday school." While she was talking to me, she was preparing Sunday dinner so it would be ready to eat when we came back. It smelled wonderful.

I admired her cooking. There weren't too many people who could cook as well as she did; at least I didn't know too many people who could. Ten minutes later, Grandma went to the basement door.

"Harry and Randy," she said to my father and Uncle, "keep an eye on these greens up here, the macaroni and corn bread is in the oven. I'm about to get ready to go to church, now." Then she shut the basement door and went upstairs.

Suddenly, the church van's horn was blowing outside. I went outside and got in the van, which was already packed. I went straight to back of the van near the back window, which was open as air flowed through nicely. If I had sat in the middle, I would have been sweaty before Sunday school, which started at 10:30 a.m. This meant that I had only slept for three to four hours. I was really sleepy.

A few minutes later, Red, Bobby, Fanny, Pooka, Mick and Gilly came outside all dressed up for church. They got on the van, packed it completely out. I laughed to myself while Deacon, Nate, and McClain said, "Praise the Lord." My cousins responded in kind, muttering in response. Everyone was sleep-deprived and cranky.

I was calm for some reason. I couldn't figure it out. I had an attitude from when I was awakened earlier. I wanted to rebel and show attitude. I realized the extra negative activity wasn't necessary. It was time for God.

We had to go sit in the church for Sunday school. We were separated by our ages and put into groups. Each group had the same level of Bible study books. We were taught the morals of some passages in the Bible in the same manner. Then we had to participate and answer Bible related questions. It was a new spiritual and educational learning experience that I enjoyed. It was another form of therapy for me.

I loved Sunday school. Being there helped to shape me morally and taught me how to make good decisions. After an hour and a half passed, we were allowed to go to the store to buy snacks.

We played with the other boys from the church and acted as if we were family. We even shared money and snacks. After we came from the store, we played and hung out, eating snack in front of the church. We only had about nine minutes before service started. On regular Sundays, the choir sang after devotional service and before the preacher was announced.

I finished my snacks and went inside for church. Service had just begun. It was starting to get warmer in the building. The church stayed packed. Suddenly I felt

Ghetto Legend Graduate
Cornelius Kinchen

fatigued. I wanted to fall asleep, but couldn't because I had to sing soon.

    I watch people clap and sing gospel songs during devotional service. I could never get into that. I wanted to save my voice for the choir. People even shouted during their testimony. I hated when people didn't know when to stop talking during their testimony, because there were other people who wanted to sing songs and testify, too. I thought that was pretty selfish. The children even testified. I had to watch other people, so I could do it correctly. So, when it was my turn to testify, I kept it simple and to the point.

    "I thank God for my life, health and strength. I thank God for awakening me in my right mind. I thank God for his mercy, my family and friends."

    Then the whole church clapped and the next child did the same.

    After we sang and the bishop preached the word of God, church was dismissed. After church, my cousins, friends and I raced to the store to buy more snacks. We wanted to get our stuff before the store got crowded. Everybody and his or her mother went to the store. I know the storeowner was happy on Sundays to have made so much money.

    We hung out and played until the van driver was ready to take us home. Twenty minutes passed and the van pulled up in front of the church to drop people off. I got into the van and was dropped off at Grandma's house. I was hungry and I wanted some soul food.

    My aunts, uncles, and cousins came over for Sunday dinner. My grandmother always made enough for the entire family. The children ate in the kitchen and the adults ate in the dining room. It always felt like Thanksgiving on Sundays after church. After I ate my food, I got dressed and stood on the corner with my cousins and waited for my girlfriend to come from church. Her church was right around the corner from Grandma's house.

    Finally, they were out of church. My girlfriend and her nieces and were coming around the corner from church walking down Straight Street. The joy in my heart to see her translated to a Kool-Aid smile on my face. When they got closer to Grandma's house, Red and I walked with them half way up the street.

    I walked beside Tiana and asked, "Do y'all have church service this afternoon?"

    She said, "Yes. Why?"

    I said, "We don't."

    We went in the house together, and Tiana's sister fixed her a plate. Deanna's mom asked, "Can I make you and Red a plate?"

    We responded at the same time. "No thank you, we just finished our food."

    Deanna and Tiana laughed because we were thinking the same thing. Jamal said, "What, y'all thinking

Ghetto Legend Graduate
Cornelius Kinchen

alike?" Then we both laughed. They ate and we chilled in their living room until it was time for them to return to church.

After Tiana ate, we went to Netta's house to chill out there and have alone time. We were able to spend at least two and a half hours together. During that time, we sat in the kitchen for a little while and talked. Then we went into Netta's room, where we were able to embrace each other and watch movies. Before we realized it, it was time for them to go back to church. I always made her late. We wanted to be together, but there was always later. We finally hugged and kissed. She went to church and I walked down the street with a smile.

When I got down the street, my family was on the porch talking to each other. My cousins were on the corner cracking jokes and playing around. I couldn't wait for Tiana to get out of church. I hoped she was going to stay the night in Paterson. I wanted to spend all my time with her.

Uncle T.D. and Roger teamed up against us to throw water on us. Mick splashed Roger and T.D. splashed Bobby and Pooka with dirty mop water. I couldn't believe it. The water was so dirty from mopping the floor. Then they chased me. I had nothing to do with their water fight. They caught me and splashed me near the church on Broadway with a cold bucket of water. Red walked down the street like he wasn't going to get wet.

Ghetto Legend Graduate
Cornelius Kinchen

Uncle splashed him, too. My grandmother and aunts laughed.

After the water fight, we sat outside and dried off in the hot air. Then we went down the street to the field to hang out. We sat on the steps and laughed about what just happened to us. We sat for a little while, and then my village boys came up Fair Street to hang with us. This time they were on bikes. Birdy was leading the crew. He rode up the street to corner. He rode down the street standing on the seat with two feet. Birdy was amazing to me. He was our size but older. He could even do pop-o-wheelies through many blocks. I tried to do everything he did, from flipping to pop-o-wheelies. I never tried to stand on the seat while riding the bike, though.

It was hard to believe that he was my friend, because he was one cool brother. He always came to the block to chill with me and my cousins. He rode up to me and said, "What's up Neal?" His boys did the same. They were six deep on bikes.

I said, "What's up Birdy? How did you learn to do that stunt?"

He smiled and said, "I just practiced and I wanted to show y'all."

"Yo, could you do it again before you leave?" He proceeded. Then he went back to the village with his crew.

My cousins and I went up the street to sit on the corner. After sitting on the corner talking, we decided to

Ghetto Legend Graduate
Cornelius Kinchen

walk to the chicken shack to buy ice cream. The Muslim owner knew my grandfather as Mandela. In fact, he called us Mandela, too. At the time, I didn't know who Mandela was. Then as I got older and wiser, I did research on Nelson Mandela. He was a political leader in Africa. He stood for non-violence and peace; however, he was jailed for what he believed in. We bought ice cream and walked back to the corner.

It was getting late in the evening, and I was still on the corner with my cousins. Tiana, Deanna, and Erica were on their way around the corner from church. They were supposed to go down south on Thursday. I was supposed to be leaving tomorrow morning. This would be my last week seeing Tiana for a while. There definitely was chemistry between us. I was totally secure and had no worries about our relationship.

As we walked up the street together, I said, "Guess what?"

"What?" she said.

"I am supposed to be leaving tomorrow."

She stopped walking. "Where to?"

"Down South."

We went to Netta's house to talk more. I explained to her that I would be down for two weeks. She explained to me that she would be leaving on Thursday for three weeks. We spent time with each other until I had to leave her at almost three in the morning to go home. I enjoyed every minute spent with her and promised her I would call her before I went on vacation. The next day, I called up the street to Netta's house, but she had left and gone home with her parents. She had to prepare to leave earlier than what I expected. I called her house in Hackensack, and her sister answered.

"She is with my mother and father shopping for clothes." I left a message to have her call me before I left. She probably returned my call, but I probably would never know.

Ghetto Legend Graduate
Cornelius Kinchen

A new environment

On a Monday evening in July 1997, a white van was rented for the trip to South Carolina. Barbara and Lawson rented the van and came back to Grandma's house with it. They pulled up to the curb and got out, and we started to put our bags into the van for the long trip down south. I was able to get permission from Grandma to go, and I was excited because I was about to experience something new. Red helped me put my bags in the car. Everyone talked about the trip for a while, and then the time came for us to get on the road. Before we left, we had prayer, then hugged Grandma. After that, we were off.

We looked out the window and talked amongst each other the whole trip until we were tired. It was a long ride; there wasn't much else to do. We stopped at a rest area on the highway in Delaware and Maryland. It was a relief to stretch our legs. We ate and played video games at the rest area, used the bathroom, then we were back on the road. I fell asleep for at least three hours.

An hour later, the sun was rising and the next stop was Virginia. I sensed a great deal of history happened there. Everywhere I looked, I saw open fields. I even saw a cornfield. The roads were long and some were made of dirt. Each house was far from the other, and surrounded by lots of land. I saw many farms with lots of animals, such as, horses, pigs, chickens, cows and roosters.

Ghetto Legend Graduate
Cornelius Kinchen

Amazed by this new environment, it was peaceful and earthly. There was a historic slave feeling resting in this earthly peace, much different from the liberal free city life up north I'm used to. I enjoyed historic museum ride.

We stopped at a breakfast buffet spot in Virginia and ate. I had no idea what a buffet was until I entered the restaurant. The place was big, clean and full of customers waiting to be seated. They were eating like they were enjoying themselves. The waiter seated us, and then we went to the bathroom to freshen up and wash our hands. There was a fresh buffet waiting for us when we came back to our table.

We paid little and got a lot. The food was good, so good in fact, that it reminded me of Grandma's cooking. Then I remembered that Grandma was from the south.

We sat for a little while to let the food digest. Then we were on our way to the bathroom. We had to take turns using the stalls.

When we finished, we left to head to North Carolina. We were on the road for hours. It was dark when we got to Aunt Carolyn's house, a nice home with a tree in front. We all got out of the van, stretched our legs, and then went up to the door. Aunt Barbara knocked.

The door opened. Aunt Carolyn burst into tears and laughed at the same time. The two sisters held onto each other like they didn't want to let go. Then we were introduced to other family members. We were invited to stay and rest until the next morning. It was already a long drive, and we needed the rest. We stayed for at least an hour talking and getting to know each other.

Then we hugged and got back into the van for the ride to South Carolina to visit Aunt Gloria, who was my Aunt Barbara's youngest sister. She lived in Columbia, South Carolina. The ride was so long, it was ridiculous. We didn't make it out of North Carolina until five hours later. When we arrived in South Carolina, we checked into a hotel. The kids shared a room and the adults had their separate rooms. We were so happy to lay in a bed and rest.

After resting and freshening up, we got back on the road and made it to Columbia that evening. It was clean and full of cars, and it was so hot outside, no one was hanging out. We parked outside of the complex door.

"Gloria is on her way from work. She is on her lunch break."

I wondered where her children were, since it was summer break for us up north. I assumed it was summer break in the south. Gloria parked her Lexus next to our van, walked over to Barbara, and they hugged.

We walked inside the complex under the central air system to cooling off. While Gloria prepared lunch, Barbara talked with her in the kitchen. We toured the house, which was big and clean.

"Aunt Gloria," I said, "where are your children?"

Ghetto Legend Graduate
Cornelius Kinchen

"They are in school. They come home at three." We hung out for a while in the living room until the lunch was ready.

Gloria gave us a rundown of the complex. "There is a pool, a tennis court and a basketball court down the street and cross the bridge." We were happy to hear that. I couldn't wait to have fun. Lunch was prepared and Gloria served everyone. We had salad, turkey sandwiches and tuna sandwiches. She made some homemade ice tea. Boy, was this down south or what?

After we ate lunch, we sat at the table and let our food digest. Gloria said, "I have to get back to work. I get off work at three. By the time I get back, Tony and King will be here. They can take you guys to the pool to have all the fun you want."

"This will give us enough time to get rested and ready to come back," Barbara said. "Don't worry about dinner, Barbara," Gloria said. "I will cook a big dinner."

So,, we got into the van and left the complex. Aunt Gloria showed us the way back to the hotel. When we arrived at the hotel, we raced to the hotel room to get our swimming trunks and towels. It was fun splashing around in the pool, and then we went back to the room and watched television for an hour and a half. We heard a knock on the door at three o'clock.

It was my Uncle Lawson. "Are y'all ready to go?" he asked.

Ghetto Legend Graduate
Cornelius Kinchen

We were ready, so we grabbed our stuff and raced to the van. Uncle Lawson locked the door behind us and came to get in the van.

Uncle Joe drove to the complex. It took us about fifteen minutes at the most to arrive at Aunt Gloria's house. There were so many convenience stores on the highway. I saw so many "South of the Border" signs on billboards, it really seemed like we were south of the border. I was curious of what the history was behind "South of the Border." I never asked.

We arrived at the complex in Columbia and parked in the spot reserved spot for Aunt Gloria. Tony and King had finished their homework by the time we arrived, and Gloria introduced us to them. They also had southern accents. We felt the warm welcome extended to us, and I was excited and looking forward to getting to know them.

After we were introduced to each other, they gave us a detailed tour of the house. The house was clean; it was nothing like being back home, sleeping in that basement with Dad and the girls. Tony was the oldest. He was the same age as me, Red, and Andrea. King was the same age as the twins, who were nine years old. They seemed happy to see us and spend time together with us. After the detailed tour, Tony said, "Did y'all bring your swimming trunks?"

"Yeah, they are in the van," I said.

Ghetto Legend Graduate
Cornelius Kinchen

"Mother can we go to the pool?" he asked his mother.

"Did you and King do your homework and chores?"

"Yes, ma'am."

"All right, go ahead," she said.

The heat was blazing when we walked out the door. We remarked about how hot it was, and Tony told us that it was usually that hot around that time of year.

"It's so hot, we can cook an egg on the roof of a car," he said. "Check this out... there are baby fish and baby lizards in the stream under the bridge."

I wanted to see them. I never got to see anything like that in Paterson. While we walked, we were getting unwanted suntans. We reached the bridge and we stopped to see what Tony talked about. I looked in the stream under the bridge, and sure enough, there were baby fish and lizards swimming downstream. I never saw anything like that in my life. I was surprised and delighted. I forgot about how hot it was, because of how fascinated I was by these little animals.

We finally reached the pool area and changed into our swimming trunks in the bathroom. As soon as we changed, King's little butt jumped into the deep part of the pool.

I couldn't believe what I just witnessed. Personally, I couldn't swim, and I was ashamed to admit it.

Ghetto Legend Graduate
Cornelius Kinchen

"If this little boy can swim, I can, too," I built up enough courage and jumped in the eight feet water. I didn't think I would drown. I just stepped out on faith.

After I jumped in the water, I went halfway to the bottom of the pool. Instinctively, I started kicking my legs. I reached the top of the water and continued to swim. I felt myself getting tired, and I swam to the edge of the pool wildly before I sank to the bottom again.

This experience became a metaphor my life. I saw God as being a source of courage and faith. In this idea, the pool is God, and the God is safe for me to jump into. Therefore, God saved me. This may not have made any sense to anyone else, but as long as it made sense to me, that was all that mattered.

When I got out of the pool, King and Tony said, "Dang!!!" Up north, the word we used was "Damn." I was proud of myself. I survived my first attempt at swimming.

My cousins didn't expect me to do such a thing. After they witness my spontaneous action, they never knew what to expect from me. We kept swimming, raced each other, and played basketball tag in and out of the pool.

We decided to stop playing for a while. All that playing made us hungry. We grabbed our towels and walked to the house. I stopped at the bridge where the little fishes and lizards were swimming and watched them for five minutes. Then I continued to walk to the house.

Ghetto Legend Graduate
Cornelius Kinchen

By time I got there, I was dry. My cousins were showering and getting ready for dinner.

I was the last one to take a shower. I got dressed and went to the table to eat, sitting between Red and Tony. As Aunt Gloria placed the dinner on the table, I couldn't help but stare, because she was extremely beautiful. Her long, silky-looking hair hung down around her shoulders.

"Neal, I see you're enjoying the environment."

"Yes, it is very peaceful and nice compared to the city life." It was true. "And life is much slower. I can think more and plan without distractions."

"You're right about that," She looked like a thick Amerie. Looking at her made me wish I was older and not related to her by marriage.

Dinner was great. We talked for a while, giving our food time to digest. Afterwards, we drove back to the hotel. The roads were so dark; we thought we saw ghosts near the trees. But I guess it was our mind playing tricks on us. I heard so many stories about slaves being lynched when I was growing up, that I was almost convinced that what I saw in the trees was real. Then I closed my eyes and forgot the nonsense my eyes thought they were seeing.

We had a good day, and now it was time for bed. We watched TV for a while, and then drifted off to sleep.

The next day, we woke up and got ready to go to breakfast. We went back to Aunt Gloria's house, and ate

Ghetto Legend Graduate
Cornelius Kinchen

what she cooked. She didn't seem to mind doing it. I think she was really happy to see Aunt Barbara. Tony and King were up, and we wanted to go outside to play with them again.

 Later that night, we went to the skating rink. It had an arcade and a big roller rink. The place was packed. The music was going, and I was skating and playing the arcades. I couldn't eat anymore, because I was full from dinner. I got tired of skating, so I bought myself a mixed slushy. I sat down and waited for my cousins to order their drinks.

 After we ordered, we sat down and watch how the people down south skated and interacted with each other. They weren't much different from the people up north, except for their southern accent which was funny to me. It sounded like a different language compared to the city accent and slang that we used. The people who spoke to us could tell by our slang that we were from the north.

 These people were so easygoing; they wanted to be our friends, especially the females. Before I knew it, was time to go. Uncle Joe was outside waiting to pick us up. Tony and King had to be dropped off home, so Uncle Joe drove them home and we went to the hotel.

 We watched movies and fell asleep. A week later, we were on our way back home. We decided stop in North Carolina to see Aunt Caroline. When we got in North Carolina, it was dark. I looked out the window and the road was pitch black. I could not believe how black it was. I thought we weren't ever going to see any lights. As we drove closer to where Aunt Caroline lived, the lights slowly began to appear.

When got to Caroline's house, Joe, Lawson, and Aunt Barbara went inside. We followed shortly after, to give Caroline a hug before we left. We hugged her, and got back in the van. While Barbara and Caroline hugged again, and cried in the doorway, we stared out the van window toward a tree forty-five feet from the van.

Andrea, the twins, Red, and Travis thought they saw a ghost hanging from the tree. I looked and I didn't see anything.

"Y'all is seeing things," I said, trying to sound convincing. In fact, I was nervous. I stared at the tree and noticed something, but couldn't make out what was it.

Soon after, Uncle Joe, Lawson and Aunt Barbara were walking toward the van. We told them about it but they didn't believe us. Then we drove down the dimly lit road. We even crossed a skinny bridge with a dim light. I thought the weight of the van was too heavy to cross. I just hoped and prayed that the bridge didn't break. There was no one insight to help us. We made it cross and I said, "Thank you, Jesus."

As I looked out the window when we crossed the bridge, I noticed a long road ahead. I hoped we would stop at a rest stop. I was really uncomfortable sitting in the van. I tried to lean against the window with my bag of clothes as a pillow, but I was still uncomfortable. I then

Ghetto Legend Graduate
Cornelius Kinchen

tried to lay my head back to rest, but I couldn't. I was ready to get out of the van and get into a comfortable bed. When we drove down here, I was anxious and happy to go on road trip to a different state. I was so happy, I ignored the uncomfortable atmosphere. I enjoyed everything except the ride home. I guess I was spooked by what I thought I might have seen hanging from that tree, and was just anxious to get home.

Hours passed and I finally got a little bit of rest. I woke up and I noticed a large hill ahead of us. It seemed to make the road look longer and further away. There were a lot of cars and trucks traveling to and from that mountain. The sun rose bright, and on the side of the road there was a field with an old wood shack. There was a lot of land around it.

I wonder what the history is behind that shack? I thought.

I stared out the window to the shack house and wondered who lived there. I wondered where the local grocery stores were. I wondered how they survived, too. I couldn't figure it out. I thought to myself, I couldn't live there. There weren't any neighbors. There weren't any police departments or fire departments near in case of an emergency.

I snapped back to reality and we were on the hill. The hill was steep. I was nervous, too. There were big tractor-trailer trucks in front of us. I hoped and prayed

Ghetto Legend Graduate
Cornelius Kinchen

their brakes didn't give out or that they wouldn't slide into us down the hill.

Uncle Lawson made it to the top of the hill and then we were on our way down the hill. It was fun going down the hill. Uncle Lawson pulled off the next exit to stop at a fast food restaurant so we could get breakfast and rest.

We all went to the bathroom and freshened up. Then we met at the fast food breakfast spot. We bought sandwiches and ate, and then I went to the restroom one more time before we got back on the road.

We all loaded the van with snacks for the road, and then we were back on the road. The ride was long and exhausting. Then all of a sudden, everyone was awake and full of life. My cousins and I talked and joked until we ran out of conversation. We were approaching the Maryland and the Delaware Water gap. My uncles explained that we were almost home.

I wanted to see my family. I had a new attitude toward life. I missed everything about the city, my family, my friends and my block.

What was ironic, I didn't even think about my mothers' problem. I didn't feel any pain from her situation. Three and a half hours passed and we were in New Jersey heading to Paterson.

Yes, we are home, I thought.

We got off the exit for Paterson, I was happy to be back in a fast-paced environment. The vacation was

Ghetto Legend Graduate
Cornelius Kinchen

worth the peace of mind and I enjoyed it, but I wouldn't trade the city life for the southern life; not ever. It was too slow and hot. Their stores were on the highway, and I could get anything I wanted conveniently here in the city, whether it was groceries or clothing; not so in the south.

When we arrived on Straight Street, all my family were sitting on the porch. I was happy to pull up in front of the house to see my family. I missed home so much; everybody and everything looked brand new. I got out the van and gave Grandma a big hug, then hugged everyone else.

After that, I went down the street to see Ali and Goya. Ali was on the porch with his cousin. I ran and picked up speed toward Ali's tree. As I got closer to the tree, I glided at least four and a half feet to the tree and hung on it. Ali was impressed. He had wondered where I was.

"Down south, chilling," I told him. "Me, Red and the Honeys were down south visiting family."

While we talked, I learned that Goya was moving away. After speaking of Goya, he came outside to be with us for the last time.

"Do you want to get a game of baseball?" he asked.

"Of course," we said. Then we went to the parking lot. My cousins and Ali's cousins followed us to the parking lot to play.

Ghetto Legend Graduate
Cornelius Kinchen

We split the teams up and played baseball for at least an hour and a half. We were having fun. Goya and Red's team won by one point. After the game, we walked up the street by Ali's aunt's house. We sat in front of her house talking about the game. We said our goodbyes to Goya and his sister Candy. They said they would come back and visit, but they didn't. They moved across town on the upper eastside.

We never saw them again. In their absence, Ali and I continued to get into mischief.

The sun was going down. We wanted to play tag through the jungle. My cousins couldn't wait until I came back from down south because they were bored. The sun went down, and we began to see the lightning bugs and feel mosquitoes biting our legs.

We started the count out from the corner of Grandma's house. I was it. I began to count and everybody ran down the street as fast as they could. I continued to count to thirty-five.

When I finished counting, I ran down the street to the Jungle to catch the first person in sight. I noticed Bobby running through the field toward the Jungle. I ran behind him. He filled with adrenalin. As I chased him, he looked back and noticed I was catching up to him. Suddenly, Bobby ran his right chin into a pole from a gate. The pole was sticking up in the middle of the field before you reach the Jungle.

Ghetto Legend Graduate
Cornelius Kinchen

It happened so fast, I didn't know what to do. He was crying. Everybody was still running. I stopped and helped him. He had to go to the hospital and get some stitches for his leg.

This time it wasn't my fault. It was dark, he couldn't see where he was running and he was having fun, so there was no one to blame.

The next day, we hung out on the side of Grandmas' house with Bobby. His leg was wrapped up. We sat on the side of the house. Somehow, Mick and I were talking junk to each other. I wanted to see who would get mad first. We were having fun until he went to the extreme and said, "That's why your mother smoke crack."

Trying to retaliate, I said, "Your father is gay." We always went back and forth in the middle of an argument. The words killed me inside, but I had to stay tough as a man and big cousin. I never cried; However, I was always about to. My eyes would get watery and I would force myself to not cry and man up.

Those were the most hurtful words a family member could say to me. I never showed my pain, nor did I let anyone see the tears streaming down my face. Eventually, we squashed the word beef. An hour later, Grandma called us inside to eat lunch. The lunch was my favorite, tuna fish on a roll, cucumbers and vinegar.

We ate and went back outside. It was very hot out, and I wanted to go swimming at Costello Pool. We

Ghetto Legend Graduate
Cornelius Kinchen

always walked up to the pool. Bobby had to stay home. All the kids on the blocked walked up to the pool. It was hot. When we walked, it felt like a hiking trip. We took short cuts where the shade was. We walked near the Great Falls, climbed up mountains, crossed paths, and climbed over and through gates to get to the pool faster.

Making it to the pool was a reward in itself. The cold shower we had to take before getting in the pool was a shock to my hot skin. That was the only part about going swimming that I hated. When we jumped in the pool, the water was like heaven.

We made a bet to each other to jump in the water at the same time. If you didn't, we had to throw you in the water. We played in the four-feet. Occasionally, I played in the five-feet. Even though the five feet was already up to my nose, I wanted to jump in the ten feet one time. I wanted to show my cousins that I could swim now.

I got out the pool and walked over to the line for the diving board. I watched at least three people jump in the ten-feet without drowning. I was fourth and behind me was a heavy-set girl.

When it was my turn, I walked to the edge of the diving board and looked backed. A heavy girl yelled, "Jump! You're holding up the line!" I thought she was going to run after me, and spare me in the pool like I stole her cheeseburger the way she said it. I jumped into the pool, and landed on my chest. The impact stung. I didn't

Ghetto Legend Graduate
Cornelius Kinchen

know how to dive and regretted trying it. While under the water, I was dealing with the pain to my skin from the lame dive.

When I floated to the top, I swam to the ladder and climbed out trying to play it off. It was too many girls there for me to act like the sting hurt. I walked over to the four feet, and sat down at the edge of the pool with my feet in the water. Ali called me out to race to the other side of the pool.

"Hold up, let me rest for a while," I said to him.

I caught my breath and raced him to the other side of the pool. Then we raced back. Man, was I tired when I got back to the other side of the pool. Ali was, too. I rested for a little while, and then I began to swim underwater with no goggles and my eyes open.

That was stupid. My eyes were burning when I resurfaced. Then I asked to borrow Pooka's goggles.

"Yeah, you can hold them," he said, passing them to me. I put the goggles on and swam under water again. This time I saw some girls in bathing suits.

It was time to clean the pool, so everyone had to get out. We rested near the pool benches for a little while. It took the pool staff at least fifteen minutes to clean the pool, and I was getting hungry again from all the walking and swimming.

"Are y'all ready to go? " I asked them. I needed something in my stomach. I didn't feel like sitting there waiting for the pool to get cleaned.

Ghetto Legend Graduate
Cornelius Kinchen

Red and Ali asked, "Why, are you about to leave?"

"Yeah, about to get dressed. I'm hungry. Come on." They followed me to the dressing room. We got dressed, and before we left the pool, I made sure everyone who came with us also left with us.

We didn't take our short cut back home right away. We walked toward the bakery. We were all hungry. Nobody had money, but we went to the bakery anyway. The bakery trucks were inside a gate, and one of the trucks was unlocked. Ali and I were the only ones who knew how to climb gates really fast, so we climbed the gate and took bread from the truck to eat before the truck driver came out the store and caught us. My cousins were the lookouts. The bread we snatched was soft rolls. We enjoyed them on the way through our little short cut.

While we were walking, I noticed the sky was getting gray. When we got to the block, we went in the house because it started to rain very hard. I was glad we left early...we made it to our houses just in time. We didn't think to bring umbrellas with us, because it was such a nice day. I decided to go to Ali's house to play Mortal Kombat. I played with Sub-Zero and he played with Scorpio. We played for at least an hour waiting for the rain to stop.

Once the rain ended, we went outside to play catch with the football. When Red came out to play, he threw the football the furthest amongst us. Ali and I

Ghetto Legend Graduate
Cornelius Kinchen

would start from the middle of the block to the train tracks and sometimes throw the ball over the train tracks. Red could throw from the corner near Grandma's house, all the way over the train tracks. I couldn't believe he had an arm like that. He threw the football at least sixty-five to seventy yards.

When we finished playing catch, we went to the Jungle to hang out. After the rain, the Jungle was a rain forest. The sun came out again and the Jungle began to dry. Then we teased the dogs that were in the backyard of Goya's old house. The two dogs were the new neighbor's dogs. They had just moved into Goya's old apartment. It was a brown dog and a huge German shepherd. The dogs couldn't get out because a gate was built around them. The gates were custom built by the neighbors. The dogs were near the Jungle. Every time we bothered the two dogs, Mrs. Joe-sefine's dogs next door barked, too.

Then we chilled on their back steps. Then I discovered we could climb the gate near the tree to get on the new neighbor's garage roof. Ali and I climbed up there and my cousins watched. They thought we were crazy. I got on the roof and looked around. We saw the dogs, Broadway and the Jungle. I thought, if we played tag or hide-and-seek, that I would climb up there to hide and no one would find me or catch me. I'm sure Ali thought the same thing.

We hung off the garage roof and jumped down. It wasn't a big roof like a house. It was a ten-foot drop. We

Ghetto Legend Graduate
Cornelius Kinchen

got down and went to the field to sit. While I sat with Red and Bobby, Ali went to his house and surprised us with four free icees from his grandmother. When he bought the icees to the field, we were cool because it was getting hot again. The icees came with perfect timing. After we ate the icees, we went to the parking lot where the dumpsters were. When Ali went inside the house, my cousins and I noticed the factory workers were throwing cardboard boxes into the dumpsters.

"Yo, let's make a club house here. We could use the cardboard boxes from the dumpster." They agreed to help.

We built the clubhouse in the field near the steps. The clubhouse was connected to the stairs where we sat. The clubhouse was great. We hung out in there until it was time to go in the house. I hoped the next day, animals didn't welcome themselves to live in the clubhouse we built.

The next day, we happy to see that no animals took up shelter in our clubhouse. We had to do minor repairs due to the wind. That was basically it. Ali was already in the club house when I got there.

"Ali, did you sleep in the club house?" I asked.

He laughed and said, "No, I just came outside to check on it." Then Red, Bobby, Pooka, and Mick came down the street to hang out in the clubhouse, too.

Later that night, Crystahl, Fanny, and the Honeys were hanging with us in the clubhouse. It was a party

Ghetto Legend Graduate
Cornelius Kinchen

spot, too. We went to the store, bought some snacks, ate and shared with everyone in the clubhouse.

Right after that, we went to catch lightning bugs. We caught some in the field where we were and in Mr. Rivers' garden. I caught over twenty-five lightning bugs and placed them in a jar. I had my own night light. When I smelled my hand, it stank like I washed my hands in poison ivory. That was the only part I didn't like. I released the lightning bugs after I played with them. Then I went to wash my hands thoroughly with soap and water.

The next day, Tiana called from down south. Grandma called me to the phone.

"Neal! Tiana on the phone!" I came running.

"Hey, Tiana, how are things down south?" I said hurriedly, after I thanked Grandma.

"Hey, Neal…things are fine, but I'm ready to come home. I miss you…I can't wait to see you and be with you."

I grinned like a fool. "I feel the same way. I liked it down there, but it was too hot. I was itching to get back to Paterson."

"I know what you mean. Guess what? I took a lot of pictures for you to see.

"Yeah? I wanna see them."

"I'll show them to you when I get back. Oh…there's something I want to talk to you about, too."

"Oh, okay."

Ghetto Legend Graduate
Cornelius Kinchen

    We talked for about twenty minutes, and because she was talking long distance and didn't want to run up her family's phone bill, we had to cut the call short. After we hung up, all I could think about was her return. I wondered what she had to talk to me about. I ate breakfast and went in the backyard to fix the chain on my old bike.

    Later that day, my father surprised me. He bought me the best bike that I could imagine. He went to his Pontiac and opened the trunk. He took a GT trick bike out. I was so happy to see it, even though he gave me a warning.

    "Listen, Neal, don't let anybody ride your bike except family. Take good care of your new bike." I thanked him, then I got on it; the bike rode smoother than any bike I ever had. It was almost too good to be true.

    My GT bike took my mind off what Tiana had to talk to me about. My cousins and I went riding all over Paterson. The bike that I fixed used to tire me out. Everybody I went riding with use to leave me behind, then had to wait for me until I caught up.

    The GT that my father bought me was fast, it had good tires and front and back hand brakes. The color was dark royal blue, black and the writing was hot peach and the seat didn't need adjustment. When I rode, I had to wait for my cousins. I was the lead rider. Also, the GT had pegs in the front and back.

Ghetto Legend Graduate
Cornelius Kinchen

I rode my bike until it was dark outside. Then I had to take my bike inside. It wasn't as easy as taking a little inch bike in the house. This bike was bigger and it had a more weight to it. The other bike was so light I could pick it up with one arm.

The weekend was near, and Tiana was on her way home. She called me on Friday night from her mother's cell phone. We talked on the phone for at least an hour. I told her that my father had bought me a new bike. I told her it was a GT trick bike, and that I wanted her to see it. She said she couldn't wait to see me.

"I will be in Paterson tomorrow," she said. Then we hung up.

The next day, I woke up in a good mood. I had a new bike and Tiana was in Paterson. I got up watched wrestling and Soul Train. Then I got dressed and went outside to ride my bike for a little. Then I got some money from my father. I rode downtown with Red and Bobby to the clothing store to buy a plain brand new shirt to wear for Saturday. On the way back, we stopped for pizza. I bought them both pizza and we played games at the arcade.

We played Street Fighter and NBA Jam until our pizza was ready.

"Bobby, get the pizza and drinks, and put them on the table."

Ghetto Legend Graduate
Cornelius Kinchen

Our pizza had cooled off by the time we had finished the game. I said, "Red, you know our girls are back in Paterson, right?"

He nodded. "When I leave here, I'm going to get dressed and go up the street to see Deanna. Her mother don't mind me as her boyfriend. She gives me anything I want."

"That's what's up," I said.

After we finished eating, got on our bikes and rode back to the block. I took my bike inside and freshened up for my girl. From riding that bike, I was musky. I couldn't chill with her smelling like the muskanator.

After I freshened up, I went on the porch dribbling the basketball working on my handle. Grandma's porch was small. While dribbling on the porch, you had to have handle, and I did have a handle. One bad dribble, and the ball will bounce off the porch and into the street and hit some car. In front of Grandma's house, the street was always busy. The street was one of the busiest streets in Paterson.

Ghetto Legend Graduate
Cornelius Kinchen

Tiana is back

I looked up the street, and Tiana and Deanna were on the porch. I smiled from ear to ear. I yelled, "Yo, Red, come on! They are up the street on the porch!"

"I'm coming now!" he yelled back. He came downstairs calm, cool and with a smile. I put the ball in the house.

They were chilling on the porch looking like fly girls with tans. We walked up the street, and when we got to the porch, we noticed that they both looked alike. I was so happy to see her, that I almost grabbed her. We kissed like we hadn't seen each other in years. Red and Deanna did the same. We didn't see each other in almost a month, and something like that takes a toll on a brother. Then Tiana pulled out the pictures for us to see. There were pictures of them at a hotel, swimming in a pool, with family, church members and on the choir singing. There were about fifty pictures with different poses. Tiana told me all about the trip while looking at the pictures. The sun was shining so bright, we had to get under a tree before I melted.

We sat under the tree in front of Deanna's house. We laughed and talked about our trip for another hour. Before you knew it, it was almost quarter to seven. Then we walked to the store for some ice cream and something to eat. Then we walked back to Deanna's house. The sun was setting and it had cooled off a little. We ate our food, then we hugged up for a little while.

Twenty minutes later, I remembered that Tiana had something to talk to me about.

"What did you have to talk to me about face to face?"

"Promise you won't get mad or angry."

"What is it? Tell me."

"I'm scared," she said.

"Of what? Is it bad news?"

"Depends on how you look at it." I was talking to somebody down south before I met you."

"Word. So you lied to me and cheated on me, too. Is that why you wanted to go down south?"

"No! He was my first. I told him about you and how much I love you. I told him I wanted to be with you. Then he kissed me unexpectedly. I'm sorry, Neal. I wanted to tell you the truth before we got deeper into our relationship."

I wanted to fight her, but I was in love with her. "Is it over between you and him?"

She had tears in her eyes. "Yes, baby, it's over. I'm sorry. I wanted to tell you the truth." I wanted to accept her honesty but I couldn't because my pride and heart was crushed. I really wanted Crystahl to fight her. I went down street and got Crystahl to fight Tiana. After we walked up the street together, Crystahl walked up to Tiana.

Ghetto Legend Graduate
Cornelius Kinchen

"I want to fight because you're trying to play my cousin."

Tiana didn't want to fight Crystahl. "I said I was sorry."

I wasn't trying to hear it. "Crystahl, eff her up."

But Tiana didn't want to fight, so we left and walked back down the street. Later that night I cooled off. I went back to talk to Tiana to patch things up.

She said, "I will make it up to you later. I am staying the night at Netta's house tonight. We can make up for lost time." Then we just held onto each other, not speaking.

It was getting dark out and we were still in front of the house. Netta yelled out the window, "Tiana, your mother is on the phone! She wants to talk to you!"

We let go of each other. She said, "Walk with me to Netta's house." Then we walked over to Netta's house. While Tiana talked on the phone to her mother, I said, "What's up Netta?" Then I sat at the kitchen table. She said, "What's up Neal?" Then she went in her room.

Five minutes later, Tiana hung up the phone. She said, "My mother wanted to know if I am staying over here for the night. I told her yes, and asked her to bring her church clothes for tomorrow."

"Are you ready to go?" I asked.

"Yeah," she said, and then to Netta, "I'm going next door."

"All right," Netta said.

Ghetto Legend Graduate
Cornelius Kinchen

When we went back outside it was still warm out. Tiana and I went to Deanna's porch to chill. Deanna and Red were in the house. While we were on the porch enjoying each other's company, Deanna looked out the window and waved her hand, smiling. Tiana and I laughed. Then she came outside with Red laughing.

When Tiana and I spent time together, we didn't think about time. We just were in our own world. It was getting late. We decided to go in the basement to see what Chris and Beonnca were doing.

When we walked into the basement, Beonnca was listening to the radio lying down under the cover. She was waiting for Chris to get back.

"Hey, my babies," she said. "Awwww, y'all look so cute together. Y'all is all in love. Don't let anybody come between y'all." Beonnca always thought I was a sincere young man, especially when she saw us together.

"Are you treating Tiana right?" she asked.

"Yes" was my reply.

"That's good." She loved Tiana just as much because she knew her first through Chris.

Minutes later, Chris arrived. He had a blue bag with beer and liquor bottles in the bag. They were about to party. This time Tiana, Deanna and Red had some liquor. They were drunk in a heartbeat. I couldn't do it. It smelled like rubbing alcohol. I couldn't believe they were drinking either. I thought they were perfect. They went to church all through the week, they sang on the choir,

Ghetto Legend Graduate
Cornelius Kinchen

moreover, Tiana's father was the bishop and he was Deanna's grandfather. I guess that goes to show you that going to church does not mean anything, because people will do what they want to do, even when God is watching. I was in shock to witness their actions. I couldn't understand it. As I got older and wiser, I realized that they were accountable for their own lives and decisions.

They partied until about three in the morning. I got up, ready to leave.

"You going home, Neal?" Red asked. "If so, leave the door unlocked."

"All right." I walked Tiana next door to Netta's house to make sure she got in the house safe. Then I walked down the street. While I was walking down the street, I remembered I didn't get a chance to show Tiana my bike. I figured I would show her another time. You know, I had to knock on the door, again. This time Grandma opened the door. I was surprised because she didn't complain. I guess she was happy that I was home safe.

"Where were you?" she asked.

"I was up the street with the Wellzes. Red is on his way down the street." Then she walked back up to her room. I left the door unlocked for Red.

I stayed in the kitchen until Red came through the door. As soon as I turned on the lights to get some Kool-Aid, there were at least two hundred roaches trying to run

Ghetto Legend Graduate
Cornelius Kinchen

for their lives. Some roaches committed suicide by jumping off the table. I tried to step on as many as I could when they landed on the floor.

Red walked through the door and straight to the kitchen to see what was going on. "The roaches are having a concert on the table?" he asked.

I laughed. "Hell, yeah, that what it looks like with all these roaches." Some roaches even jumped off the ceiling fan. Red helped stomp on some. Then they quickly cleared the table. Some roaches got away and some were massacred by the bottom of our sneakers.

After all that stomping, I was really thirsty. We drank some Kool-Aid, and then went to bed. The following day was Sunday, so we had to get up and get ready for church.

I was tired, sleepy, and didn't want to be bothered. My grandmother yelled down in the basement for me to get ready for church. I didn't understand why I couldn't sleep on Sundays.

"Y'all got to give God some time and praise for His mercy and grace on our lives. Without God, nobody would exist on earth. God breathes life into us every day. Every time you wake up, it's another chance to ask God to forgive you for your sins. Take advantage, because you do not want to go to the lake of fire for eternity."

I listened to her for the moment. Everything she said made sense. My heart wanted to praise God. I freshened up and got dressed, wearing the same suit from

Ghetto Legend Graduate
Cornelius Kinchen

Easter Sunday. I didn't care as long as I had something clean to wear to church. I felt presentable to God, now I could go give Him some praise.

I was hungry for the Word in Sunday school as soon as I got there. I really didn't like church service too much. The bishop screamed through the mic, people jumped up and shouted like they were crazy, and most importantly I never understood the sermon that was preached. There were too many distractions in church to learn what the sermon was about. I learned from Sunday school lessons. I understood the moral teachings and parables better there than I did when the preacher was preaching.

After church, I went to where my cousin Crystahl and Kevin stayed on East Nineteenth Street. Kevin's mother was cooking when I got there, so I ate with them. Kevin, his little brother Jarrett, and I were in the back room playing Street Fighter. Kevin and Jarrett had a well-trained light brown and white pit-bull name Quanah. My cousin Wilbur trained this dog like he was an expert.

We played the game for at least an hour, taking turns playing each other. It was loser off and the winner stayed on. After we played the game, we played double tag in the building. This meant two people were it. There were four floors to play on. It wasn't easy trying to catch someone, running up and down four flights of stairs. In the building there were long hallways, the three

Ghetto Legend Graduate
Cornelius Kinchen

stairways, the three exits and the laundry room. We couldn't go inside apartments.

When we played, it took some time trying to catch someone. The game was fun, but tiresome. After playing for a while we went to Food-town Supermarket to hustle some money. Kevin, Damon, and I were in front of Food-town helping people carry bags to their cars. Wilbur suggested that we make some money by doing this, after we asked him for some.

"Money doesn't grow on trees. Y'all can go right around the corner to Food-town and make some money. Help people with their grocery."

After doing this for an hour, we made at least seven dollars apiece. After the supermarket closed, we walked to the store that had the arcade game on Nineteenth. We played a couple of games for a while until it got dark. Then I walked home. I was familiar with the 'hood and the kids that lived around there. I went to School 6 with them.

When I got home, I called Tiana. While I was talking to Tiana on the phone, another call beeped through, I clicked over, and it was Mother Warner from the church. I loved Mother Warner because she was the only one who understood my painful relationship with my mother. She was really concerned about how I was doing, emotionally and spiritually, and I admired her for that. She contributed to my inner strength and self-esteem that I possess today. I clicked over and told Tiana I would

Ghetto Legend Graduate
Cornelius Kinchen

call her back. I gave Grandma the phone and went downstairs to the kitchen

    Mick and Red were in the kitchen, so I cleared the table to play football. I asked, "Who wants to play paper slide football?" Red was first and Mick wanted to play the winner. We played up to seven touchdowns including field goals after each touchdown. I beat Red forty-two to twenty-seven. Then I played Mick. I beat him forty-two to forty-one. He missed one field goal and loss by that field goal.

    After the game, we went outside on the porch for fresh air. It was cool outside, and nobody was hanging out. We sat outside until we got bored, then we went back inside. We went upstairs to play Sonic in the attic. Red, Bobby and I took turns. We competed to see who would get the highest score. Red stayed on the game the longest and got the highest score.

    It was too late to talk to Tiana like I wanted to, so after Grandma finished her call, I called Tiana back, and wished her a good night. I told her I was sleepy and to call me tomorrow. She was fine with that because she was sleepy, too.

Ghetto Legend Graduate
Cornelius Kinchen

End of summer

It was the last week of summer. I want to have the most fun this week before school started. I wanted to ride my bike with my cousins, go swimming, and be with Tiana on the weekend. Things were looking good.

On Monday, I woke up happy. I freshened up and went upstairs to the kitchen. Grandma was showing Red how to cook breakfast. All my cousins came downstairs to the kitchen to eat. Grandma made the biscuits and sausages, while Red made the eggs and cinnamon French toast for everyone. They came out great. I couldn't believe it. This was his first time cooking in the kitchen with Grandma. There was plenty to eat, and we all enjoyed it.

Aunt Kate and Uncle Benny came from East Nineteenth with all my cousins in the car. Aunt Doris came over to help with breakfast. Grandma was fixing plates. There were about twenty-three grandchildren in the house. The children were in the kitchen and the adults were in the dining room eating breakfast.

After breakfast, we went in the backyard and watched Uncle Benny hook up the grill for the cookout. He set the grill up and placed charcoal in it. He put lighter fluid on the charcoal and lit the fire.

Then we went down the street to buy twenty-five cent icees from Ali's grandmother, and sat in the field on

Ghetto Legend Graduate
Cornelius Kinchen

the steps talking. I wanted to have a little more fun. I wanted to play something everybody could play.

I went back to Ali's house and asked him if he wanted to play baseball in the parking lot. He said, "Yeah." Everybody helped with the baseball equipment. This time we included the girls, since they also wanted to play. We even had the little cousins and friends play. The game was evenly matched. We played for at least two hours. The older kids were teaching, helping and having fun with the little kids. We had a lot of fun. My cousins and I worked up an appetite for the cookout, which had just started, although we were not sure if the food was ready yet.

After we played baseball, we walked back up the street to see if my Uncle Benny put the food on the grill. He had just brought the food out; because he had to let the coals get hot first. My father brought out the radio. Aunt Kate made the sauce for the ribs and put the burgers and hot dogs in an aluminum pan. While we sat in the back yard, Uncle Benny got frustrated because he felt crowded by us. . He told us to go play until the food was ready. Grandma worked on the fried chicken, collard greens and rice.

I walked in the front of the house to chill on the porch. My cousins followed. We sat on the front steps. After playing all that baseball in the parking lot, I couldn't wait until the food was done. I was sure my

Ghetto Legend Graduate
Cornelius Kinchen

cousins couldn't wait, either. We were bored out of our minds.

The girls decided to play jump rope. The boys watched for a good ten minutes, then Red said, "Let's build a basketball court on the side of the house. By time we finish building the court, maybe Uncle Benny would call us for our food."

"Cool, come on," I said. We walked to the supermarket to get a milk crate to build the court with. It was hot walking to the supermarket, and we were all sweating. Crystahl said, "After the cookout Rita is going to take us to Costello Pool to go swimming later."

I said, "Now, that sound better than cooking in the heat."

"Yeah, I can't wait to jump in a cold pool," Red said.

Bobby said, "I'm going to be the first person in the pool."

"Yeah, right!" said Mick. "You're going to be scared of that cold water."

I picked the milk crate to build the court. It was the smallest milk crate there, but it was big enough to shoot the basketball through. That was the main focus. After I picked up the milk carton, we walked back to the block. Red, Bobby, Kevin and Mick went in the backyard to get the wood to build the court on. We needed a backboard, so I asked Mr. Rivers for a piece of wood. He went to the back of the garden to get it.

Ghetto Legend Graduate
Cornelius Kinchen

It took him at least four minutes to bring it to us. I said, "Mick, go and get the nails and hammer from the basement. Ask my father where the tools are." He said, "All right." He walked in the backyard to ask my father, as I watched. My father got up from his seat and went to the basement to get the hammer and nails. He came back outside with a brown paper bag with nails in it and the hammer. I watched my father give Mick the stuff for the court.

Mick walked down the steps and to us. I said, "Bobby get the hammer and break the bottom of the crate." He took the hammer and tried to break the crate. It took him long too long to break the crate, so, I decided to help him with the other half.

"I'll kick out the bottom of the crate, it will be faster." He said

"All right, do it," I said. He did. It seemed easy for him because he was heavier than I was. If I would have done it, it would have took me the same amount of time it took Bobby.

After Red was done, I had to bang the nails in the backboard Mr. Rivers gave us, to the ten-foot pole we got out the backyard. After we did that, we put the crate in the middle of the backboard. We all took turns banging nails into the court.

In the back of my mind, I knew Red wasn't going to break the court down like Shaq because the court was placed higher than he could jump.

Ghetto Legend Graduate
Cornelius Kinchen

    When we were done, we all helped lift the court up and placed it against Mr. Rivers' gate. We had to be careful not shoot the ball over the gate. Whoever shot the ball over the gate, had to climb over and get the ball. That meant you had to have shooting skills.

    As soon as we began to play, Uncle Benny and my father were calling us to the backyard to get our food. While my cousins lined up in the backyard waiting to be served, I shot the basketball around.

Ghetto Legend Graduate
Cornelius Kinchen

Sasha

While we were shooting the ball, a very pretty girl walked up the street with a bag in her hand. Sasha, 4'5', 80 pound, Indian brown skin, long black Indian hair, brown eyes and beautiful: noticed Crystahl eating a hamburger and said, "Hi, Crystahl. What are you doing down her?"

"What's up, Sasha?" she said to the girl. 'Where are you coming from?'

"From downtown... had to buy something to wear for this party later on tonight."

While they were talking, I was all in their conversation. I wanted to get with Sasha. She looked at me shooting and listening to their conversation.

"Who is that cutie?" I heard her say. I kept shooting as if I didn't hear what she said.

Crystahl said, "That's my cousin Neal." I said in a loud voice, "What's up? Do you want to play? Because you are looking like you can play basketball."

"Yeah, I can play for a little while," Sasha said. That was how we met and began a relationship.

While my cousins were getting their food, Sasha and I were going at it in a basketball game. Crystahl watched for a while. In the middle of the game, she went to turn the jump rope with the girls. Sasha was a good ball player. I couldn't believe she knew how to play. She played with heart. The score was twelve to nine in my

Ghetto Legend Graduate
Cornelius Kinchen

favor. We exchanged numbers, and I told her I would call her later.

"Bye, y'all," she said to us, and walked up the street. I had no idea where she lived. I just watched her walk up the street.

I said, "Yo, Crystahl where do you know her from?"

"We graduated from eighth grade together," she replied.

"I just got her phone number. She wants me to call her."

"Call her... I never saw her with a boyfriend. I thought she was a tom-boy: she is never dressed up, and she played basketball for School 21."

My cousins finally walked from the backyard across the street. I started a game of twenty-one, and kept knocking down baskets.

Crystahl and Sasha are going to high school in the fall, I thought. *I will only be in eighth grade.*

I continued to shoot the ball. After I won the game, I went and got something to eat. While I ate, I watched my Uncle Benny put his special sauce on the ribs. He was the best at cooking on the grill. Aunt Kate passed him the special sauce and seasoning, and then she went back in the house and continued cooking the greens and macaroni salad.

Ghetto Legend Graduate
Cornelius Kinchen

After I ate, my cousins walked in the backyard and waited until the ribs were done. When we waited long enough, we were back and forth through the house to the front porch.

An hour passed, the food was ready. Everybody was on line for a plate and Uncle Benny's special ribs. I hated the wait for a plate of food. Nevertheless, I waited. Grandma excluded no one. The little kids were served first, the teens were served second and the adults were served last.

After the cookout, my father, my Uncles Benny, Randy, and Darnell, and their friends sat in the backyard drinking, smoking and listening to old school music. They were having a good time. Meanwhile, Grandma and her daughters were in the front talking about family and church business.

The next day, I called Sasha. I asked her to visit me a little later so we could play basketball. She agreed. I couldn't wait. I wanted to see her skills in detail. I arranged to meet her halfway, which meant walking down to the Boulevard.

Finally, it was time for me to leave. I walked up Hamilton Avenue, and I noticed a girl from afar. I wondered if it was Sasha. I got closer, and realized that it was her. Her hair was done in a style; maybe she was trying to impress me.

When we met, we hugged. "Hi," she said. "What's up?"

Ghetto Legend Graduate
Cornelius Kinchen

"Nothing." We walked together back to Grandma's house. When we got there, I went in the backyard to get the basketball. We played each other, the best out of three games. The person to win two games is the series winner. Of course, I allowed her to win the first game. I won the second game and the third game was close. I won the series. I wasn't going to allow a girl to beat me on my block.

After the game, we sat and talked over a glass of ice-cold water. I told her I was going to the eighth-grade.

"You're younger than me? It doesn't seem like it."

"Yeah, well, it is what it is."

"But you're mature for your age."

"Thanks...I think."

"Well, I'm going to Eastside High in the fall." When she mentioned that, I thought I was a Mack. Then she said, "I have a curfew."

"What time do you have to be home?"

She said, "Seven-thirty."

"That's kind of early."

"My mother is stricter on me now that I'm older. She doesn't allow me to walk home while it's dark. She's over protective of me."

"Do you have any brothers and sisters?"

"I am the only girl and I have a little brother." It was getting late and I walked her more than halfway home. I walked her past the Boulevard.

Ghetto Legend Graduate
Cornelius Kinchen

"Where do you live?" I asked.

"On Tenth Ave, next door to Highway Church of Christ."

"Oh, word? I use to go to that church with my family. Have you ever attended that church?" "Yeah, a couple of times. I enjoyed myself the last time I went. I enjoyed my time with you today."

"Yeah, I enjoyed being with you, too." She walked up to me before we split and kissed me sincerely on my mouth. Then we tongue kissed. I was in shock. We hugged and we said our good byes.

I had to turn around and walked that long way back home. I wish I rode my bike. The distance to Grandma's house was more than three miles from where I was. I was happy. I got a kiss from my new girlfriend. I forgot about Tiana just that quickly. This girl was crazy over me to give me a kiss on our first chill.

Twenty minutes passed and I was on my way down Fair Street headed towards home. The block was clear. When I got home, my aunts and uncles were on the porch talking. My cousins were on the side of Grandma's house hanging out.

They wanted to play Four corners. Four people were in four corners and one person in the middle. The person in the middle had to say corners to rotate the players on the actual corner. To eliminate players, the middle person had to race and beat the individual to the corner they're racing to, then their positions were

Ghetto Legend Graduate
Cornelius Kinchen

alternated. We played under the streetlights for at least an hour and a half. Then it was time for my cousins to get in the car and go home.

I had to help bring the chairs inside, this time Grandma helped me. I was surprised. She called my sister, "Esha, come on now, it's time for my drops." That job was fairly easy. Also, Esha was paid allowances to help Grandma with her eye drops. Grandma had to have her eye drops when she woke up and before she went to bed. I noticed at times, she used them when her eyes were dry.

Esha came from the basement to give Grandma her eye drops. I went downstairs to bed.

The next day, I woke up feeling like the summer was almost over. In reality it was. I had a couple of more days to have fun and enjoy the rest of the summer.

I will be in eighth grade and one more school year before I go to high school, I thought.

I freshened up, put on my shorts and went upstairs. Doris was in the kitchen with Grandma giving her a needle in her arm.

What is going on? I wondered. The needle thing freaked me out. I hated needles, and hated to see Grandma getting insulin from my Aunt Doris on a daily basis even more.

"Don't look so sad," Grandma said. "I have diabetes and I need insulin and orange juice to maintain a certain awareness and conscience level. Eating too many

Ghetto Legend Graduate
Cornelius Kinchen

sweets and salt may cause my sugar and blood pressure to go up."

I looked with a tragic look and sad expression of disappointment.

I went and got my GT bike to ride for a little while. I lost my appetite for breakfast, and wasn't sure I wanted lunch. I rode down the street to find Ali. I went inside and asked if he wanted to ride for a little while.

He said, "Yeah." He went to get his bike and bought it outside.

We rode around the block and up and down the street. Then we stopped by the field. I asked, "Yo, do you want to build a jump ramp on the sidewalk?"

"Yeah, come on," he said. We rode to the parking lot and found some wood. We had to cut the wood down. It was too big to be a jump ramp.

We rode to get the saw under my back porch. Then we raced back to the parking lot on our bikes to cut the wood. We rode to get crates to place under the ramp. We placed rocks under to secure it and jumped it. He tested it out. Then I followed. We jumped for a while. Then we rode back up the street from under the train tracks. We left the ramp under the train tracks in the sidewalk. He went to his house and I went to my house for a little while.

Ghetto Legend Graduate
Cornelius Kinchen

My new bike is gone

It was a little after noontime and I went inside with my bike to get lunch. Grandma offered leftovers from last night's cookout. I wanted a plate of food because I hadn't eaten breakfast. I ate and went back outside in the front with my bike.

My cousins were outside hanging out on the porch. It was approximately three in the afternoon, and it was cloudy out as if it was going to rain. We saw my drug addict cousin Terrance walking down Straight Street. I had just walked my bike down the steps and was listening to my cousins talk. Terrance walked up to the porch.

"What's up, cousins?" he said.

We all said, "What's up?" He asked me, "Neal, can you ride me to the Fabian Movie Theater?"

"I can't go that far with my bike," I said.

"I will give you some money."

It didn't take long for me to make a decision. "All right."

"It will be fast," he said. "This is a fast bike. AGT. You ride on the pegs. I will ride us; it will be faster." So I did.

We sped down Ellison Street until we got to the Fabian Theater. When we got there he said, "Neal, wait right here and I will be back with the money." I was

Ghetto Legend Graduate
Cornelius Kinchen

hesitant to give him the bike, but the way he spoke to me was very convincing.

"I will be right back, I promise, cousin." I believed and trusted my cousin Terrance to come back. I waited in front of the Fabian Hotel for at least an hour and a half.

He never came back. I ended up having to walk back home, depressed.

I was still depressed when I got home. I told my father and Grandma. They were pissed off and felt bad for me, but they couldn't do anything about it. They didn't know where to find Terrance. He ran the streets all the time chasing his happiness like my mother. I was so sad. I wanted to cry. However, I was strong.

The next day, I wondered who was going to buy my school clothes. I didn't have many clothes the years before that. I was sharing clothes with my cousin Red. I was getting tired of that poor stuff. My father was getting cheaper and cheaper when it came to school shopping.

Red said, "Did you see the new Columbia boots?"

"What boots?"

"My mother and my Aunt Booby are taking me to the store to buy the boots."

I said, "Why will I go to watch you get new boots?"

"I will ask my mother to buy you some, too."

"Really? Then ask first."

Ghetto Legend Graduate
Cornelius Kinchen

"I'll ask my mother. My mother gets paid on Friday, but my Aunt Booby is going to use her credit card to buy the boots. On Friday, my mother is going to pay her back. The boots are selling fast. We will be the only ones with the Columbia boots in School 30."

It was getting late in the evening, and the stores would be closing soon. At 4pm, Aunt Booby and Aunt Barbara came and got us from in front of Grandma's house. Red said, "Ma, can Neal come with us and can you buy him some boots too?"

"I don't know, Tyreik (Red)," she said. "I'll see...come on now, before the store closes."

It took us about ten minutes to walk to the sneaker store on Straight Street and Park Ave. When we got there, Red walked over to the boot section and said, "Neal look, here they are." I looked and picked up the boot.

"These boots are dope!" I exclaimed.

"I want the yellow and black ones, Ma," Red said.

His mother asked the store associate, "Do you have these in a size eight and a half?"

The store associate said, "Two pair?"

She said, "Yes." Then he walked to the back of the store to check. I really didn't expect my Aunt Barbara to say yes. Neither she nor Aunt Booby was obligated to buy me anything.

Red and I sat and waited. Five minutes later, the sales associate bought out two boxes. He gave Red the yellow boots. When I reached for mine, he explained,

Ghetto Legend Graduate
Cornelius Kinchen

"The yellow boots are sold out. We only had a 9 ½ in blue and black." I took the boots and tried them on. I didn't care that they were a size and a half bigger than what I actually wore.

I will grow into them, I thought.

I knew this opportunity would never come around again. I knew my father wasn't able to afford a pair of hundred dollar boots. We took the boots off and took them to the counter. My Aunt Booby took her credit card out and paid two hundred dollars for two pairs of boots. Red and I thanked Aunt Booby over and over. We walked out of the sneaker store carrying our purchases.

Booby said, "All right, Bee. I will chit chat with you later." She left. Barbara, Red and I went back to Grandma's house. Barbara said, "All right, do not put those boots on until school. When you get to the house, put them up until your father comes. Do you hear me?"

"Yes," we said in unison.

When we got to the house, we put our boots in the trunk of Uncle Lawson's car. We couldn't show the Honeys because they would get upset that we went shopping first. I was so happy to have something for school.

After we put our boots away, we hung out on the side of the house. We were shooting the basketball for a little while. Uncle T.D. and my cousins came outside to play with us. I didn't think T.D. would play with us. He even had a jumper. I was surprised. We played twenty-

Ghetto Legend Graduate
Cornelius Kinchen

one skutter. He scored fifteen points. I was determined to win. Eventually, I did. Then we shot the ball around from long distance. Red and Uncle T.D. had their shot down packed and consistent, too.

Aunt Doris yelled from the back porch, "Neal, telephone!" I ran through the backyard and to the kitchen. I picked up the phone and said, "Hello."

It was Tiana. "What are you doing and why didn't you call me?"

"I was busy having fun. Plus, my bike got stolen yesterday."

She said, "I missed you, and I'm sorry your bike got stolen. I'm staying over the weekend and I want to spend time with you before we go back to school."

"All right, I will see you this weekend. It's hot in this kitchen and mad flies in here."

"Okay. Bye."

"Bye," I said, then I hung up the phone and went back outside.

Everyone took a break except for Mick and Torrie. They were still shooting the ball. I blocked Mick's shot, took the ball and tossed it up. Then I shot until I missed. After I missed, I went down the street and jumped on Ali's tree, hanging on it for a while. Then Ali ran down the street and jumped on the tree. Then I did it a second time.

After that, I sat in front of Ali's house for a little while. I gave Ali a quarter to get me a coconut icee. The

Ghetto Legend Graduate
Cornelius Kinchen

icee helped to cool me off. He killed his coconut icee, too. Then my cousins walked down the street and all wanted icees.

While everyone was getting icees, Aunt Kate and Uncle Benny were driving down Fair Street. They rode down the street past us beeping the horn. They made a u-turn under the train tracks and rode up Fair Street and parked near the corner of Grandma's house. Crystahl got out the car looking down the street to see who was hanging out on Ali's porch besides me. Crystahl's nephew, Corey, got out the car right after her. Aunt Kate walked toward the front and Uncle Benny got out and walked toward the backyard.

Crystahl and Corey walked down the street to get an icee and hang with us. We all sat in front of Ali's house eating our icees and planning to buy roller blades. We talked about starting school and Crystahl starting high school.

"Crystahl, what high school are you going to?"

"Paterson Catholic," she replied.

"I have one more year before I can graduate."

Ali and Red both said, "Yeah, me too," then Ali admitted that he wanted to go to Passaic County Technical Institute to play baseball. I was undecided about what high school to go too. I wasn't sure if I wanted to go to high school.

Bobby, Mick, Pooka and Fanny were talking about rollerblades. They said their parents were going to

Ghetto Legend Graduate
Cornelius Kinchen

get them some soon. I thought to myself, *I wanted to get some rollerblades, too.* But I wasn't sure my father would give me the money to waste on rollerblades.

Ali walked across the street to hang out in the field, a train rode through speeding. Red, Ali, Bobby, Kevin, Pooka, Mick, Torrie, Corey, and I threw rocks the size of tennis balls at the train. We were surprised the windows didn't break nor that the cops weren't called.

After the rocks were thrown, we walked down the street under the train tracks and hung out for a while. It was getting dark, and I knew the street lights were about to come on soon.

So I thought to walk to the village, and my cousins followed. The sun was setting fast as we walked to the village. When we got there, Birdy and the fellows were hanging out on bikes, riding them back and forth in the village middle section. Also, in the two parks in the middle section of the village were right and left. We were able to chill and play there. There were lights in each park that came on when it got dark out.

After my cousins and my boys spoke to one another, we hung out in the village for at least an hour and a half. Kevin and I walked in the park on our right. There were two girls in the front next door where Nas lived. I went up to the girls and Kevin followed.

"What's up?" we said to them.

"What's y'all's names?" one of the girls asked.

Ghetto Legend Graduate
Cornelius Kinchen

I said, "My name is Neal, and this is my cousin Kevin." They introduced themselves as Che-Che and Kim. We hung out and talked for a few minutes, acting like we were shy.

Che-Che asked, "Do you have a girlfriend?"

Lying through my teeth, I said, "No."

She pointed to Kevin. "What about you?"

"No."

I wondered if Che-Che and Kim had a boyfriend. I asked, "Do y'all have a boyfriend?"

They laughed and said, "No."

"Then we can chill?"

"Yeah, we could chill," Che-Che said. "I'll be here every weekend with Kim. I'm from Lincoln Park." I asked for her phone number, and she went inside Kim's house and wrote the number down on a piece of paper, then brought it out and gave it to me. She was from another town, and I was happy to get her phone number. I told her I would call later. Kim gave Kevin her number as well.

While Kim, Che-Che and Kevin were talking, I went in the back where the park and monkey bars were. I noticed the bigger boys and some adults were back there drinking and smoking. The dim orange street lights made it look like their batteries were going dead.

I got on the monkey bars, and swung across them. Suddenly, Birdy got on the monkey bars, stood on top of them, and started to follow me across. He shocked me

Ghetto Legend Graduate
Cornelius Kinchen

again with another stunt. I wanted to try it, but I didn't want to fall and break bones. He then sat on the monkey bars for a little while until he decided to hang through the monkey bars and jump down.

Kevin came in the back. "Neal, are you ready? Crystahl and them is ready to go back to Grandma's house."

I got off the monkey bars. "Yo, Birdy, I will holla at you later."

"Peace, Neal," he said.

As Kevin and I walked toward the front, we saw the girls again. "Y'all leaving?" Che-Che asked.

"Yeah, we will call y'all later."

"Okay, bye, y'all."

My cousins and I walked back home. We were excited to have gotten another girl's number at such a young age. When we got to Grandma's house, it was time for everyone to go home. I was looking forward to Tiana coming to see me this weekend.

I didn't mind having other females to hang out with, but I really was in love with Tiana. She was my main girl, the one I really wanted to be with.

I slept late on Friday and woke up early Saturday afternoon. I knew that Tiana and I would be up all night anyway, so it was no big deal. I was sweaty and sticky, so I got up and cleaned myself up, changed my clothes and went downstairs to ask Grandma for a dollar.

Ghetto Legend Graduate
Cornelius Kinchen

She gave me the money and said, "When you come back and finish eating, I want you to vacuum the living room and dining room." Before I went to the store, I did both chores. Then I went to the store to get my food. I didn't want to hang in the house or Grandma would have found me other chores to do. It took me about ten minutes to do them.

I walked to the store: Che-che and Kim were walking out the store.

I smiled. "What's up, ladies?"

Che-che said, "Heyyy."

"Where is Kevin?" asked Kim

"Wow, you remember his name."

Kim laughed and said, "Shut up. Yeah, I remember his name."

"He didn't come to Grandma's house yet," I said. "But I will definitely tell him you asked about him."

Kim nodded. "Tell him to come visit me."

Che-che said, "Yeahhh, you come too."

"All right, we will come chill with y'all later." They walked to the village.

I got my snacks, then went back to Grandma's house. I walked past Ali's house and noticed the Guyanans playing soccer in Mrs. Joe-sefine's driveway. I watched as they kicked the soccer ball and did tricks with the ball. They were cool with my uncles. There were four brothers and two sisters who lived in that light-green house.

Ghetto Legend Graduate
Cornelius Kinchen

Their mother wasn't as strict as Mrs. Joe-sefine when it came to property. I continued to walk and watch them play. I couldn't believe as dark as their skin color was, that they were able to kick a ball so well. They kicked constantly and consistently without allowing the ball to touch their hands. I thought only people from Germany and Italy played soccer.

Ali wasn't home when I got there. I thought to myself that I was wrong about that stereotype, but I couldn't understand it nor accept the fact that Guyanans loved soccer.

I walked off the porch after no one answered. I went and sat on the Guyanans' porch. While I watched them play soccer, I ate my butter roll, chips and drank my juice. All I could hear was Guyanans talking and the kicking of the ball.

Red came outside from the back of Grandma's house, and walked across the street to ask me, "Neal, do you want to play baseball in the chicken store parking lot?"

"I don't care," I said. "What time is it?"

Red said, "It's almost three."

Ghetto Legend Graduate
Cornelius Kinchen

Fight with Red

    I wanted to play baseball in the parking lot. We loved to play in the parking lot next to Grandma's house. Sometimes we were able to smack the ball on the roof, and the ball was able to roll off the roof into the backyard or back into the parking lot from the bounce. Also, we needed extra balls, just in case a baseball got stuck on the roof. Sometimes the balls were hit as home runs into Mr. Rivers' garden; if it was hit hard enough.
    An hour later all my male cousins were at Grandma's house ready to play. We walked down the street toward the chicken store. We had all our stuff together, and we argued who would get a chance to bat first before we even got near the dumpsters. We had to open the garbage dumpster gate to get in the chicken store parking lot. Anyone as skinny as I was could easily fit between the gates. Anyone fat, such as Red and Bobby, had a tough time squeezing their gut through the gate.
    We all got through and chose teams. The teams were pretty much matched with great pitchers and hitters on both sides. I had to set things off by hitting a grand slam homerun with men on first and second base. After Mick hit the ball, he made it to first base. It was Ali's turn to bat: Red threw a fastball as hard as he could, and Ali hit a home run into Grandma's backyard.

Ghetto Legend Graduate
Cornelius Kinchen

We stopped the game to get the ball. While Mick and Ali scored, Kevin went and got the ball from the backyard. He was on Red's team. They were getting hot under the collar and blown out by us. In addition, we had no outs. Even Mick and Corey got a hit from over hand slow pitches from Red. We played until we shut them out with a score of thirteen to zero.

Red had a temper problem and it was hard for him to keep his cool. It was my turn to bat again, and he threw a curve ball with the bases loaded. He threw me two strikes. On the third pitch, I smacked the ball over Grandma's roof into Mr. Rivers' garden. All my teammates walked home slowly taunting Red and his team. They didn't get a chance to bat and that was the last ball.

After that last run, we quit, not giving them a chance to come back and compete. Red lost his temper and hit me with a brick on my right leg. I went up to him to fight and by this time the argument escalated to a bigger argument. Mick was the first to Grandma's house. He told Grandma Red hit me with a brick.

When we got to Grandma's house, she watched and heard Red and I arguing. She said, "If y'all can't get along with each other, get in the backyard. Now!" With watery angered eyes, I wondered why she had us get in the backyard. So we went. It was hot and the backyard was dusty. Grandma stood at the top of the back porch and said, "Fight! Y'all always arguing now fight." I

Ghetto Legend Graduate
Cornelius Kinchen

looked around, my cousins and friends watched as me and Red fought. We threw punch after punch after punch. He missed and I landed very swiftly and out of fear. I even clipped him in the dust off. He was dusty and so was I.

After five to ten minutes of scrapping and getting dusty, Grandma said, "Stop, now peace it up." Red was so mad he didn't want to peace it up with me. He looked me in my eyes and still wanted to fight me. I stopped and listened before Grandma got angry with me. When I looked at her, I noticed how proud of me she was for holding my ground after all these years of being bullied and scared to fight Red.

While I was trying to catch my breath, my cousins were amazed that I stood up to Red. He was making all types of growling and grunting noises with tears coming from his Red eyes in anger. He had bumped me in the process of noise making and anger.

"Grandma, could you tell him to stop?"

Grandma said, "Red, if I got to tell you again to stop. It's going to be me and you. Now, go sit down."

After a half hour he finally relaxed his temper.

I left out the backyard and went down the street under the train tracks. All my cousins followed except for Red. Mick laughed and said, "Yo, you beat Red up." Then my friends and other little cousins laughed, too.

I was proud of myself. But Red still was my cousin. I felt like a hero and role model to my little cousins. I sat and rest for a while until I got bored. After a half an hour, I went up the street. Tiana walked down the street. We hugged and walked up the street together.

"How are you doing?" she asked.

I said, "I'm good. I just had a fight with my cousin."

"Who?"

"Red."

"Why?"

"He got mad because we beat them in baseball. Then he hit me with a brick!"

"Oh, my God. Are you all right?"

"Yeah, I'm good."

She grabbed my hand. "Come on." We went to Netta's house for a little while to watch a movie. When we walked through the door, the air conditioner was on in Netta's room. The cool air felt so good. We were alone. Just the two of us, Netta was at work. She was about to get off work.

We watched the movie *Seven* on cable. It was pretty good. We watched it with our arms wrapped around each other, kissing and what not. I respected Tiana enough to wait until she decided that she wanted to be intimate, so I made it a point to keep sex out of my head.

Netta was about to get off work soon. Tiana said, "Let's go outside for a little while."

Ghetto Legend Graduate
Cornelius Kinchen

"All right, come on," I said. She took my hand and we went in the backyard. Then we continued to hug on the back porch.

A few minutes after five, Netta walked through the backyard and noticed us hugging. "Why are y'all back here in the heat? The air conditioner is in the house?"

"We didn't want to be in your room when you got off work." Tiana explained.

"Girl, you know I don't mind if you are in the room with the door open and the air on."

"Oh…okay, no problem," Tiana replied.

Netta spoke to me, "Hey Neal."

I said, "What's up Netta? How was work?"

"Fine… y'all come in the house under the air, it's hot out here."

"We're coming." The door closed. We smiled at each other.

"Are you going to church later?" I asked.

"Yeah, I have to sing with the choir. If I don't go, my parents won't let me spend the night, and I will be put on punishment."

"Your parents are strict like that?"

"They can be if they choose to. But do you want to finish watching movies and chill over here before I go to church?"

"Oh, yeah, no doubt."

We went inside, Netta was preparing dinner.
"Tiana, who dropped you off?" she asked. "My mother and father."
"You going to church?"
"Yes." We went to Netta's room. Twenty minutes later Netta called out, "Tiana, are you hungry?"
"I will eat later, thank you, Netta."
"Neal, did you eat?"
I said, "Yes, before I came up here. Thank you, Netta."
Tiana turned to videos. We watched music videos until she had to get ready for Friday night church service at her church.
Time went by quickly. It was time for Tiana to get ready for church. While Netta occupied the bathroom to prepare for church, Tiana got up and walked me to the door. She kissed me and said, "I will see and be with you after church."
"All right," I said, and left.
When I walked off the porch and from the backyard, Mike was smoking a joint and talking to Beonnca and her cousin Yvette. Beonnca smiled and hugged me.
"Where is my baby at?"
I said, "She is in Netta's house getting ready for church. What's up, Yvette and Mike?"

Ghetto Legend Graduate
Cornelius Kinchen

In a sweet little girl voice Yvette said, "What up, Neal?" Mike gave me dap. I walked off saying, "I will holla at y'all later. I'll be back later." Beonnca said, "All right boo, I will see you later." Yvette smiled and said, "All right Neal." Mike just continued to smoke.

As I walked down the street, the streetlights were on and it was dark outside. It was humid from the heat earlier, but it was cooling off slowly but surely. I figured Kevin and I could walk to the village to check Che-che and Kim until Tiana returned from church. I got to the corner across from my Grandma's house and saw Kevin walking out the house.

"Yo, come on lets go to the village," I yelled. He came over to where I was.

"I was waiting for you to come down the street," he said.

"Yo, I saw Che-che and Kim earlier at the corner store. Kim asked about you."

"What did she say?"

"She asked where you were and to come check them tonight. It is night and we are going to check them."

We walked down to the village and kicked it for a little while. Kevin asked, "What were you doing?"

"Yo, I was with Tiana up the street. She is feeling me."

"Word, I was talking to her. I thought she was feeling me."

I laughed. "We will ask her to choose later."

Ghetto Legend Graduate
Cornelius Kinchen

"I think Kim wants me to be her man."

"Holla at her, I think she likes you. I am going to holla at Che-che."

When we arrived at the village, there were kids riding bikes and adults in the middle section getting some air. My boys from the village were in the middle section talking junk to each other about sports. Kevin and I gave the fellows dap and we went to see the girls. I knocked on the door. The little sister came to the door looking like Kim.

I asked, "Is Che-che and Kim here?"

"Hold on," she said, and closed the door slightly.

We waited in the front. We heard the smaller version of Kim relay the message, "Neal and Kevin is outside." Kim came to the door first. Che-che was right behind her.

"Come in." I don't know about Kevin's black self, but I was cooking in their house. It was very hot, like they had the heat on. I didn't see how they could deal with it. But they wanted to chill in the living room. They walked in the living room first. We waited in the kitchen until they called us.

Then I heard Che-che whispering, "Let's chill in the living room with them because Gee-hay is outside." I heard that while I was in the kitchen. These females thought they were slick.

Ghetto Legend Graduate
Cornelius Kinchen

Kim said, "Kevin, y'all come in here." We walked to the living room and sat down next to each other. Che-che asked, "Are y'all hot?"

I said, "Is that a serious question?"

She laughed and said, "Ohh, smart-aleck, are we?"

"Open the back door and I will turn on the fan," Kim said. They did just that. Che-che was nervous because her boyfriend Gee-hay was somewhere around in the village, and she would rather burn up with a cracked door and a little bit of breeze than to get caught by her boyfriend Gee-hay.

"Uh-uh, close the door a little more," she begged.

It was obvious Kim didn't like Gee-Hay. So Kim opened the door to be spiteful. Che-che was about to cry.

I said, "Yo, just chill, Che-che… you're with me now."

"Yeah, just chill. He does it to you." I knew what Kim was talking about, and I didn't care. I wanted to chill until Tiana came home from church. The time was ticking and Che-Che was wasting time. I wished that her boyfriend would come through the door and see me with her. I also noticed that all Gee-hay's boys were outside and watched Kevin and I go inside to chill with them. After an hour, I got up because I wasn't feeling Che-Che or the situation. I went outside, Kevin followed. We didn't say bye or that we would holla later. We went through the back door where the crowd was. There were so many people.

It was really crowded. The village was live from the talking of Birdy, Sean, Gee-hay and Shy in the backyard. It seemed like a party was going on outside. U-God was back there, too.

A Wu-Tang song was playing, and he had to almost yell to make himself heard. "What is your name? Aren't you related to T.D, Ivory, Neaka, and Hobo and them?"

I said, "Yeah. My name is Neal. This is my cousin. Kevin." He gave me and Kevin dap in the midst of talking. Then he continued to work out on the swinging park bars. Birdy and Sean were swinging upside down on the bars, flipped off, and landed on their feet.

These brothers is wild, I thought.

U-God got on the medium bar to do pull-ups. He did twenty like; it was so easy. Then Shy did some pull ups, too.

"Yo, let me try," I said. I got on and pulled up five times. I jumped down and said, "That is hard to do."

U-God said, "That's because you're pulling your body weight. I can get you use to it if you come work out every day with me."

"Yeah, I will come down," I said, "but what time?"

"Anytime after three-thirty."

Ghetto Legend Graduate
Cornelius Kinchen

    I gave him dap. "I'll holla at y'all. We are out."
    Kevin and I left and walked toward the front of the village. As we walked, out Che-Che and Kim were in the front of their house. They were supervising their little cousins and Kim's little sister. Kevin and I walked right by them saying nothing and laughing. They watched us. Their facial expressions showed that they were confused about our meeting and relationship front that point. Kevin and I didn't care; we still had other girlfriends to chill with.
    We walked back to Grandma's house. It was almost ten o'clock at night, about the time that Tiana would get out of church. Kevin and I walked up Hamilton Avenue. I noticed people were getting out of church, talking to each other and walking to their cars. It was always crowded at Friday night church service at Tiana's church.
    We walked at a pace to wait for Tiana's presence. By time we hit the corner on Straight Street and Hamilton Avenue, Tiana still hadn't come out of church and I didn't want to show up unannounced. Therefore, Kevin and I continued to walk toward my Grandma's house.
    When we got there, Kevin and I stood on the corner waiting. Tiana, Deanna, Erica, and Jamal had just turned the corner on Hamilton Ave walking toward us. I smiled and watched them walk closer with their church clothing on looking like little Christians. They were happy about church or getting out of church.

Ghetto Legend Graduate
Cornelius Kinchen

I waited for Tiana and her cousins to get on Fair Street. When they were about to turn the corner, I said, "Kevin, let's ask her who she wants to be with."

He said, "All right...come on." We walked across street and met with them.

I spoke up. "Tiana, I have to ask you something."

She stopped and turned around. "What is it?"

"Weren't you talking to my cousin first?"

"Yeah, but I like you." "

So who do you choose me or him?" She said, "You, Neal. Are you coming up the street?"

"Yeah, I'm coming."

"Come on then." I gave Kevin dap and walked with Tiana up the street. Kevin turned around and walked across the street to Grandma's house.

Tiana and I walked up the street. I asked, "How was church and did you pray for me?"

"It was fine. I did think about you. What was that about back there?"

"I wanted to know the truth about us and our relationship. Plus, I didn't want you to lead my cousin on."

"And I told the truth back there. I'm with you and I love you now."

We continued to walk. When we got up the street Beonnca, Chris, Yvette, and Mike were hanging out in front of Netta's house. They were putting in money to get some liquor from the store and some smoke. Beonnca smiled and said, "Awwww, look at the love birds." Then she hugged us.

After Beonnca hugged us, we went to Netta's house through the back. I waited in Netta's kitchen for Tiana to change her clothes. Deanna came out a few minutes later.

"Whatcha gettin' all cute for, Red?"

Deanna smiled and said, "You like what I got on?"

"Yeah, you're fine. Speaking of Red, here he comes now. Neal, don't start." Tiana and I looked at Deanna's face when she noticed Red walking up the street; she looked like she just saw an angel from heaven.

Tiana and I were hugging when Red came up on the porch. I had to make sure he wasn't going to sneak me. So I stared him down. He gave me a smirk.

"Yo, my bad," he said, giving me dap, "for hitting you earlier.

"Yeah, no doubt." I said. "It is squashed."

He hugged Deanna, then they kissed like porn stars. Tiana and I watched. Then we waited for Chris and his friends to walk to the liquor store. While we waited, Tiana's parents rode up the street to say good night, then they drove off to Hackensack.

Chris, Beonnca, Mike, and Yvette walked to the liquor store. While Tiana, Red, Deanna and I waited for them to come from the LQ store, Terrance pulled up in his black Volvo. He got out drunk.

Ghetto Legend Graduate
Cornelius Kinchen

"What's going on, y'all?" he said.

"You started early," Tiana responded. "Chris, Beonnca, Yvette and Mike went to the liquor store to buy drinks."

"Oh, yeah? I will wait until they come back. Where is Sheri?"

Deanna said, "She is inside the house getting ready for bed."

Minutes later, the crew came around the corner with a blue bag with the liquor in it. They were having a conversation laughing and joking amongst each other. When they got to the porch, Terrance spoke to them.

"I see y'all got the party in the bag," he said.

"Yeah," Chris said, "we are about to go in the basement, and you know the rest."

Chris and Beonnca led the way through the house to the basement. We went around the back to get to the basement. We didn't want to disturb Chris' moms. The basement was dark. The girls rushed Chris to turn on the light. Chris walked to the back and turned on the light. We were all right behind him. When he turned the light on, Beonnca turned on the radio. We partied and listened to Hot 97 half the night until the a.m.

Tiana surprised me when she started drinking. When she started, she drank a cup and held her liquor like an adult. I thought she was going to throw up. Deanna held her liquor, too. After Tiana drank her liquor, she wanted to dance with me. Therefore, we danced to the music. She was a little off beat; she danced like she never danced before, but she was happy to dance and get loose. We were having fun laughing and dancing while everybody watched and smiled at us because they knew we were in love.

Red looked at me and asked, "You want some? It will put hair on your chest."

"It'll put hair on your nuts," added Chris.

"No, I'm good," I said. "That's nasty. How can y'all drink liquor? Liquor doesn't have a sweet taste."

They laughed at me. I was the only one not smoking and drinking. I didn't mind being the outcast. I still had fun watching them chill and have a good time. I enjoyed my dance with Tiana. We spent a little more time together, then I had to leave.

"Tiana, I gotta go…it's two forty-five."

"All right." We got up and walked to the door. I kissed her, then I left.

Ghetto Legend Graduate
Cornelius Kinchen

Life in the hood

I wanted to go with Dad to Jimmie's, but after three hours of sleep, who would really feel like getting up that early? So when he asked me, I declined.

"Dad, I'm sleepy. Can you bring me some breakfast?"

He said, "Yeah, I'm going to McDonalds. Go back to sleep."

After he left, I dozed off again. I had the little let-out bed to myself, so I was comfortable. Dad returned at eight thirty with two bags from McDonald's with breakfast in them. I woke up, turned on our little color television and put on cartoons.

I ate, then I laid back down. Then I realized I couldn't go back to sleep because the sun was shining through the basement windows, and I wanted to go outside and play.

I went upstairs to take a shower and get dressed, then came downstairs into the kitchen. "Good morning Grandma," I said. She was cooking breakfast.

"Good morning Neal. Can you take out the garbage? Your lazy cousins see the garbage piling up and they will not take it out. The garbage on the second floor, too."

"Sure, Grandma, I'll take it out." When I went upstairs, Mick was standing in the hallway.

"Want me to help you?" he said.

Ghetto Legend Graduate
Cornelius Kinchen

"Yeah, come on." We took the garbage out, then cleaned ourselves up. I had already eaten, so I wasn't hungry.

"Y'all come and eat. Your breakfast is ready," Grandma called out.

"Grandma I ate already," I told her.

"I didn't," Mick said. "I want grits with ketchup on them, sausages, eggs and two biscuits."

"Malcolm, go wash your hands."

Later that day, I went outside. Red and Aunt Barbara were just coming back from downtown. Red had a big bag in his hand, and I wanted to know what was in it. We walked in the backyard together. Red started opening the bag.

"Look at what I got for us." It was a basketball hoop for us to hang just about anywhere.

"Wow, we can play anywhere," I said. We took it out the bag and began to set it up. I went inside and got a screw driver from Dad.

When I got back on the back porch, Bobby, Mick, Pooka, Torrie, and Ali were there waiting to play.

"Where did y'all come from that quick?"

Ali said, "I just walked up the street."

"Hurry up, Neal. You just took too long to get the screw driver."

"Yeah, right."

While Red took all the parts out of the box, I started reading the directions on how to put the basketball

Ghetto Legend Graduate
Cornelius Kinchen

hoop together. A few screws here and there, and it was together and ready to be played with. The game rules were there couldn't be any dunking on the court, because the backboard was wood with screws in it. Also, whoever dunked on it and broke it would have to pay for a new one. We didn't have money for a new hoop. Therefore, we all agreed to the rule, including Red.

After we set up the court, we took it down the street under the train trestle. We hung the basketball court on the wood fence. It was a perfect location in the shade so we played at that spot. I won three out of five scutters. Red and Mick won and split the other two one a piece.

Suddenly, I looked up Fair Street and saw my boys from Auburn Street walking toward us. They wanted to play us in basketball.

"What's up?" they said.

"It's all good," I said. "What's up with y'all?"

"Y'all want to play us?" Chuck asked.

Yeah, come on. We got ball first."

He said, "Let's shoot for it. Whoever makes it takes the first."

I shot the ball and made it.

"You're lucky."

"No, I'm nice," I replied.

"Don't dunk on my court," Red warned.

We played and we were tied up on the score. Suddenly, Shy'mir dunked on the court and broke it. He

Ghetto Legend Graduate
Cornelius Kinchen

ripped the basketball rim off the backboard, and then started celebrating with his teammates.

Red was pissed off. He walked up to Shy'mir and started punching him in his face until he slid down the wall near the basketball court. The only thing on the ground was pieces of the backboard, the basketball court, and Shy'mir.

"I told you not to dunk on the hoop!" he yelled, still punching Shy'mir in his grill.

When Shy'mir got up, he ran up the street, crying. "When I come back my cousin is going to f*ck you up! Watch!"

Red responded, "Go get whoever you want to!"

Red beat up one of my boys, I thought to myself. *Now the weight is going to fall on me.* I knew it was beef now. They were going to jump me when I went around the corner.

We waited for thirty minutes. They came back with Andre, who used to bully me when I was younger. He bumped my head on the ground one day after school. It was in front of my crush Angel, too. I was embarrassed for a while because of that. Then we got cool.

Andre was mad. "Whoever jumped my cousin have to fight me."

"Yo," I said, "nobody jumped your cousin. It was a one on one. He broke my cousin's basketball court after we told him in the beginning that it was no dunking. Then Red beat him up by himself."

Andre asked Shy'mir, "Do you want a rematch with Red?"

Shy'mir didn't say a word.

Sighing heavily, Andre told him, "Yo, don't call me no more to waste my time if you don't want to fight." Then they walked back up the street.

"Sheesh." I did not feel like fighting.

While they walked back to their block, I could hear them arguing about the situation. That was that. We couldn't do anything about the hoop. I was happy that Red stood his grounds. We laughed and joked about Red's victory over a street person.

We walked up the street and walked into the backyard, still talking about it.

I never saw that side of Red before. He had street heart like me, and wasn't afraid to handle business in the street.

The sun was going down, and we would have played tag, but no one wanted to play. Therefore, I said, "Red, let's go up the street with our girls."

"Come on," he said, smiling. We walked up the street. When we got to Deanna's porch, our girls were waiting for us.

"What took y'all so long?" they asked.

Erica walked out the house. "Red, Deanna was talking about you all day," she said. Deanna grabbed her and put her in a head lock.

Ghetto Legend Graduate
Cornelius Kinchen

Tiana agreed. "Yes, she was, Red. I mean all day long. She was wondering where you were, when were you coming up the street to be with her. She was getting on my nerves."

That swelled his head. Red smiled and said, "Word." Then Deanna finally let Erica go from the head lock. Red hugged his girl, then put her in a head lock for doing the same to Erica.

"That's my little sister, don't put her in the head lock for telling the truth." When he let her go, she punched him in the arm.

Changing the subject, I said, "Guess what? Red just beat up Shy'mir."

Tiana said, "The boy from Auburn Street?"

"Yeah. How do you know him?"

"They all tried to talk to me, trying to get me to be their girl. I told them that I go with you, and they started hating."

Deanna asked, "When was this fight?

"It was just before we walked up the street."

Tiana laughed. "That's funny! They tried to talk to me before they walked down the street. They were deep. Y'all wasn't scared when they walked down there to fight y'all?"

"No. Shy'mir punked out of the second fight. He didn't want any more of Red's punches to the face."

Tiana said, "Did you fight, too? Don't lie."

"No, it was a fair one," I said.

Ghetto Legend Graduate
Cornelius Kinchen

"Oh, okay."

Jamal had come outside while we were talking about the fight. "Y'all bad and y'all always fighting," he said.

Red said, "They broke my new basketball court. We told them before the game even started not to dunk on it."

"That's how the fight started?"

"Yeah," he replied. Suddenly Deanna hugged him, feeling his arms and his hands. She wanted to see if he was all right.

Tiana and I were still holding each other as all of this was going on. Erica walked off the porch and said, "Love birds." Jamal followed her to Netta's house. Some dude walked out with curly hair and a fresh shape up. I found out it was my girl's brother.

"Hi, brother," she said to him.

He said, "Hey Tiana. Mommy and Daddy are about to come from Hackensack. So keep your eyes open for them."

She introduced us. "Neal, this is my brother Bill. Bill this is my boyfriend Neal."

He shook my hand and said, "What's up? You are related to T.D, Chubby, and J right?"

I said, "Yeah, those are my uncles.

"It be lots of people down there every day and night," he remarked.

Ghetto Legend Graduate
Cornelius Kinchen

"Yeah, that's all my family that come visit my Grandma," I replied.

"Oh, like Big Mama from 'Soul Food." He laughed.

"Yeah, something like that. There's a lotta love in the place."

Deanna said, "Uncle Bill, This is Red."

He turned to Red. Then he shook his hand. He said pointing to me, "Y'all are cousins right?"

"Yeah," Red confirmed.

Bill said, "Nice meeting y'all. Y'all are some cool kids. Tiana, don't they remind you of Chris Cross?" They both laughed.

Approximately thirty minutes later, Tiana's parents turned the corner and drove slowly down Fair Street. We immediately split apart out of respect for her parents, but they still saw us. They pulled up next to Bill's car and began to hold a conversation with him.

"Hi, girls," Tiana's mother called out. 'Aren't you going to introduce me to your boyfriends?"

All of a sudden, I got nervous. I asked Red, "What's with that silly smirk on your face? Are you nervous?"

He had a cheesy grin on his face, "Yeah."

"You're first up," I said, pushing him towards the car.

"Uh-uh, you're first," he said, pushing back.

Ghetto Legend Graduate
Cornelius Kinchen

Tiana was so proud to have me meet her parents, she had tears in her eyes, "Mom, this is my friend, Neal. Neal, this is my mother, Mrs. Wellz."

I reached in to hug her through the car window and said, "Nice to meet you," we said at the same time. Her perfume was nice, and it clung to me after I let her go.

Deanna said, "This is my friend, Red." Mrs. Wellz shook his hand.

"They are handsome and well-mannered," she said. "Good to meet you both. Do y'all go to church?"

"Yes, ma'am," I answered. "We attend church."

"That's good," she said, nodding. "You're welcome to our church, too. Stop by to visit us one Sunday."

"Yes, ma'am. Thank you for the invitation. Nice meeting you, Mr. and Mrs. Wellz."

"Same here, Neal." Red and I walked back to the porch. Tiana talked to her mother for a few minutes, then came to me and whispered in my ear,

"My mother likes you. She said you are a gentleman, and that she could tell from the way you greeted her."

"She just met me," I said. "How can she tell?"

Tiana shrugged her shoulders.

Bishop and Mother Wellz were about to leave. "Bill, we will see you in the morning," said the Bishop.

Ghetto Legend Graduate
Cornelius Kinchen

To the girls, he said, Girls, we will see y'all tomorrow in church. Bye, Neal and Red, hope to see you soon."

"Yes, sir," we said in unison. Then they drove away.

We hung out in front of Deanna's house until it got dark. The only thing I thought about was the message from Tiana's mother. I was amazed. It was obvious that Tiana's mother loved her a great deal. I found myself wishing that my mother and I could have that kind of relationship.

Tiana could tell that something was on my mind. "What are you thinking about?"

I sighed. "My mother."

"Where is she? Can I meet her?"

"Yeah, one day. Whenever she come around to check on me like a mother should."

She put her arms around me. "Don't worry, Neal... everything will be fine."

"I will try not to. Thank you." On that note, I went home and got ready for church the next day. I could feel her eyes on me as I walked away.

I got home earlier than usual. I helped my Grandma bring the chairs in off the porch. She thanked me and said, "Neal, it's some watermelon inside the refrigerator. You can cut you a piece."

"Yes, Grandma, thank you." She walked in the kitchen, washed her hands and cut me a piece. She didn't

Ghetto Legend Graduate
Cornelius Kinchen

know how I felt about my mother's absence; but even the simple act of cutting me a piece of watermelon made feel better. If no one else loved me, I knew Grandma did.

I thanked her and went in the basement. It was dark going down those steps, so I turned on the lights. Dad was passed out drunk, lying on the floor. I tried to wake him up, but he wouldn't respond. I panicked.

I shook his shoulder hard. "Dad! Dad, are you okay?"

He said, "What? What, Neal?"

"Dad, are you all right?"

He said, "Yeah, just sleepy man."

"Why are you on the floor?" I pulled out the folding cot, and said, "Dad, get off the floor and lay here." He got up, laid in the bed, and fell asleep; so did I. There was nothing else to do. Besides, the exchange between Tiana's mother and me was still fresh in my mind, and was still there when I finally drifted off.

I got nothing out of the message from Sunday morning service. It was too hot to concentrate on the preacher. All I can think of is the preacher walking up and down the aisle preaching and sweating on the microphone. I couldn't wait until service was over, so that I could change clothes and play on my block with my cousins.

Ghetto Legend Graduate
Cornelius Kinchen

Last day of summer

This was the last day of summer vacation. School officially started tomorrow. I couldn't wait to wear my new clothes and see my friends at school. On top of that, I knew I had the hottest boots in Paterson. I was ready to wear them to school and show off a little.

The first day of school was the most exciting for me. I didn't feel like I was the only one with hand-me-downs on. I felt a higher level of acceptance from my peers based on the way I was dressed. The way I looked built up my self-esteem. Wearing other people's old clothes made me feel insecure and dirty. It also made me a little paranoid, thinking somebody was talking about me. This kind of thinking interrupted my focus.

When I got to Grandma's house after church, my uncles were on the porch.

"Neal, get my slippers for me, would you, please?"

"Yes, ma'am." I went to get them for her, and she slipped them on her feet and started to prepare dinner for the family.

Aunt Doris showed up with banana pudding. Aunt Kate relieved Grandma so she could change out of her church clothes. Grandma put on her same comfortable house gown. Falling into this routine was a comfort for my tortured soul, which still missed my mother and wished she was here.

Ghetto Legend Graduate
Cornelius Kinchen

The Bishop Payne and his wife came over to visit in their new Mercedes Benz. I don't know if he was showing off, or if he finally decided to come and try Grandma's cooking.

We were well aware of how to behave when company came over. So as not to embarrass my grandmother, we went outside and left the adults to their conversation.

All the while, Grandma was keeping an eye on the food, walking back and forth to the kitchen. Finally, dinner was ready. She fixed our plates first, because she believed that that was how it was supposed to be. Then she fixed plates for the adults.

After I ate, I went outside to catch some fresh air. Tiana, Deanna and Erica were coming down the street. I was on the corner waiting for them when they got there. I got my customary hug from my girl.

Deanna said, "Hi, Neal. Where is your cousin Red?"

"I think he just went in the house to eat his food," I told her.

"Can you go get him for me?"

"Yeah." I ran in the house and said, "Red, Deanna is outside, come on."

"All right." He got up and followed me out the front door.

Ghetto Legend Graduate
Cornelius Kinchen

Erica pulled me to the side when I came out. "Neal, who is that?" she asked, pointing at my cousin Corey.

"That's my little cousin. Y'all are the same age. Would you like to talk to him?"

She said, "He is cute."

"I'll call him over. Yo, Corey, somebody wants to meet you! C'mere."

I introduced Corey to Erica, then they went off to talk. Tiana and I hugged up again after being interrupted by Deanna's request for Red.

She was leaving early today because she had to get ready for school tomorrow, too. As long as I was able to see my girl for any amount of time, I was fine with it.

"Are you going to call me later?" I asked.

"Yes, I will call you later. I will see you on the weekends and during school breaks, too." "All right," I said, then whispered in her ear, "I love you."

She whispered back to me, "I love you, too." Her parents were up the street waiting.

"Hey, y'all," she said to the girls, "my mother and father are waiting for me. I'm going home to get prepared for school."

Deanna and Erica said, "We'll walk you up the street, Auntie."

Ghetto Legend Graduate
Cornelius Kinchen

Tiana said, "Okay, come on. Bye, Neal. See you later, Red." Red and I stood on the corner and watched them walk up the street.

I said, "Red, tomorrow we are going to rock our new boots."

"Yeah, I can't wait until tomorrow to wear mine."

The Bishop and his wife left after the spread Grandma laid out. They obviously enjoyed themselves. After they left, I walked to kitchen to get some Kool-Aid. My little cousins had made a mess on the kitchen table. There were plates with a little bit of food on it, cups of left- over Kool-Aid, and some aluminum pans with macaroni and cheese and corn bread in it.

After I got my cold drink, I went out back and said to my cousins, "Whoever was sitting at the kitchen table clean your mess before Grandma yells at y'all." They ignored me, so I left and went around to the corner.

I saw Kevin crossing the street. I gave him dap and said, "What's up? Did you hear from Kim and Che-Che?"

"We were on the phone earlier," he said. "Che-Che is down there and she wants to see you."

"Oh, word? That's what we'll do later, unless you want to go down there now."

"Let me go get something to eat real fast before we go to the village."

Ghetto Legend Graduate
Cornelius Kinchen

"Yeah, you better hurry up before the food is gone." He walked in the house. I stayed outside on the corner.

I looked down the street, and low and behold, it was Che-Che and Kim. I assumed they were walking to the chicken store to buy ice cream.

Che-Che stopped within inches of my nose. "What's up, Neal? You mad at me or something?" She was acting kind of low key this time. I made up my mind that I was not going to speak to Che-Che until she spoke to me first. I felt some kind of way from the last visit.

"What's up with you, Che-Che? I ain't mad, but I don't like being put to the back or the side. You probably do, because, your man does that to you all the time." That must have struck a nerve, because she had no answer to that.

Kim asked, "Where is your cousin?"

"Would you like to see him?"

"Where is he?" she asked again.

I said, "Come with me."

We walked through the house to the kitchen, and Kevin was sitting at the kitchen table eating his food. Kevin looked up with a mouth full of food and was surprised to see Kim standing there. He laughed.

Kim said, "You so nasty. Why are you laughing?"

"We were just talking about going to visit y'all in the village."

Ghetto Legend Graduate
Cornelius Kinchen

"We just talked y'all up. That's crazy. Where were y'all going?"

"We were going to buy ice-cream and something for my aunt from the chicken store. We decided to stop by to visit."

"Wow, you changed, Che-Che."

"Yeah, you're right, I've changed, Neal. Do y'all want to walk with us to the village when we come from the store?"

"Yeah, we were going to walk to visit y'all anyway," I said. "Go ahead to the store and we wait for y'all on the corner."

"I'm going to finish my food," said Kevin. "I will see y'all when y'all come back from the store."

I walked them back outside, and watched them as they walked down the street. I waited on the porch thinking of something to talk about when they came back, and couldn't come up with anything. So I figured we would just chill at their house and go with the flow.

Kevin came outside. "Did they go to the store?" he asked

"You know they went to the store, no point in asking me that."

"What if we are waiting for them to come back, and they walk down Broadway and forget all about us?" We both laughed, knowing that was not possible.

Ghetto Legend Graduate
Cornelius Kinchen

"If they do that, I will never say anything to them again." I put him in a head-lock for even suggesting that, and we laughed harder.

Fifteen minutes later, they were walking back down the street towards the house. I went upstairs to get Kevin.

"Come on, let's see if they are going to stop for us." We went into Grandma's room to look out the window. We hid behind the curtains to make sure they didn't see us.

A few seconds later, Aunt Doris called upstairs for us. "Neal and Kevin, your little girlfriends are here for you!"

"Okay, Auntie," we said, and went downstairs. As soon as we got to the porch, Kim said, "Y'all knew we were coming back and y'all going to make us look for y'all."

I said, "Never mind all that. Are y'all ready to go?" They bought what they came to get, so we all set off towards the Village. When we got down there it was crowded with people from different parts of the Fourth Ward. It was like a block party.

It was after five, and the sun was still shining bright. Kim's house was quiet when we got there, because her brother and sister were outside playing somewhere. We waited for her to give her mother the ice cream, then we all sat in the living room on separate couches and watched Video Music Box. Then my favorite video came on with Puffy and Mase. I wanted to be like them, successful and feeling like I was on top of the world. They represented a world that I wanted to be a part of.

Che-Che said, "That's y'all right there, Paterson's version of Puffy and Mase." I was souped up after hearing that. I smiled from ear to ear. My life goal was to be a superstar, someone who was successful and could motivate other people to be successful as well. Wu-Tang Clan's video *Chess Box* was next.

"Oooohh," Kim said, "U-God always listens to Wu-Tang, right Che?!"

"Yup. He always does."

"U-God from out here?" I asked.

"Yeah," Kim said, "he always has a radio out here on the bench or in the back on the monkey bars working out."

"Yeah, I know him. I met him the other night we were down here. I'm supposed to work out with him in the back on the monkey bars."

"Neal, Are you are trying to get buff on me?" Che said.

"A little sumpin', sumpin'."

We stayed for a few hours, then we had to leave. First day of school was tomorrow, and I wanted to get my rest to be fresh for the first day of learning. We hugged each other and said our good-byes until the weekend.

Ghetto Legend Graduate
Cornelius Kinchen

"Call me," Che-Che said as we walked out the door.

"I will," I promised. Then we left.

We walked through the center court feeling like players. I wondered if Che-Che and Gey-ahh were over. It really didn't matter to me, because I had a girlfriend. It felt good to have her on the side and many others on standby. If one girl got out of line, I would move on to the next one. I had this mentality since grade school. Part of me enjoyed being a mack. The other half of my ego was thinking, my mother should be here teaching me about females from her experience.

Ghetto Legend Graduate
Cornelius Kinchen

Momma on my mind

I did my best to keep my head up. My soul felt ripped apart because my mother chose drugs over her kids. My sisters could have benefited from her being around to teach them how to grow up and be responsible young women. I felt that my life was incomplete without my mother.

However, in spite of everything that was going on, I still managed to keep a positive outlook on life. I would tell myself that my mother would be at my graduation, and that eventually she would want to get off drugs.

I wanted my parents to be proud of me. Dad never finished school, and had to drop out in the seventh grade to work at a job that didn't pay much. There wasn't much I could do to help, because I was a kid. Someone had to pay the bills.

I didn't feel that what I wanted was out of selfishness, I believed that any normal child would want the approval and the love of his mother. I wasn't looking for a fairy tale family, I just wanted my mother, and her absence was felt keenly.

For a little while, I had moved back to Grandma's house. Some of my clothes were still at Aunt Barbara's, since I would be going back to School 30. I wanted to see if my mother would come back around; I hadn't seen her in two months, and I missed her terribly.

Ghetto Legend Graduate
Cornelius Kinchen

So, the next day, Dad got me ready for school. I was wearing old clothes with a pair of new boots that were too big for me. Even though my feet were comfortable inside, I wasn't.

A light rain had started by the time I made it to the bus stop to catch either the 712 or the 704. I made it just in time for the bus, and got on it, heading to school. Fifteen minutes later, the bus pulled up in front of School #30. I looked out the window and noticed the students were in the front of the building waiting to go to their assigned classes. I got off the bus and walked toward the school. Students were going inside to the café for instructions. I was anxious to start this school year off the right way.

I sat in the café for a little while until things got organized. The principal announced over the loudspeaker that the teachers should meet in the café to pick up their students. A few minutes later, teachers flooded into the café with their list of assigned students for their respective homerooms. One at a time, they called names on their lists, and I listened carefully for my name to see what homeroom I was in.

After twenty minutes of roll call, I finally heard my name. I was placed in a music homeroom. I got up from the lunchroom table and got on line with my assigned homeroom teacher Mr. Parks. We walked in a straight line through the hallway on the first floor to our homeroom.

Ghetto Legend Graduate
Cornelius Kinchen

Mr. Parks reminded me so much of my Uncle Gilly. I thought they were family. They had similar features. They both had a funny-shaped head, an effeminate way of speaking, and other ways I couldn't understand, and never wanted to.

He approached me after roll call. "Are you related to Tyreik and the twins?" he asked.

I said, "Yeah."

"Then you are related to Montell Gilly."

No kidding, I thought. "Yeah."

He laughed and said, "We were on the band and on the choir together. That's weird to be teaching his nieces and nephews." One of my new classmates, a kid named John, made fun of Mr. Parks' female-inflected voice and the whole class laughed.

Mr. Parks was quick to respond. "John, I'm not having any of your nonsense this year, am I? I will get your mother on the phone so quick, your head will spin. Do you understand me?"

Sarcastically, John responded, "Yes, Mr. Parks." It was funny to see John make fun of the teacher on the first day of eighth grade.

What a way to crack the ice, I thought.

We stood for the flag salute and listened to the announcements welcoming the new staff and students. I had already obtained my class schedule. When the bell rang, I went to my first class, which was English.

Ghetto Legend Graduate
Cornelius Kinchen

I saw Red in the hallway talking to a few students. I knew most of them from last year, so I walked over.

"What's up, Red?" Then I proceeded to give my boys dap and the ladies a hug. After that, I made it to my first class, and got there just as the bell rang.

When it came to my education, I did not play. My English teacher had my full attention, and my only thoughts were to make every effort to get good grades this year, and each year following. Each day, that was exactly what I did, and it felt good to know I was making the right choice. I couldn't wait to get my report card for the first marking period. Getting good grades during the semester, and the idea of seeing Tiana on the weekends, was icing on the cake.

After school, and before Red and I walked home, we told Marquise, Will and the home boys that we would come over after we finished our home work to play them in basketball. We gave them dap and walked home.

While walking, we saw Tiya, my rap star partner, beating up Y-Nita, another friend of mine. She had Y-Nita's hair in one hand, penned against the gate, hitting her in the face with a closed fist. I had to intervene.

"Tiya, what the hell are you doing?"

Breathing hard and still swinging, Tiya said, "She was talking smack to me in class, trying to get me in trouble on the first day!" Nita was wailing, trying to protect her face from another hit, but failing miserably.

Ghetto Legend Graduate
Cornelius Kinchen

"Tiya, let her go!" I yelled. "Get your hand out of her hair! Y-Nita, is this true?"

Her face was bruised, and her lip was bleeding. "Yeah," she admitted, "it is true. But I was just playin'!" That earned her another hit to the face from Tiya.

I caught Tiya's fist before it connected again, then said, "Tiya, leave her alone! Some teacher might see you and get you in trouble." During the entire exchange, Red said nothing, but stood there with a big smile on his face.

Still breathing heavily, Tiya said, "You're right, Neal." Then she let Y-Nita free. "You're lucky to have a friend like Neal to save your ass." She turned on her heels and walked away.

Y-Nita wiped blood from her mouth with her sleeve, and the tears from her eyes with the back of her hand. Her face had started to swell. Her mother was not going to like this.

"Nita," I said to her, "go home. And stop starting stuff." She walked away, still crying and wiping her face.

Red thought the whole thing was hilarious. "Y-Nita does start trouble with people and act innocent. She has a slick mouth in school, but after school she runs straight home. I guess today she got caught."

"They are both my friends, Red. Do you have a lot of home work to do today?"

"Nope. Why, what's up?"

"Nothin, just asking. Red, the weekend is going to be off the hook when we see Tiana and Deanna."

Ghetto Legend Graduate
Cornelius Kinchen

"Yeahhhhh, you're right. My mother is supposed to get us a phone."

"That's what's up," I said, "then we can call our girls."

"Guess what? Tamara likes you," he said. Tamara was a dark-skinned girl in his homeroom. She had long hair and was very pretty.

I said, "Hook me up."

"Tomorrow when I see her in homeroom...and Tasha likes me. She is always up on me."

"Ask them to come to the house so we can chill together."

"Yeah, that's a plan."

We finally made it to the house. Aunt Barbara hugged both of us and said, "Dinner will be ready shortly. Take out your homework."

Red asked, "Mom, can we go to Marquise's house after dinner?"

"Yes, ask your father, too." So he did and got the go-ahead.

We were done with homework and dinner in forty-five minutes and out the door by four o'clock. When we got to Marquise's house, he was already in the backyard shooting around with some of the fellows from school. We were ten to twelve deep in his backyard. We played for a little while and joked for a little while. After I won a game of twenty-one, they gave me respect. I loved it.

Ghetto Legend Graduate
Cornelius Kinchen

It was about to get dark soon, so we left after giving daps to the homeboys. Everybody else was leaving to go home, too. When we got in the house, everybody had taken their showers for the next day. Red and I took turns in the shower, then we watched a little television and got in the bed.

The next day, after school, Red convinced Tamara and Tasha to come over to the house. Boy, I was excited to see Tamara. We were relaxing in the house with the girls, while my Aunt and Uncle were in the bedroom watching television. Tamara and Tasha got bold and started getting close to us. We started kissing and feeling on each other. We wanted to have sex, but the twins were running back and forth getting on our nerves. While my hands were in her pants, I was paranoid that my aunt would bust in on us, so Red and Tasha went in the closet. The door was cracked and we could see them while sitting on the bed.

I couldn't believe how down they were to hang with us. My hormones were raging. We couldn't do anything because of the chances of getting caught were high. I did not want to get caught and risk losing my privilege of living with my aunt and uncle, so we cut our visit short and walked them to Tamara's house down the street.

We didn't stay long because we had to go home and get ready for dinner. This was my first time touching a girl's private parts. I smelled my finger and it smelled

Ghetto Legend Graduate
Cornelius Kinchen

like wet powder. I put my finger to Red's nose and said, "Red, smell this."

He smirked and put his finger to my nose and said, "Now, *you* smell *this*."

It smelled like he touched a wet dog. I immediately jerked my head back.

"Man, we have to wash our hands."

The aroma on my fingertips turned me on. I felt a stirring in my groin, and it made me want to have sex with Tamara. I was clueless, and didn't know the first thing about sex, and had no one to talk to about it. After dinner and my shower, I went to bed thinking about Tamara, and how exciting this afternoon was with her.

The next day, I went to homeroom. John stopped me just after walking through the door.

"Tamara was just here looking for you, her and Tasha."

"Ohhh, yeah? What did they want?"

"They just asked 'where's Cornelius?' I told them you didn't get here yet. That was it. Then they said to tell you they were looking for you."

In no small amount did I feel my swag. Just before my first period class, Tamara met me at my locker. She smiled and said, "What's up, baby?"

"What's up? I heard you were looking for me."

"Who told you that? Oh, I know...John's black ass."

Ghetto Legend Graduate
Cornelius Kinchen

"Yeah, he told me as soon as I walked into homeroom."

"Yes, baby, I was looking for you. I wanted to kiss you."

"What are you waiting for?" Then she looked at me with hearts in her eyes and kissed me like I was the love of her life. It was a long one. We both came away breathless.

"I will see you later," she said, "I have to go to class."

"Yeah, me too. See you later," The kiss had my toes curling. I couldn't wait to see her again.

I did see her before I went to lunch. We walked to lunch together. People recognized that we were going out together. Some smiled and some hated. When we got in the lunchroom, she went with her girls and I went the fellas. The boys and I had planned to play basketball in the gym, because it started raining outside. When I sat at the lunch table, Tiya and Tryheim wanted to rap. She walked over to my table and said, "Neal, give me a hot beat to freestyle to."

I gave her a freestyle beat followed by the beat from Puffy's *All About the Benjamins*. She rapped off the beat like a pro. Everyone crowded the table. The lunch monitors thought it was a fight and ordered some students to sit and some to line up for lunch. We had time because the lower grades were first in line to eat. The eighth graders were last to line up and eat lunch.

Ghetto Legend Graduate
Cornelius Kinchen

Ten minutes later, we got our lunch trays and ate together. While we ate, we talked about the intramural basketball league the school sponsored every year for the seventh and eighth graders.

We talked about who were going to be on teams. It was definitely Tryheim and I on teams and whoever else. He played like Reggie Miller, and I played like an all-American. We planned to bring our A-game to whoever wanted a challenge.

After we ate, we walked to the gym to ball. Each team captain picked who they felt were the best basketball players to be on their team. I wanted Li'l Vernon and Tryheim. Vernon was a great point guard to play with because he made smart plays. He was the coolest little person.

Seven people were picked to be on each squad. Two had to sit out until someone got tired. I always gave a person on the sideline a chance to play. We had a short period to play, too. The girls watched and talked like sports commentators.

We played for a good twenty-three minutes of hard basketball until the bell rang. We didn't have much time to get prepared for our next class. I had to go to the bathroom to wipe myself down with paper towels because I was sweaty. I grabbed nineteen rebounds like Anthony Mason from the New York Knicks, and made five points with seven assists. I was the talk of the game.

Ghetto Legend Graduate
Cornelius Kinchen

    I went to my locker, and got my books for class with Mr. Muasby, my social studies teacher. I couldn't wait to go to his class, he was a great teacher with a sense of humor and made learning fun.
    The day didn't go by fast enough. All I could think of was the weekend. I really wanted to see Tiana. I didn't even want Tamara as bad as I wanted Tiana. I really could not call her as much, because calling Hackensack would run the phone bill up. I definitely didn't have a job to pay any bill. Therefore, I waited until the weekend to see her and talk to her.

Ghetto Legend Graduate
Cornelius Kinchen

Can't wait to see Tiana

Finally the weekend was here. I wanted to see my future baby's mother. I thought she would be the perfect mother to my child because of the way she treats me. Moreover, her parents were leaders of a church. I felt they would support and love our child like they supported the church ministry.

It was Friday and the school day went by smoothly. No fights and no confrontations with anyone today was a sign that this weekend was going to be the best. After school, Red and I went to the house and ate some chocolate chip cookies and drank milk. Soon after, Red and I hung out and waited for my Uncle Lawson to come home from work.

Meanwhile, we listened to a DJ Clue's mix tape in the living room. We turned it up halfway. Aunt Barbara wasn't liking it.

"Are y'all deaf? Turn that radio down some."

We turned it down. I said, "Red, I'm going to ask my father for some money to buy a Sony or a Panasonic Radio."

"How much do they cost?"

"I think they are fifty dollars downtown. We will have some sounds to listen to walking to Grandma's house or around Paterson."

"Yeah, that's a good idea."

Changing the subject, I said, "I can't wait to hang with Tiana. Did you do it to Deanna?"

He hesitated. "Yeah, that's why I can't wait to go hang with them, too." Red was sneaky.

Uncle Lawson walked through the door ninety minutes later. "Hey, y'all. Is everybody ready to go down the hill to Grandma's house?"

Indeed, we were ready. He went to use the bathroom. When he came out, we were already in the front of the house claiming our seats and windows. Three ended up sitting in the front and four in the back. We got in the car and pulled off.

It took ten minutes to get to Grandma's house. When we got there, Red and I ran inside and spoke to Grandma.

"Hi. How is school?" she said.

"It's fun and we are learning, Grandma." I responded.

"Oh, Neal," she said, "a girl name Tiana called for you this week more than twice. Red, Deanna called for you earlier."

Red and I looked at each other. Then we walked out the door and up the street. He knew Deanna was up the street because she lived there. I couldn't wait to ask Deanna to use her phone to call Tiana. I wanted to know what time she was coming to Paterson.

Ghetto Legend Graduate
Cornelius Kinchen

When we walked up the street, the sun beamed on my back. Erica had just walked in the house. She noticed us and said, "Hi, y'all."

"What's up?" I said. She ran in the house. I guess she went to inform Deanna that we were coming up the street. Then Deanna walked out on the porch and down the steps to meet Red and me, and the two of them hugged.

"What's up, Deanna? When is my girl coming to Paterson?"

"What's up Neal? She should be on her way. We have to sing tonight."

"Oh, okay, because it's been a long wait. I didn't see her all week."

"I know, right? I thought I wasn't ever going to see Red. But she is definitely staying over my house for the weekend."

Red and Deanna went in the house to chill for a little while. I went inside and waited as long as I could. Red and Deanna went to the kitchen to talk, so I followed. I spoke to Rachelle. She spoke back.

Rachelle's boyfriend walked in and I was introduced to Mike. I gave him dap and said, "What's up?" He was dark-skinned and looked like a bum. He hung out by the liquor store with people he knew. I saw him out there a couple of times. His breath smelled like beer someone took a dump in. Then he walked in the kitchen to meet Red. He felt Rachelle's kids were his

Ghetto Legend Graduate
Cornelius Kinchen

kids. He wanted the best for them and he tried to keep things in line around the house. I respected him for that.

We hung out in the kitchen talking, laughing and joking with each other. Forty minutes went by and I went outside to see if Tiana was on her way over. As soon as I walked outside, Tiana and her parents were pulling up in their car. I waited on the porch until she got out the car. I waved and said, "Hello Bishop Wellz and Mother Wellz."

They waved back. "Hi Neal," said Mother Wellz. "Where is my hug?" I walked down the steps and gave her a hug. I shook Bishop Wellz's hand.

Tiana got out the car and said, "I will see you at church Ma." We walked inside Rachelle's house. Her parents waited outside in the front, waiting to see Rachelle, who walked past us towards the front of the house. "Hey, Tiana," she said.

"Hi Rachelle," Tiana said. Mommy wants you. Her and Daddy is outside."

When we were alone, Tiana put her bags down, and hugged and kissed me. She looked me directly in the eyes.

"I missed you," she said, kissing me again.

"I missed you, too," I said. "I was waiting for this moment." She took me by the hand.

"Walk with me to Netta's house. I need Netta to do my hair for church later. Deanna, is Netta home?"

Ghetto Legend Graduate
Cornelius Kinchen

"Yeah, Deanna said, "she is home." Tiana seemed to notice Red for the first time and said, "What's up Red?"

"Oh, I thought the cat had your tongue," he replied.

Tiana laughed. "No, I thought the cat had *your* tongue."

When we got outside, we walked toward Netta's house. Before we got there, I stopped Tiana, looked her in the eyes and asked her something I never asked anyone.

"Tiana, I want you to have my son. Will you have my son?"

I could tell that she was not expecting to hear this, but she answered without hesitation. The look in her eye matched mind.

"Yes, I will have your baby."

I was elated. "When?"

"Whenever the time is right. But try to keep it down a little; my parents didn't leave yet."

"All right," I said. We continued to walk to Netta's house.

When we got there, Netta came to the door and opened it. "Hey love birds," she said.

I said, "What's up Netta?"

Tiana said, "Can you do my hair for church, Netta?"

"Sure. Do you have your stuff with you?"

Ghetto Legend Graduate
Cornelius Kinchen

"Yes."

Netta said, "Whenever you're ready." We sat in the kitchen. I looked her in the eyes.

"You're serious about what we talked about outside?"

"Yes." To me, it felt like the right time to have a baby boy.

"Having a baby is something serious, Neal. I just want to be sure this is what you want."

"This is what I want. I love you, I am in love with you, and I want you to be the mother of my child."

"Okay, baby." We sat and held each other's hand, looking into each other's eyes, just feeling the love. It was almost like you could touch it. Minutes later, Netta walk into the kitchen.

"Are you ready?" She asked.

"Yeah, I'm ready. Neal, are you going to wait here for me to get my hair done or you need to go down the street?"

"I will wait for a little while until I get bored."

I waited for about ten minutes; I was bored. I stood up. "Tiana, I'm going to get something to eat. Are you hungry?"

"Where are you going to get something to eat from?"

"From Grandma's house."

"I will come and get you when I'm finished."

"Cool. I will see you in a little while."

Ghetto Legend Graduate
Cornelius Kinchen

I walked down the street to Grandma's house. When I got there, my family was on the front porch talking. I made my way through everyone.

"Excuse me Grandma, is there something to eat in the kitchen?"

She said, "Yeah, your plate is in the oven."

I walked to the kitchen and looked in the oven. There were five plates in there. I picked a plate, washed my hands and sat at the table to eat. After two scoops of food, I poured a glass of Kool-Aid with ice. I ate and enjoyed my dinner.

At least fifteen minutes passed, Red walked through the door with Tiana. I ate the last bit of food on my plate. Red opened the oven and grabbed a plate, too. Tiana looked at me and said, "Hungry, are we?"

I laughed and said, "Yeah, I was hungry. Your hair looks great!"

She said, "That didn't take long right?"

"Not at all. I was in here grubbing on my food. You should have come earlier, I would have let you taste it."

"What were you eating?"

"Fried chicken, cabbage, rice, and macaroni and cheese."

"You had the works."

Red said, "I'm about to grub, now that your done."

Ghetto Legend Graduate
Cornelius Kinchen

Tiana laughed and said, "Yeah we know you're about to grub, you're a big boy."

"Yo, where is Deanna?" I asked.

Red said, "She is in the front talking to Grandma."

"About what?"

"I don't know," he admitted.

Tiana moved towards the door. "It's almost time for me to get ready for church." That was my cue, so I got up from the table and walked with Tiana up the street. We walked through the back and around to the front to walk up the street. I didn't want to be put on the spot with a million questions from my family. We left Red in the kitchen, eating.

When we were crossing the street, Deanna was still on the porch talking to my family. We didn't want to interrupt, so we kept walking. I walked Tiana to Netta's back door. We hugged each other again. Then I asked, "Tiana, are you going to have my son?" I wanted to be sure, it wasn't like I wanted to pressure her.

With no hesitation she said, "Yes, Neal. I will have your son. Are you going to meet me after church?"

"Yes, I will meet you in front of Deanna's house."

She kissed me. "I have to take a shower and get dressed."

"Yeah, do your thing. I will wait for you later."

"I love you and I will see you later."

"Okay," I said, then I left.

Ghetto Legend Graduate
Cornelius Kinchen

    I walked down the street feeling strong about our relationship. I couldn't wait to have a son that I could love and care for unconditionally. Not once did I think about how I was going to take care of this child. I was living with someone else, no job, no money, and didn't even finish elementary school. The love was blinding realism. I lived in a puppy-love world while with Tiana. For me to think about something so grown up, mental, emotional and financial; stability didn't cross my mind. All I thought was that having a son would give me something to live for. Without my mother's love, I felt I had nothing to live for at times. I thought having a son would allow me to live and be loved unconditionally.

    I couldn't wait to make a baby with Tiana. Her answer to my question of having my son proved her love to me in an extremely special way. I felt for her to agree to this, she really was in love with me. I couldn't wait for that day.

    I walked down the street to chill with my cousins. Deanna and Red stopped me while before I got to Grandma's house.

    Deanna said, "Where is Tiana?"

    "She is at Netta's house getting ready for church," I said.

    She said, "Yeah, well, I'm on my way up the street to get ready for church, too. We have to sing tonight. You and Red should come."

Ghetto Legend Graduate
Cornelius Kinchen

"Maybe one day. But we have to help my Uncle Gilly load up the sound system for church."

"Y'all started a church?" she asked.

"It's been about a year and a half. But I have to go now."

She said, "All right I will see you later, Neal."

Red walked down the street. I waited for him to come back. When Red crossed the street, that was my clue that the girls had gone to church. "Did they leave?" I asked.

"Yeah," he said. "They walked through the field."

"Through the short cut?"

"Yeah." Then he helped load the equipment in the car.

Grandma called me to the telephone, so I went inside and took the call.

"Hello, who is this?"

"It's me, Sasha."

What's up, Sasha?"

"Do you want to come to my house?" she asked. "I can have company now."

I smiled and said, "Now?"

"Yeah, I will meet you have way."

"Okay, meet me half way." I hung up and went outside.

"Yo, Red. I will be right back," I said. "Sasha wants me to come to her house."

Ghetto Legend Graduate
Cornelius Kinchen

"All right, what do you want me tell Tiana if they get out of church before you get back?"

"I will be back before then."

I walked to meet her. I met her on East Eighteenth Street and Hamilton Avenue. We walked to her house on Tenth Avenue. She lived right next door to Highway Church on the second floor. Her apartment was hot and humid. The fans were blowing warm air, making me feel sticky. I was introduced to her mother and little brother. I knew she had a curfew, so I couldn't stay long. We listened to music and talked for at least an hour and a half.

We listened to 'Kissing You' by Total. Then her mother went to the store and left us alone. Sasha had the song on repeat. I loved Total's songs. They were part of the Bad Boy family in music. We sat in her living room. She decided to be like Total and started kissing me. I stopped the kiss. The reason why is that I felt hair on her lip, like a moustache.

Why are girls always coming on to me and kissing me? I thought. I couldn't believe what was happening to me.

Her mother came back with snacks for her son and had bought us sodas. I said, "Thank you."

"You're welcome," she said. "I like him, Sasha. He has manners and he's handsome."

"Thank you," I said again, smiling.

Ghetto Legend Graduate
Cornelius Kinchen

"You can come over anytime. Did Sasha tell you her curfew?"

"Yes, she made that clear to me."

"Yeah, I got to have rules for my children to follow. Do you have a curfew?"

"Yes, ma'am…, I have to go in a couple more minutes."

"That's good," she said. "There is nothing wrong with being obedient to your parents. You will live longer."

It was almost time for the girls to get out of church. I gave myself enough time to walk home. Sasha walked me to the end of the block near the church store. I hugged her and said, "I will come visit you another time."

She said, "I will call you. Can you come see me tomorrow?"

"I will let you know on the phone."

"All right, I will call you tomorrow." Then I walked home. It took me thirty minutes to get to my block.

When I was walking down Fair Street, Tiana was on the porch with Erica, Chris, Deanna, Mike, Jamal and Terrance. They were mimicking people from the church that were singing and shouting. They were laughing and joking about it. I went on the porch. I gave dap to everybody except the ladies. Tiana still had her church dress on. So did everybody else. Terrance laughing and

Ghetto Legend Graduate
Cornelius Kinchen

walking to his car said, "I got to go home and get changed. I will see later."

Tiana and I went inside. Deanna followed us and asked, "Where is your cousin?"

"He should be on his way up here," I said. "After y'all get dressed, we will walk down the street and get him."

Deanna smiled and said, "Yeah, let's do that."

They got dressed and we walked down the street to find Red. He was on the corner with Roger listening to the radio. I heard the radio all the way from up the street.

When we crossed the street, I noticed Che-Che and Kim walking from the Chicken Store. My heart raced with adrenaline. I wondered, what I would say to them while my girl was standing there. They walked passed and said, "Hi, Neal." I said, "What's up?" They kept walking.

Tiana said, "You have a fan club?"

"No, I know them."

For a second, it looked like Tiana was getting jealous. "I don't want to stay down here to see and hear other girls talk to you. Deanna are you ready to go up the street?"

Deanna, Red, and Roger laughed. Then Deanna said, "Yeah. I think Chris and Mike went to get some LQ. They should be back by now." We walked up the street.

As soon as we got up there, we chilled on the porch. The Bishop and the First Lady dropped Rachelle

Ghetto Legend Graduate
Cornelius Kinchen

off at the house and said good night to us. We waved good night and they pulled off.

As soon as they pulled off, Chris, Beonnca, Mike and Yvette walked around the corner. Terrance had just pulled up, too. We got together and went to the basement of Deanna's house to party.

When we got in the basement, Chris turned on the lights. Terrance and I talked about the weights and getting bigger. I lay on the bench and said, "Terrance spot me and make sure the weights don't fall on me."

He said with a southern accent, "Yeah, Neal go ahead." I lifted several times. Then he got under and I spotted him. When he lifted, it was like he was about to perform on the television show *World's Strongest Man*. I couldn't believe how strong he was. He stopped after doing twenty lifts. I quit after that. He out-lifted me.

He went to the back of the basement where the party was. I followed and when I got back there, the party had already started. Everyone, including Terrance, had a cup of LQ. I didn't want to drink that stuff and was the coolest without it.

Hours later, they were drunk. I was the only one sober. The best part was we were safe. We worried about Terrance because he had his mother's car. We didn't want him to drive like that. I asked, "Terrance how are you going to drive?"

Ghetto Legend Graduate
Cornelius Kinchen

"I will stay the night over here if I'm too drunk to drive. I don't want my mother to scream at me and lose my privilege to drive."

"Yeah, good answer."

Tiana said, "That made a lot of sense." Everyone laughed.

It was time for me to go. I mentioned it to Tiana and she said, "Yeah, I think I had enough to drink. Neal, walk me to Netta's house."

"Come on." We said, good night to everyone and we walked out the back door from the basement. When I walked Tiana over and into the house, we kissed good night. Her breath smelled like LQ.

I said, "Good night and I love you." She said the same to me. I walked out of Netta's back door, and at the same time, Red and Deanna came up from the basement door. I continued walking slowly to wait for Red. When I got to the front, Red said, "Yo, hold up. I'm coming." When I looked back to see what he wanted, he left Deanna with a hug and a kiss good night.

I felt I was ready to lose my virginity, and I wanted it to be with Tiana. Red said, "Deanna and I had done it already."

I smiled and said, "Word!"

He smiled. "Yeah, we did it in Deanna's basement." I said, "I want to try it. No wonder Deanna always wants you."

Ghetto Legend Graduate
Cornelius Kinchen

First encounter

September1996, Saturday, Today while I was chilling with Tiana on Deanna's porch, By'ron and Rob walked around the corner. They walked up to me trying to regulate (roughhouse) me in front of my girl.

They struggled to get me to the ground. When they did, it was hard for them to keep me on the ground. I was still a tough play fighter. They beat my knees up. I took it like a soldier to remind them I was still hard-body. I proved myself by fighting back. When I fought back, I made them quit. While they were hitting me with their hardest punches, I couldn't feel any pain when I thought of comparing the pain to my mothers' drug addiction. They were impressed with my mental toughness and strength.

They ran off a short distance after I got my punches back. Then they walked up to me and gave me dap. Rob said, "What's up? I thought you were a traitor for a minute."

"Nah, you know I transferred to get a fresh start."

By'ron said, "Neal, are you coming back to School 6?"

I said, "Yeah, I'm going to come back the third marking period."

He said, "Yeah, we will see if you are a man of your word."

"That I am," I said.

Ghetto Legend Graduate
Cornelius Kinchen

Rob said, "Is that your girlfriend?"

"Yeah. Why?"

"The fellows around the corner tried to get with her at a party on Auburn."

I said, "Did it work?"

"Obviously not, you're with her. She doesn't even speak to nobody around the corner anymore."

I said, "Yeah, definitely the third marking period. Y'all will see me again. I want to graduate with y'all. Y'all two is like my brothers."

They agreed, gave me dap and said, "We are going around the corner. We will see you third marking period."

"Aight, one." They walked up the street and around the corner.

Tiana had moved to the side during the time of rough play. She did not want to get hit by jumping in or in the way of punches thrown. When she walked back on the porch from inside Deanna's house, she said, "Neal, y'all play too rough. Are you all right?"

"Yeah, I'm all right."

"Are you thirsty?"

"Yeah, can you bring me some water?" She went inside and bought me some ice cold water and some napkins for my face. I was hot and sweaty.

Tiana said, "I have to call my father."

"For what?"

"I have to go home and get my changing clothes for tonight."

"Come on then." We walked to Netta's house and she used the phone. I waited on the back porch while she made her call.

When she came out, she said, "They are in Paterson at the church. They will be here to pick me up in ten minutes. Just wait here with me, Neal." I drank my water slow and continued wiping my face.

"I will wait with you," I said.

Ten minutes later, her parents pulled up. I walked her to the car. I said, "Hi, Mrs. Wellz and Bishop Wellz." They said hi, and Tiana got in the car and said, "I will be back later." I said, "Bye, I will see you later." They pulled off and I walked down the street with a cool Diddy bop.

When I got down the street, Roger was on the corner listening to the radio. I went up to him and said, "What's up, Roger?"

"What happened last night player? You almost got caught out there."

I laughed and said, "Yeah, almost but I played it off. That's why we went up the street. She got jealous a little."

He laughed. "I know, but you're smooth, B. You got that off."

"Yo, it's more in school who is on my jock."

"You are too cool, B." Then I had an idea.

Ghetto Legend Graduate
Cornelius Kinchen

"Roger, let me hold your radio to go to this other girl house on Tenth."

"When, now?"

"Yeah, I will be back."

"How long are you going to be over there?" "Not long," I said. "She has a ten o'clock curfew."

"Yeah. Just be back by ten o'clock."

"I will be back before then.

I went inside the house to call Sasha. I called and asked her if I could visit her. She got permission from her mother. I went back outside and got the radio from Roger. This was the coolest thing he had ever done for me. We got cooler, right at that moment.

After giving me the radio, he said, "Don't drain the batteries out and be careful."

"All right." I was happy and felt like the man. I continued to walk up the street with the radio on blast. I received so much attention when I walked with the radio so loud. The hood was parting on me and the music I was playing. At this point people couldn't tell me I wasn't cool.

I got to her house faster than I thought I would. When I got in front Sasha's house, I turned the radio off and rang her doorbell. Her mother answered the door.

"Hello," I said.

She said, "Hi," and welcomed me into her home. It was even humid in her hallway. Also, it smelled like cooked doo-doo. I waited in her living room. I couldn't

Ghetto Legend Graduate
Cornelius Kinchen

believe what I smelled. Ten minutes later, Sasha walked in the living room happy. She gave me a hug. Then she sat down beside me for a couple of minutes. Her mother had left to go to her friend's house. Sasha took me to her room, turned on her favorite song and got horny for me.

She pulled me in her room and threw me on the bed. I was surprised. I couldn't get in to it. She tried to kiss me. I felt she dookied and I was immediately turned off. She was grinding on me with her clothes on. Then she proceeded to take her clothes off. When she did, I noticed that her crotch had a bush that needed to be landscaped.

I said, "I can't do this, because I have never done this before. Plus we don't have protection." Suddenly we heard the door slam.

Sasha jumped off me and said, "Go in the living room my mother is coming upstairs."

I walked into the living room and sat down. When her mother got upstairs she said, "Sasha, get the air freshener and spray in here, because it stinks and you have company." She got the spray and sprayed. That didn't help the scent because it was so muggy in there.

When she did that, I said, "I have to go now. My cousin wants me to bring his radio back now." She looked embarrassed.

"My mother is trippin'; I will call you later."

"All right, I will see you later."

Ghetto Legend Graduate
Cornelius Kinchen

I left and went back to Grandma's house laughing at the situation. When I got back to Grandma's house, I went upstairs to Roger's room and gave him back his radio.

He said, "You are back earlier than what I expected."

"Yeah, the broad was trying to give me the kitty."

He smiled and said, "My niecee (sarcasism) got some poon-tang! All right!"

I gave him the radio and went back outside. I hung out on the porch for a couple minutes. I thought about what had happened at Sasha's house. I laughed to myself. I didn't want anyone to find about this situation. I kept the details to myself. I looked up the street, and I noticed Bishop had dropped Tiana off again.

The sun went down. I waited a couple of minutes before walking up the street. A dark-skinned teenager with a radio in his hand walked up to me and asked, "Is Roger here?"

I said, "What's your name?"

"Black." He wasn't lying about that.

"Black, he is upstairs getting ready to come out. What kind of a radio is that?"

"This is a yellow Sony radio." His radio had a knock to it. It was hot and I wanted one just like it.

I went inside to get Roger and we both went outside. He left with Black and I walked up the street. It was getting darker outside; I looked in the sky and noticed a full moon. I went to Rachelle's house and knocked on the door.

    Mike's drunk ass answered and said, "What's up Neal? Tiana! Neal is here to see you. You can come in if you would like to."

    "I will wait outside."

    "Then suit yourself." He meandered back into the house.

    Tiana walked on the porch, I said, "What's up? I thought you weren't coming back to Paterson."

    "What made you think that?"

    "You took long to come back."

    "I had to take another shower and get my clothes ready for tonight."

    "Oh, okay," then I asked. "Did you get everything you needed?"

    "Yes, I think so. I don't think I forgot anything."

    "What do you want to do tonight?"

    "Whatever you want to do."

    "Okay, that's cool." We hung out on the porch hugged up facing each other. I proceeded to give her a hicky on her neck. After I gave her one, she gave me one, too. Then she wanted to go inside Rachelle's house. But I wanted to stay on the porch, I didn't want to hear Mike's voice and smell his garbage breath. So we stayed on the porch, hugging.

    I didn't hang around too late because I had to go church. I didn't want to witness Tiana getting drunk again. I said, "Tiana, I would like for you to stop drinking."

She looked at me with a smile and asked, "Neal, are you serious?"

"Yes, I am. Especially if you are planning to carry my baby boy."

"You know what, you're right. I will stop, just for you."

"Not for me. For the baby, and for you."

I left it at that and said my good night three hours later.

Ghetto Legend Graduate
Cornelius Kinchen

Thanksgiving

    The weekends went on the same until Thanksgiving. I walked back and forth, in and out of Grandma's house. I thought about the night before, how my Aunts and Grandmother started preparing food for thanksgiving.

    The day of Thanksgiving, I thought about my team record for PAL East, we were one game away from the football championship. We had to play PAL West for the championship on Sunday.

    Also, I couldn't wait to see Tiana today. When I spoke to her earlier in the week on the phone, she said she knew Bell the PAL South cheerleader coach. She had a meeting with her to try out for the cheerleader squad. I was hoping she would keep me updated.

    It was little before noon. I walked in the kitchen. Grandma was mixing the sweet potatoes pie around for the pie. Aunt Doris was mixing the corn bread with the blender. Aunt Kate was making the stuffing. Aunt Beava was putting the cream on the cakes. Aunt Branda was putting the macaroni and cheese in the oven. I loved the smell of soul food. The kitchen smelled so good, I wanted to fix my plate. After I walked in the kitchen and looked at everyone, I walked right back out and got out of the way of the best soul food cooks that I knew on this earth.

    I went up the street to be with Tiana. When I got up there no one was there except Deanna, Erica, and

Ghetto Legend Graduate
Cornelius Kinchen

Jamal. Mike asked us to watch the house while he was gone. Rachelle was gone, too. Tiana and I went into Rachelle's room. I looked up at the time and it was 11:49a.m.

Tiana and I started kissing slow. Then we were horny and wanted each other. We took each other's clothes off and lay down.

This was it! We were finally going to make love for the first time! Since I didn't really know what to do, I had to go slow. We were making true love. We would stop and start again. It was so fun; I wanted to keep going without eating Thanksgiving dinner. We did keep going until about seven o'clock when we took a break.

Deanna knocked on the door and said, "Neal, Red wants to know if you are hungry."

I said, "Yeah, is the food ready?"

"I think so."

"Deanna, tell Red to bring me something to eat. Tell him to wrap it up for me and bring it up here."

"All right we got you. Tiana did you want something to eat, too?"

She said, "Yeah, bring me a little bit."

"All right," she said, then left.

When they left, we were at it again. We didn't use any protection... Nothing else was on my mind except for having a baby with her and raising a family. I knew I had to wait until high school to have a baby. At the time, we discussed it.

Ghetto Legend Graduate
Cornelius Kinchen

On the other hand, I didn't think about AIDS, crabs, syphilis, gonorrhea, or any other sexually transmitted diseases. I was young, and blinded by love and sex.

Now that I think about it, I wish I had someone to talk to about sex to abstane until married. Many people have lost their lives because of having unprotected sex and contracting a disease they could not get rid of. Life is the most precious thing that God could have ever given to man, and it is too bad that many people don't take it more serious by not having sex until married.

On the other hand my life hadn't ended, it just began. I wasn't a virgin anymore. While I was contemplating this, Deanna and Red bought the food back up the street.

They knocked on the door. We opened the door with sheets wrapped around us. We grabbed our food and ate in Rachelle's room. Tiana and I didn't stop making love until twelve o'clock that night.

Finally, we got dressed. I was ready to tell Red what happened. We heard Mike's drunk mouth talking to Red. I walked out the room ready to leave. Mike walked in the house with green breath and said, "What's up, Neal? You leaving already?"

"I need some air."

He laughed and said, "Yeah, the heat is kicking in here like the projects." He walked into the kitchen.

Ghetto Legend Graduate
Cornelius Kinchen

Tiana and I went outside. We hung out on the porch with Red and Deanna.

"Y'all were in that room for a long time," Deanna remarked.

Tiana laughed. "I will talk to you later." I looked at Red and he smirked.

"Who was down the street?" I asked.

"Everybody. Oh, Kevin was looking for you, too."

"Is people still down the street?"

"Everybody just left not too long ago."

"King Jah, dark skin, built like a monkey, from Guayana wanted to play football earlier. But everyone wasn't at Grandma's house yet," Red said.

"I'm glad you didn't interrupt me. I would have said 'no,' and you know why, Red."

Deanna laughed and said, "Yeah, Tiana we know why." Tiana laughed along with her.

"Yeah, Deanna. You are funny."

I hugged my girl, and put my lips close to her ear. "I will talk to you on the phone when I get down the street," I whispered. "I love you."

"All right, I love you, too. Call me at Netta's house. I will be waiting by the phone." We kissed, then I walked down the street. Red stayed with his girl. Rachelle would be gone until Friday evening; she went south for Thanksgiving.

Ghetto Legend Graduate
Cornelius Kinchen

I went down the street, when I got there, the pie was in the refrigerator. Grandma was going upstairs to get ready for bed. The phone was already plugged up in the kitchen. She said, "When you're done with the phone unplug it and bring it upstairs."

"All right," I said I cut two slices of sweet potato pie, sat at the dining room table and ate. I called Tiana and talked to her for two and a half hours. When I was done talking, I took the phone back upstairs to my Grandma's room.

The whole entire weekend, Tiana and I spent as much time together before she went back to Hackensack. I was on top of the world, knowing I wasn't a virgin anymore. Our love had become more intense after having sex. I wanted to be there for her, and she wanted me around more and more. She was extremely emotional about our situation.

The situation was, we were young; fourteen to be exact. We used no protection and we only cared about living in the moment. The love was powerful; it took over our minds, bodies and souls almost from the moment when we met. *We were* deeply in love. Experiencing her body was fun. We felt like adults in teenage bodies, and were trying to come to terms with how we felt about each other.

The emotional changes enhanced our relationship. We continued to love and support each other genuinely. I always wanted to be with her.

Ghetto Legend Graduate
Cornelius Kinchen

I went to visit her one o'clock the next afternoon at Netta's house. I had football practice at five o'clock that evening.

"Tiana we are in the championship on Sunday. I know you can't make it because you have to go to church. But I will play my heart out for us."

"Awwww, that is so cute." She kissed and hugged me closer. "Who are y'all playing against in the championship?"

I said, "PAL West. Why? Do you know players from that team?"

"Yeah, Sharky and Smoky."

"Yeah... we are playing them in the championship."

"I wish you luck and I hope y'all win."

I said, "Thank you."

We talked and hung out for three hours; all too soon, it was time for me to go.

"Well, I have to get ready for practice." I was reluctant to leave, and she knew it.

"What time do you have to be at practice?"

"At five o'clock."

She said, "Go and get ready. I'll be here when you get back."

"All right." I walked down the street, got into uniform, and walked to the field house at Eastside. It was getting chilly, but it was a great day to practice with the energy I had from the night before.

Ghetto Legend Graduate
Cornelius Kinchen

In practice, we worked very hard during the defensive drills and offensive drills. I was in rotation at fullback and halfback. I ran for a practice touchdown twice. Each time Little D tried while I was on defensive, I caught him before he could explode through the hole. Little D was the starting running back. He was fast and savvy on his feet, and could shake from a possible tackle.

It was dark out after an hour of being on the field. Coach Cassius called a dive play for Little D to run, and I had to block.

Set-hut!

I burst through the A gap right followed by Little Donald with the football and I blocked the first guy in sight to open up the hole for him. The next guy had grabbed Little D's ankle and tackled him. He got upset with me. Before he could get in my face while saying, "If I would have twisted my ankle, I would have fucked you up."

I looked at him straight in the eyes. "Yeah, right. That will never happen." He was known for his intimidation and his boxing skills. However, he wasn't familiar with my fighting skills. Trying to get to me and held back by other teammates he said, "What! Let's fight then! You have a lot of mouth.

I said, "Come on. Bring it!" After the coach intervened, we continued to practice.

The next play, I was sent on a screen. When I jumped in the air to catch the ball Schoharie was at

Ghetto Legend Graduate
Cornelius Kinchen

corner and he cracked me in the back. That shit hurt me bad. I had to sit out for a couple of plays. I wanted to display how tough I was, but it hurt too badly. I got over it and continued to practice.

After practice, I went to visit Tiana in my football gear for a while. I kept in mind that I had a big game tomorrow. When she saw me, she was impressed.

"Y'all have Eastside High School colors, too?"

"Yes we do."

"You look sexy in those football pants," she said. I grinned.

It was getting late, and I had to go. "Tiana," I said, "I will have to talk to you tomorrow after the game."

"Call me in the morning," she replied. "I know you have to get some rest for the game tomorrow."

"Yeah, I will do that." We hugged and kissed. Then I went down the street to get ready for the big game.

Ghetto Legend Graduate
Cornelius Kinchen

The big football game

    The big day was here. Championship Sunday, PAL EAST vs. PAL WEST at Hinchcliffe Stadium in Paterson, and I was souped. Dad and my little brother Torrie, Uncle T.D., Randy, and Donell came out to support me. They drove me there, then got seats in the stands. I wanted to show my skills at defensive end. This was the first game they had ever come to see me play.

    I was nervous and scared, I wanted to show off my skills and make my family proud. Most of all, I wanted to help my team win a championship. PAL WEST was our rivalry like the competition between the Eastside Ghosts and Kennedy Knights football teams. We were the eight-grade Ghost orange-navy-white team colors and they were the eight-grade Knights red-black-white team colors.

    We played first. The sun was shining bright and the turf was warm. We were warming up on the field, while the other team was just running onto the field to warm up. While I was warming up, I looked to my right to see if Dad and my uncles were watching me get ready to perform. I felt like I was in the NFL. The support from my family was appreciated, and I would choose this over a million dollars any day. It would have been complete if my mother was there. Just once, I wished that she had been there for me, especially that day in my young life.

Ghetto Legend Graduate
Cornelius Kinchen

    If she had been there, she might have been inspired to put down her rock addiction and want to see more moments like this one. She failed to know or want to know of my accomplishments on that day. She knowingly was heading towards her death, being addicted to crack.

    Both teams headed for the sideline to begin our championship game. We were on the visitors' sideline. Technically, we were on their field. They had the advantage with a sixth man to give them extra momentum.

    The captains were on their way off the field. We kicked the ball and they received. They ran the ball to the thirty-eight yard line. I started in my position as defensive end. I got close to the quarter back several times, but I didn't get a sack. I stopped several runs and forced them to pass. Little D was at safety. They couldn't run the ball, however, they passed the ball to Little Donald's side several times for pass completions.

    Little D was four foot ten, but he had skills as a running back and speed at safety position. I was taller than him, standing five-four. Sharky and Smokey were the same height, five-six. They had two advantages: height and speed. One could see and throw over our defense and the other could catch over the defense to score touchdowns.

    I asked the coach to switch Little D and me for a better defensive scheme, but he wouldn't. He just ignored

Ghetto Legend Graduate
Cornelius Kinchen

me. They did the same play on our weak defensive line throughout the game to obtain the victory over PAL EAST.

They won the championship in a skilled fashion. The score was twenty to thirteen, in favor of PAL West. We showed good sportsmanship by shaking their hands to congratulate them on their championship.

Most of all, I was happy to have my father at the game. His presence meant the world to me, and I would never forget it. When we went home, my Uncle T.D. complained about the coaching on defense having recognized the problem in the secondary, which was Little D's height. It wasn't our fault that the coach decided to ignore a good idea.

When I got home, I packed up my equipment. I had to return it to the coaches at our football meeting on Wednesday. I wanted to keep my football helmet and jersey, since this was my last season playing for PAL EAST.

Even though I wanted to, I didn't see Tiana after the game; she had to go home and get ready for school after church. I had to do the same.

Hours after the game, I sat on the front porch. Grandma and family had just got out of Sunday service. As they were walking in the house, the phone rang,

Grandma said, "Neal, answer the phone. It might be your little girl friend." I picked it up, and sure enough,

Ghetto Legend Graduate
Cornelius Kinchen

it was Tiana on the phone. For a minute, I thought Grandma was psychic.

She told me she couldn't make it this weekend and asked about the game. I told her we lost.

Don't worry; as long as you made it to the championship, you must have done something right. Did you get in the game?"

"Yeah," I said, "I played the entire game on defense. My father came to the game with my uncles to see me play."

"Were you nervous that they were there?"

"Yeah, this was the only game they attended throughout the season."

"Ohhhhh, okay."

I could hear her sister Trisha in the background asking to use the phone really quick. My phone beeped and she said, "My sister wants to use the phone. I will call you back in five minutes. Stay near the phone."

"Okay." I clicked over and it was Mother Warner on the phone. We spoke for a little while before I gave the phone to Grandma.

"How are you doing, baby?"

"I'm fine." At that moment, I was anything but fine, but I wasn't going to tell her.

"You miss your mother, don't you?"

I said, "Yes." My heart dropped into my shoes, and ached at that moment, but I would not let her see my pain.

Ghetto Legend Graduate
Cornelius Kinchen

"I know, baby. I will pray for her. Don't you worry about her; she is in God's hands, okay, baby? Just keep on praying and doing what you are doing. Go to school and make something of yourself. And I love you, and I am proud of you, Neal."

The dam burst. I cried because Mother Warner was so sweet, and loved me enough to care about my feelings. She wanted the best for me and I loved her for that. While wiping my eyes, I said, "Thank you, Mother Warner, for the love and encouraging words."

"I love you. Anything you want to talk about, I am here for you, baby, okay?"

"Yes, ma'am," I said, still wiping my tears away. "I love you too, Mother Warner. Hold on, I'm going to call Grandma to the phone."

"All right baby, bye," she said. Then I called Grandma to pick up the phone.

I went to the bathroom to wash my face. Afterwards, I went outside to catch some fresh air. I walked around the block and sat in front of the church before I walked up Fair Street. I felt like God had spoke to me through Mother Warner. He had comforted me in the time of need. The pain and neglect had me in a sad and lonely frenzy before she called. It was a good thing to cry and talk out problems. Revenge and rebelling isn't the answer.

Ghetto Legend Graduate
Cornelius Kinchen

Needing love

February 1997 rolled around, and I hadn't gotten a hug or any kind of affection from neither my father nor my mother. I thought parenting was about loving, caring and providing a safe-secure environment for your child by any means necessary. I guess I was wrong.

My birthday rolled around again. It was early, and I was getting ready to catch the bus to School 30. I was dressed and ready to leave. My Uncle Gilly walked down the steps and noticed my unhappy spirit. My father didn't acknowledge my fourteenth birthday nor did he wish me a happy birthday. I never recalled a birthday party either. Not even a card or cake. I explained this to my uncle.

He did the unthinkable. He knew it was my birthday. He walked downstairs to wish me a happy birthday. While I cried, he gave me encouraging words of strength and made it relevant to his situation growing up without a mother. He understood my neglectful pain. He gave me a hug and fifty dollars for my birthday.

God sent more comfort to me on time, again. I loved God for His on-time actions and for His will. I cheered up, then went to school. At the time, I couldn't understand. I could only put up this macho façade but for so long. Things bothered me more than I realized, and pouring my heart out and releasing my pain, even if it was for a little while, helped me a great deal.

Ghetto Legend Graduate
Cornelius Kinchen

It was getting closer to graduation. Four months until the big show, and two days away from the third marking period. I told Grandma and Aunt Barbara that I wanted to go back to School 6 to graduate with the friends I had from kindergarten. They understood and transferred me back to School 6 in the middle of the third marking period.

I was placed in Mrs. Rizzo's 8-3 class. It felt good to be back with my original friends and class. I didn't care about what class I was in, I just wanted to continue to do good academically. I want to broaden my opportunities of getting accepted into a great high school. This would only be possible based on my academic performance every day in the classroom. I understood that with respect for myself, my education, the staff and students, I would reach the goals that I had set a long time ago. I followed these mental and physical guidelines to ensure my future success.

When I got back, I felt welcomed. I surprised my friends at lunchtime--Rob, By'ron, Frank, Allen, Joe-sef, Jay, and the girls. The headlines were about my return, and who was going to the prom in May with whom. As usual, I was feeling my swag at School 6. I was the front-page headliner with the girls, until we graduated.

Ghetto Legend Graduate
Cornelius Kinchen

Prom time

    I was focused. I wanted to go with a girl named Stacey to the prom. She was dark-skinned with a baby face, long black hair, and was shorter than me by four inches. I waited to see who would ask me. Some girls in 8-1 and 8-2 asked me who I was going to the prom with, and I said that I didn't know yet.

    After lunch, it was time to go back to class. Mrs. Rizzo had to settle our class by yelling in a loud screaming voice. "Shut! Your! Mouth!" We all settled down.

    Tina laughed and asked, "Mrs. Rizzo are you upset? Why are you screaming at us? We didn't do nothing wrong, we just came from lunch. Give us a chance to settle down."

    Mrs. Rizzo apologized for the outburst. "Okay, Tina…, it is entirely too loud in here, I can't even hear myself." We sat at our desks quietly waiting to go to our algebra class with Mr. Fitzgerald. He was an excellent teacher, and made sure we were prepared to go to the next level.

    After his class, it was back to Mrs. Rizzo's for dismissal. I walked home with By'ron and Rob. We stopped on Auburn where the block money flowed. By'ron's house was right on the corner. They had easy access to the money, if they worked out there. First, they had to watch.

Ghetto Legend Graduate
Cornelius Kinchen

Then I told them, "Yo, I'll get up with you later. Stop by my house."

After my homework, I went to work out with my Uncle T.D. in the backyard. I wanted to lift weights and get stronger; moreover, I was going to high school in the fall. I went in the backyard to prepare the weights. He went to his car and got the boxing pads and gloves to teach me how to box.

This was my recreation. First, he had me start lifting twenty-five pounds on each side of the weight bar to warm up. Second, he had me lift thirty-five pounds by adding ten pounds to each side. Lastly, he had me lifting forty-five pounds on each side.

After we worked out, he put the pads on, and I put on the gloves. He taught me a three-piece combination, as we continued he taught me a total of thirty-two punch combinations. He taught me everything I know about boxing, including bobbing, weaving, ducking and footwork, too. I enjoyed it. Every time I would complete the combination, he would say, "You have power and speed behind your punches." This motivated me more. Also, I was able to air out my frustration physically. When I finished, I felt great about myself. I felt like nothing or no one could touch me.

After the intense workout, Rob and By'ron came to visit. I couldn't wait to test my new boxing skills on them in slap-boxing. We slap-boxed in the middle of the street and on the side of Grandma's house. Rob and

Ghetto Legend Graduate
Cornelius Kinchen

By'ron were up first. Rob slapped up By'ron for at least five minutes until By'ron had ran out of breath. Next, I gave Rob a breather before I slapped him up. After his breather, we were out in the middle of the street. Uncle T.D. watched from the backyard. He yelled out the combinations and I performed them on Rob. At this point, Rob couldn't touch me as easily. We stopped and went in the backyard. I went inside the house to get water for all three of us to drink.

We sat in the backyard, and we laughed about the slap-boxing matches between us. Rob mentioned, "By, you and Neal have to slap-box." I drank my water and came off the steps ready to slap By'ron up.

I said, "By, come get some." He got up and we began right there in the backyard. He bought the Brooklyn back aka the windmill slaps. He caught me three times in the face.

I didn't expect him to do that. Uncle T.D. said, "Neal, sit on it and send a straight right hand." I did just that. Before By'ron could hit me two more times, I had stopped his windmill slaps with my combinations. I did a twenty-piece punch combo to By'ron's' face until he quit. Rob souped it up and teased By'ron about getting slapped up worst than him.

We sat a little while longer and drank water. After a while, they had to go home and get ready for school. I went in the house ate dinner and got ready for school, too.

Ghetto Legend Graduate
Cornelius Kinchen

The next day, we picked up each other to walk to school together. On the way to school, Rob asked, "When are you going to ask Stacey to the prom?"

"I'll ask her today," I said.

"Yeah, right."

By'ron said to Rob, "When are you going to ask Shannon to the prom."

"Today," Rob said, "only if you ask Jamaican Mateasha."

I was surprised. "By, you are going to the prom with Mateasha?"

"Yeah. I'm going to ask her cousin, too."

"You can't possibly pull that off!"

"Watch me, son," he said,

"If you don't have both girls on your arm on prom night," I said, "I am going to 'Johnny Gill' the mess out of your neck. Bet?"

Rob said, "I am in on that bet, too." Then we all agreed to the bet and shook on it.

When we arrived at school, we went to separate classes and said we would see each other at lunchtime. I went to Mrs. Rizzo's class and they went to 8-1, Mr. Steve's class.

When lunchtime came, we got together and played basketball in the gym. It was 8-1 versus any class, including mine. We played until lunch was almost over. Ten minutes before we went to class, I went to the playground to find Stacey. I found her with her girls from

Ghetto Legend Graduate
Cornelius Kinchen

her class. I asked her in front of all of her friends, "Stacey do you want to go to the prom with me?"

She said, "Are you serious?" "Yes," I said.

"Yeah, I will go with you. Come to my house after school to talk about what we are going to wear."

"Okay, but I have to do my homework first."

"Bring it to my house so we can do our homework together." That wasn't a bad idea. I told her so.

"I will see you later, then."

"Yeah, meet me in front of the school so we can walk together."

"All right," I said, smiling.

Then I ran to tell By'ron and Rob. "Yo, Stacey said she will go to the prom with me. What's up with y'all answer?" They hadn't even gotten the courage to ask yet. Therefore, I didn't even worry about them after they told me no results. I figured as long as I had my prom date, I was good to go. From there, I went to my class.

Before I knew it, class was out and school was dismissed. I couldn't wait to meet with Stacey in front of the school. She probably thought I was bluffing, based on my player type persona. I caught up with Stacey in front of the school. She was waiting with Frank and his brother. We walked toward Franks' house. Stacey opened the gate, and Frank and his brother followed. I knew Frank lived on Carroll Street, but I didn't know they lived

Ghetto Legend Graduate
Cornelius Kinchen

next door to each other. Moreover, I didn't know they were cousins. When I got there, Stacey's mother had just walked downstairs.

Stacey said, "Ma, this Cornelius. Cornelius, this is my mom."

I said, "Hi, how are you doing."

"Fine," she responded. "Cat, he is handsome."

"Ma, he asked me to the prom," Stacey said. "I am going with him to the prom."

"What color do y'all want to wear?" her mother asked.

"I want to wear a baby blue dress to the prom."

To me, Stacey's mother asked, "How is baby blue?"

"It's cool with me," I replied. "I can wear a white tuxedo with the baby blue bow tie and under vest to match your dress."

"Don't worry about the transportation, I have that under control and paid for. Y'all is going in a limo. Plus I have a camera."

"All right," I said, smiling. "Then we are all set. I'll let Grandma know."

"Did you still want to do your homework?"

"Sure," I answered, "come on." We went inside and her mother went next door to Frank's house.

Stacey and I went upstairs. Her sister Chrissy was upstairs doing her homework, too. We sat down at the kitchen table and did our homework. I flirted with her the whole time. She enjoyed my presence. It felt like I was her dream come true. She was so happy to be around me, especially since this was our first time talking and hanging out together. I felt like I made her happier because I felt the same way about her and us.

    We were done with our homework quickly. Then we went outside to chill and catch fresh air. We sat on her porch for an hour just hanging out, talking and flirting with each other. The time was going by fast; it always seemed to do that when I was enjoying myself. I had to go home before Grandma worried about me.

    Before I left, I said, "Stacey, I enjoyed your company. I will talk to you in school tomorrow."

    "I enjoyed being with you, too," she admitted. "I hope to see you and talk to you tomorrow, too."

    "You will. Have a good night." Then I walked home.

    When I got home, it was quarter to five. I walked in the kitchen, and dinner was being served. I said, "Hi, Grandma, guess what? I found a date to go to the prom with in May."

    Her face lit up. "Hi, Neal... is that where you are coming from?"

    "Yes, ma'am. I met Stacey's mother and we discussed the color we are wearing to the prom."

    "Is she pretty?"

    "Yes. I want to wear a white tuxedo and baby blue bow tie and under vest."

Ghetto Legend Graduate
Cornelius Kinchen

"What color is Stacey wearing?" said Grandma.

"She is wearing a baby blue dress."

"All right… we will make arrangements to get you that tuxedo. I made some tomatoes, rice, and corn. Are you hungry?"

"Yes, ma'am," I answered. She fixed me a plate and I ate. I then went outside in the backyard to let my food digest. Uncle T.D was waiting for me so we could practice boxing.

I got up from the steps and put the gloves on. We worked on the three-piece punch for two minutes. Then we followed up with the ten-pieces, which included ducking, bobbing and weaving. When I didn't pay attention or I messed up on a punch combination, Uncle T.D. would hit me in the head or the face. So the next time I got it down to perfection. We practiced for an hour and stopped.

The next day, after school, Uncle Gilly surprised me by taking me to get measured for my tuxedo. We went to a men's clothing store in Passaic on Main Avenue. When we got there, it was crowded with parents and their kids. I guess they were preparing for their prom early, too.

I was excited about getting measured for my tuxedo. I felt extremely important, feeling like I was going to be fly and fresh prom night. I knew I was handsome, thanks to Mother Warner and from the girl talk headlines at school. As my uncle and I waited in the

Ghetto Legend Graduate
Cornelius Kinchen

waiting area, I looked around the tux shop and I noticed a black tux and a white tux on the mannequins. I grabbed a tuxedo magazine advertisement off the little table in front of us. I looked through it while we waited.

I saw different styles that I liked for my future high school prom. Then as I looked through the tux advertisement book, I noticed the white tuxedo with the baby blue cummerbund and bow tie. I held the book over to my left and said, "Uncle Gilly, look... this is the tux and the color I want."

"Oh, yeah... that is a nice color for you. Your date is wearing a blue or white dress?"

I said, "She is wearing a baby blue dress."

"That will look real nice," he said.

In the middle of the conversation, an associate walked over and said, "Good evening. How can I be of assistance to you today?"

Uncle Gilly said, "Yes, my son is here to get measured for a tuxedo for his eighth grade prom."

"When is the prom, sir?"

"May thirtieth."

He said, "This is the perfect time to get prepared. We usually get a lot of customers getting measured a week or two days before prom. You guys have perfect timing. Could you stand up, please?"

Ghetto Legend Graduate
Cornelius Kinchen

When I stood up, he pulled out a measuring tape. He measured my neck, arms, chest, waist, and leg length. Then he wrote on the pad.

"What color tuxedo would you like?" I pulled out the advertising book and showed him the tuxedo.

"Cool." He wrote everything down that we requested, including white shoes and the right size on a receipt to give to the cashier. "You guys are all set" he said, "and your tuxedo will be ready in seven days. Thank you and have a nice day."

Uncle Gilly said, "Thank you." We walked to the cashier and my uncle left a deposit, then we left.

The sun was still shining bright. When we got home, I was planning to go to Stacey house to tell her where I went. After we drove home, I got out the car and began walking up the street.

Uncle Gilly said, "Where are you going?"

I said, "To my prom date's house to talk and chill with her on Carroll Street."

"All right, as long as somebody knows where you are." I continued walking and passed Deanna's house. Jamal, Bill, and Tiana's other brother Neil were on the porch.

Jamal laughed. "I knew it was you from a block away. I know how you walk."

Bill agreed and said, "It's your cool walk, that's how I knew, too."

Ghetto Legend Graduate
Cornelius Kinchen

I laughed and said, "Thanks. What's up with y'all?"

Bill said, "Just got off work. We were just kicking it. Where are you headed? Around the corner?"

"Yeah," I said. "I just got measured for my prom."

"Oh, yeah. I forgot…, Deanna, Red and Tiana have a prom to go to. What high school you are going to?"

"I have no clue, and Eastside isn't on my list either."

"Yeah," Bill said, "I heard its nothing but trouble up there."

"But I would go to Rosa Parks High school for creative writing," I said.

He didn't seem the least bit surprised "That's cool man. If you can go, go."

But Jamal was surprised, and said, "You write stories?"

I said, "I love writing. I just don't tell a lot of people. I'm into writing short stories and essays."

Jamal was impressed. Not often did anyone from the 'hood hear about someone who wanted to write. "I heard that's a hard school to get in."

DD said, "You can play an instrument to get into Rosa Parks, too. You would just have to watch out for the gay kids up there."

We all laughed at that. On that note, it was time for me to leave.

"I have to go. I will holla at y'all later," I said.

"All right," they said in unison.

I continued my walk toward Carroll Street heading to Stacey's house. When I got there, I saw Frank in the front with the dealers.

"Frank, what's up? Is Stacey home?" I asked.

He said, "I think she is upstairs. Do you want me to go up and check for you?"

"Yeah, no doubt." He ran up the stairs. A minute later, he came back down and said, "She is coming down now." Stacey's sister walked outside behind Frank to chill in the front, too. I chilled with them until Stacey came out.

While my back was turned, I heard Stacey's voice.

"Hi, Neal." I turned around and she was on the porch. "Come up here." I opened her gate and went up the steps to her porch.

"What's up?"

"Nothing much. What's up with you?"

"I had no idea you would surprise me. I thought Frank was lying to me. He does play too much."

"Guess what, my uncle took me to the tuxedo shop a little while ago to get measured."

"And what else?" she said.

Ghetto Legend Graduate
Cornelius Kinchen

"I was surprised to get measured. I didn't expect to go today and so soon." It will be ready in a week. What's up with your dress?"

"It's getting custom made," she said.

"Did you get your shoes?"

"No not yet. I don't know what kind of shoes to get without my dress. I am waiting for my dress to be made, then I'll pick out my shoes."

"Were you busy?"

"No, not really," she said. "I just finished my homework."

"What class you had homework in that took so long?"

She laughed. "Mr. Fitzgerald's math class."

Now I understood what took her so long to come downstairs. "His class is challenging right?"

She sighed. "It's hard, because I don't like math. So did you like the tuxedo and the colors?"

I said, "Yeah, I like it. It was my first time seeing a real tuxedo. I only saw them on people on TV."

"Well, guess what? Soon you will be in that tux with me at the prom,"

I liked that idea. "Yeah, I can't wait, we are going to be so fresh on prom night."

We chilled a little while longer on her porch, talking about this and that. "Where is your mother?" I asked.

Ghetto Legend Graduate
Cornelius Kinchen

"She went to the supermarket to get us some dinner."

"Oh, okay. Well, I have to get going. Tell your mother I said hi."

"All right." She went upstairs and I went home. When I got there, Uncle Gilly was setting up his keyboard. I followed him into the living room.

"What are you doing?" I asked.

"I am getting ready for Bible study."

"Are you going to church for Bible class?"

"No, I'm having it here. Are you coming?"

I made an instant decision. "Yeah, I'll help load the equipment to the car. I want to learn how to play the piano like you, Uncle."

"All right. We are about to leave as soon as we are finished loading. I have to pick up Mother Warner, and some more people."

At the time, I thought he was courageous for starting a church on his own. I didn't understand exactly what he was doing, but I felt proud of him for doing so. I went to the kitchen and got some water to drink. I sat in the kitchen for a while and he began to play pleasant church music to warm his fingers. I wondered would he continue to play for Highway Church.

I went back in the living room to watch him play for a while. The music sounded so heavenly. I couldn't believe it was coming from my uncle. His fingers flew

Ghetto Legend Graduate
Cornelius Kinchen

across the keyboard gracefully. I wanted to learn to play like that.

Forty minutes later, it was time for Bible class to start. Grandma and Mother Warner started a praise and worship song. It was a beautiful slow worship song to begin with, followed by a prayer from Grandma. Uncle Gilly followed the song on the piano easily.

After prayer, my Uncle Gilly taught Bible class in detail, almost like a professor would at Harvard. His passion and knowledge of the Bible was admirable.

After Bible class, I went up to him. "I enjoyed Bible class," I admitted.

"Oh, really? So I will see you more often in Bible class?"

"I guess so," I said, "I want to learn more."

"Then don't hesitate to come."

After he said that, Mother Warner called me to her. I went over to say hi. She gave me a big hug with a big smile, showing the little bit of teeth she did have. The hug was very welcoming. After the hug, I went outside on the front porch to catch some fresh air. As soon as I went on the porch, people who attended Bible study came outside to go home. My uncle came outside and asked Bobby and I to ride with him to drop the saints off.

The first one to get dropped off was Mother Warner. She lived right around the corner. She had so much faith, if she could walk around the corner to Grandma's house for Bible study and church, she would.

Ghetto Legend Graduate
Cornelius Kinchen

We dropped her and the rest of the saints off, then came home to get ready for bed. When we got in the house, I went to the basement to get my clothes to take a shower. Man, the line was long to take a shower. My cousins and I had to wait on the steps. Whoever was there on the step first waiting for next went in. Grandma was first to shower. By the time Bobby and I got back, Grandma, Branda and Fanny had taken their showers already. Pooka and Mick were next. I was after them. Then Bobby was after me.

When I finally got in the shower, the water was warm. It was about to get cold. I loved a hot or warm shower. I couldn't stand the cold showers. After I took my shower, I got dressed and walked out to the hallway.

"Bobby," I called out, "I'm out the shower, but the water is cold. You have to wait like fifteen minutes to take a shower."

"Yeah, because we got here too late," he said. "I'll take a shower in the morning."

"Yeah, tomorrow fat boy," I said.

On my way downstairs with my dirty clothes in my hand, Bobby said, "You need to eat more, boney boy." I laughed, then went to the basement and got in the bed.

During recess the next day, my boys and I were in the gym playing basketball. Cantrell's little brother ran down the gym steps and said, "Yo, its some boys from Eastside outside. They want beef."

Ghetto Legend Graduate
Cornelius Kinchen

"Right now?" Before Carnell little brother could answer, we were walking up the gym stairs and out the door. When we got outside, we saw that it was Mr. Steve's all-boys' class who graduated the year before us. The boys that tried to bully us while they were here at School 6. We weren't having it then, and we sure weren't having it now!

There were five fights going on: Rob, By'ron, Frank, and Cantrell were each fighting a boy, and Shy'mir and Shy lee were jumping another boy. There were about to be six fights; when I went to get involved, I was sucker-punched twice from behind.

When I turned around, I said, "Who hit me?" I noticed Big Albert with his fists ready.

I know I don't have to fight this gorilla, I thought. But, I put my hands up fast to fight him. I hit Big Albert with a fast two-piece, and he ran. Frank needed help with his opponent. He was fighting Keshawn for at least eight minutes near the School 6 gates on the Hamilton Avenue side. I ran at full speed, punched Keshawn into the gate, and damn near through the bottom of the gate. He fell holding his jaw. Mind you, in the middle of this, our girls were watching us and our heart was the key to our victory.

After Keshawn got up from the playground, he and his Eastside boys ran out off our playground and up Hamilton Avenue. We chased them toward Rob's grandmother's house.

Ghetto Legend Graduate
Cornelius Kinchen

They ran fast and cut through alleyways to get away from us, we stopped running in the middle of Hamilton Avenue. Then we all turned around to go back to the playground. The cops were called, arriving after the fight. We were nervous, because we had to report to the auditorium as requested by the principal, Mr. Phillip.

I just knew I was in trouble. I promised Grandma that I would not get into trouble when I returned to this school. My ear was hurting from the fight, so I rubbed it.

We walked to the auditorium. I sat down in the same row as my boys. Mr. Phillip walked in the auditorium ten minutes later. Folding his arms, he looked at each of us in turn.

"What happened on my playground?'

I spoke up. "Mr. Steve's all-boys' class from last year came up here wanting to fight us. They came up here to our playground starting trouble with us. We were minding our business until they came up here starting with us." My boys nodded their heads in agreement.

"Are you guys all right?"

We kept nodding. "Yeah, we're good." I said, "We ran them out the playground."

He relaxed his arms. "I am glad somebody whooped their behinds."

We looked at him in surprise. We were sure we were all in big trouble.

"They are always starting trouble with you guys. None of you are in trouble. Settle down and return to

Ghetto Legend Graduate
Cornelius Kinchen

class. I will call your teachers to have you excused from any kind of detention."

At this point, I couldn't believe my ears. I got excused from the biggest fight I'd ever been in. I thought we weren't going to attend the prom tomorrow. We got up and went to class. In the hallway, we laughed and talked about the fight, and about how we beat the charges after fighting.

When we returned to class, Mr. Phillip was on the phone talking to our teachers about the fight. I felt a little cocky after the fight. After meeting with Mr. Phillip, I felt like we were cool.

I walked in my class, victorious. The girls looked at me, smiling like I defended them. I took my seat next to Tina, who asked, "Cornelius, are you all right after that big fight?"

I smiled. "Yeah, I'm good."

"I heard you, By'ron, and Rob were in Mr. Phillip's office. Did you get in trouble?"

"No Tina we didn't even get in trouble."

She said, "You are still going to the prom right?"

"Of course. I'm going to be fresh and fly."

She laughed. "Conceited, now, are we?"

"Yeah, you're damn right."

She still found it hard to believe. "Y'all didn't get in trouble at all by Mr. Phillip?"

"Nope, they came here starting trouble with us."

Ghetto Legend Graduate
Cornelius Kinchen

Mrs. Rizzo picked up on the conversation and said, "Cornelius, who were the guys that were starting trouble?"

"It was Mr. Steve's last year all boys class. They walked from Eastside High School to fight us elementary school boys."

"That is bad," she said. "They were troublemakers when they were here. Mr. Phillip did call and excuse you, so you are fine.

"Is everyone going to and prepared for the prom tomorrow?" she asked.

The entire class responded, "Yes." We started talking to each other about how fly we were going to be for the prom.

Mrs. Rizzo sat at her desk. "Now that we got that settled, take your books out for the next class." We did what we were told.

When I got into that fight, I almost lost my chance to go to my prom and graduation fighting with those boys. It seemed as if Mr. Steve's all boy's class tried to set us up. How? They came here to start a fight with us just before the prom and graduation, moreover, to get us in trouble with Mr. Phillip. They knew he was a strict principal and he didn't tolerate nonsense. They figured they'd get us to fight, so we would get into trouble and not have an opportunity to have fun and enjoy the rest of our eighth grade ceremonies. Now, how unfair is that?

Ghetto Legend Graduate
Cornelius Kinchen

Throughout the whole situation, God made a way for us. God had the principal excuse us from any suspensions, allowing us to go to the prom and participate in graduation.

After school, I walked home to meet Uncle Gilly. We had to go to Passaic to pick up my tuxedo. When I got home, I had to wait for him, so I sat on the porch. Time was ticking and I was ready to pick up my tuxedo.

While I waited, I did my algebra homework and I checked it to make sure it was done right. While I checked my homework, I heard a horn. I thought it was traffic. On Straight Street it can get very busy after three o'clock. Therefore, I ignored it. I continued to check my homework. My Uncle Gilly walked in the kitchen saying, "Neal, you didn't hear me blowing the horn for you? The tuxedo shop is going to close if we don't get there in time. Let's go!"

I put my books away and then we left. I followed my Uncle outside to the car. I got in and we pulled off into traffic. I thought we weren't going to make it before five o'clock.

Twenty minutes later, we arrived in Passaic at the tux shop. We went straight to the front desk with our receipt in hand. Uncle Gilly had the money and the receipt. When we got there, there were two people on line waiting for their tux, too. We waited on line patiently.

Ghetto Legend Graduate
Cornelius Kinchen

Finally, it was our turn to give our receipt to the cashier. Uncle Gilly gave it to the cashier, who said, "I will be right back." He went to the back to get my tux.

While we waited, I looked at the catalog. A few minutes later, he came out.

"Here is your white and baby-blue tuxedo sir. If that would be all, your remaining balance is one-o-three ninety-five. When you return the tux, you will receive seventy-five percent of your money back, sir. Is that all, may I assist you with anything else today?" When I looked up, I saw the tuxedo bagged on a hanger, and my uncle giving the cashier the money. I put the brochure down and grabbed the tuxedo bag.

"No, that's it. Thank you and have a blessed day."

"Thank you. You have a nice day as well." We walked out the tux shop and to the car. I was full of gratitude.

"Thank you, Uncle Gilly," I said, smiling. I couldn't wait to try it on.

"You're welcome, son." Then we pulled off into traffic on our way back to Paterson. On the way home, all I thought of was the prom and that I had my tux. Now I needed some shades.

"Can we stop to a store downtown to buy some shades for tomorrow?"

"What store downtown?"

"Any store, it doesn't matter."

Ghetto Legend Graduate
Cornelius Kinchen

"Yeah we can do that." We went downtown Paterson and bought shades. Main Street was full of people. We just bought shades and went to the house. When we got there, Grandma was on the porch talking to my aunts and waiting for my Uncle John to arrive. I got out the car carrying my tux.

"Hey Binky," Grandma said to Uncle Gilly, "where you coming from?"

"We just came from the tuxedo shop," he explained. "We had to pick up Neal's tuxedo for the prom." He kissed her on the cheek.

"Thank you, Binky."

"No problem, Mommy."

"Hi, Grandma. I have my tux."

Grandma smiled and said, "I see you have your tux. I can't wait to see you in it. Let me see that tux, boy." I unzipped the bag and held the tuxedo up for Grandma to see.

"That is very nice, Neal," she said in approval. My aunts also loved my tux.

I zipped the bag back up and began walking in the house. Grandma said, "Neal, make sure you put your tuxedo up." "Yeah," Aunt Kate said, "you don't want your tuxedo to get stains on it. Make sure the zipper is closed. You're going to be sharp tomorrow."

I said, "I 'm going to put it up now." I took my tux downstairs to the basement and hung it up. Dad looked up from listening to his oldies.

Ghetto Legend Graduate
Cornelius Kinchen

"What's up?" He said.

"My prom is tomorrow. This is my tuxedo."

"Who took you to get that?" he asked.

"Uncle Gilly." He said, "Oh." He looked at the tuxedo and said, "It's nice. Don't get anything on it. Hang it up."

I hung it up and went upstairs. I relaxed in the living room for a little while, thinking about the prom. I figured I would be doing a lot of dancing at the prom tomorrow, so I decided to take a shower early. Afterwards, I sat on the porch with Grandma and my aunts and listened to them talk for a little while. Grandma was back and forth to the kitchen fixing dinner. While I waited for the food to finish cooking, Aunt Doris and Kate ask me to go to the store for soda and snack cakes for them, and they gave me a dollar for myself.

When I came back from the store, the dinner was ready. Grandma had already eaten and had fixed my plate. When I walked in the house, she was coming back outside. I left the bag with my aunts on the porch, then I went inside and ate my food.

It was getting dark outside. It was almost time for me to go sleep. After I ate my food, I went downstairs anticipating prom night. When I got downstairs my father asked, "Is the food ready?"

"Yeah, I just ate."

"Turn to channel fifty for the lottery at eight o'clock," said Dad. Then he went upstairs. I turned to *The*

Ghetto Legend Graduate
Cornelius Kinchen

Simpsons. I had just enough time to watch the entire episode.

At ten minutes to eight, I turned to the lottery. My father had just walked downstairs from the kitchen with his food. He had to fix the antenna on the black-and-white TV. The lottery came on and he put his plate down and pulled out his lottery numbers. In addition, he pulled out his pick-it Bible to see if the numbers called on TV were in that book.

After the numbers were called, I didn't know whether or not my father hit the pick-it or not. He was so calm all the time, except for when he had to slap me in the head for being hardheaded. Disobedience and backtalk were two things he never tolerated from me. After the lottery went off, my father stayed up looking at his numbers, and I went to sleep.

Ghetto Legend Graduate
Cornelius Kinchen

May 1997, prom day!

  We had a half day, so the eighth-graders could prepare for the big night. When I went to school and to class, my classmates and I were in class discussing what we were going to wear at the prom. Who was going to dress the best to impress the ladies. Moreover, who was going to be named prom king and queen. We debated over that. Before we knew it, it was time to go to lunch.

  At 11 o'clock we lined up and went to lunch. It was a beautiful day for the prom. Some eighth-graders were being picked up from school early by their parents to get ready for the prom. The others, including myself, hung out near the auditorium on the steps with their friends. We were at the top of the steps looking at the girls on the playground. We had the door open to the auditorium while Mrs. Nelson, the music teacher, had a class in session.

  We must have been making too much noise, because she asked, "Eighth graders keep the door close, thank you." We were respectful and closed the door. We didn't want to mess up our chances to attend the prom.

  After lunch recess, we went upstairs for a little while, and sat in the class until dismissal at one o'clock. But when we got upstairs to the class, it was twelve-fifteen. We sat in the classroom with the lights off. While Mrs. Rizzo provided crossword puzzles for each student to complete, we sat and talked quietly.

Ghetto Legend Graduate
Cornelius Kinchen

    The time went by really fast after completing the crossword puzzle. Before we knew it, it was time for dismissal, and it was time to go home and get ready. I couldn't wait to get dressed up in my tuxedo. I wanted to show off and get a lot of attention from the girls. I wanted more attention than my boys.

    Rob, By'ron and I walked home together. When we got to Auburn Street, we went our separate ways home. I walked fast to get home. When I got home, Uncle Gilly was waiting for me to arrive from school.

    "Neal you have to get your haircut from Rob on Carroll Street."

    "Oh yeah. I almost forgot about my haircut!"

    "You can't put a clean tuxedo on without a fresh hair cut," he said.

    "You're right."

    "Come on. Get in the car."

    We got in the car and went to Rob's Barber Shop. Stacey lived right across the street from there. I had no idea that it was that close to where she lived.

    When we pulled and parked in front of the barbershop, I looked across the street to see if Stacey was outside. When I didn't see her, I figured she went to pick up her dress. When my uncle and I got out the car, I said, "Uncle Gilly, my prom date lives right in that gray and Red house with the stairs."

    "Oh yeah?"

Ghetto Legend Graduate
Cornelius Kinchen

When we walked into the barbershop, there was a little boy in the chair getting his haircut. Rob was straight hood and self-educated. He knew his African American history from reading a lot of books. He could have been a professor at any college or university if he wanted.

While Rob talked about Malcolm X, Martin Luther King, Marcus Garvey, Harriet Tub man, Rosa Parks and Brown vs. the Board of Education, I learned things from him that were, at the time, not properly discussed and elaborated on in the Paterson Public School system, except during Black History Month. I was interested in all of Rob's topics including civilization in Africa.

While Rob was talking, Uncle Gilly introduced me to him. Rob knew me as my uncle's son for years. He also knew my father, having grown up with my uncles that hustled drugs in the eighties. He knew my mother, too.

After we were introduced, he finished the little boy's haircut. It was my turn.

Rob said, "What's up?"

"It's my prom tonight," I said, proudly.

"Oh yeah? Who are you takin'?"

"Stacey."

"From across the street?"

I said, "Yeah."

He placed the sheet around my neck and said, "Neal, your education is your way out of the 'hood. The

Ghetto Legend Graduate
Cornelius Kinchen

more educated you are, the more powerful you become. Knowledge is power. Once you have that power, you are a threat to the majority of today's society. Believe and listen to what I'm saying. This street life will land you in jail or in the ground."

"I'm listening."

"You look like you are going to be smarter than these other guys out here. You look like a leader. Stay in school and read lots of books."

I thought, *God is talking to me through Rob*! I received that advice wholeheartedly. My faith in God and belief that I was able to do anything I set my mind to would allow me to be a positive light to the youth just as Rob was for me!

It took Rob only twenty minutes to cut my hair. The results were on the money. My hairline was straight and my hair was wavy. Rob knew how to cut some hair.

He dusted the hair off my face with a brush, cleaned my hairline and sprayed oil sheen on my haircut. When I got out the chair, he gave me dap and said, "Any time you need to kick-it, come holla at me."

"All right, I appreciate it." When I was leaving out the door he said, "Enjoy your prom little bro."

"I will. Thanks, Rob." Then my uncle and I left the barbershop.

Once I got home, I went to the basement to get my shower clothes. When I got upstairs, Grandma said with a smile, "Neal, it's your night...and I want you to

Ghetto Legend Graduate
Cornelius Kinchen

have a lot of fun tonight. I really want you to enjoy yourself at your prom. Do you hear me?"

I said, "Yes, Grandma."

"You can get dressed in my room. Leave your shower clothes and go get your tuxedo and lay it on my bed. When you get out the shower everything will be ready for you." I put my things down on the bathroom sink. Then I ran downstairs to get my tux, came back up to Grandma's room with it and placed it on her bed along with my shoes.

After I got out the shower and put on the tux, Grandma went inside her purse and gave me thirty-five dollars for my pocket. She handed me the money and said, "Here, don't spend it all in one place. Put it in your pocket."

I said, "Thank you, Grandma."

I went downstairs to the living room to wait for my prom date Stacey. I sat in there playing with my shades for ten minutes. Uncle T.D. walked in the house and said, "Hey, Mommy, is Neal here? A limo is out here for him." Then I heard a lady's voice when I walked to the door.

Uncle T.D. said, "Oh, never mind he's right here."

When I got to the door, it was Stacey's mother.

"Wow, you look sharp, Neal! Stacey is in the limo." I smiled my thanks to her, and then I followed her out to the big car. Stacey got out the limo. It was a black

Ghetto Legend Graduate
Cornelius Kinchen

funeral home limo with clear windows, gray seats, three rows inside and three doors to decide which row we were going to sit on. I couldn't believe it. I was embarrassed. I did not want to get inside of that ugly funeral home limo. Plus, it didn't have any air conditioning in it.

Stacey got out of the limo and gave me a hug. I said, "You look beautiful in your dress."

"Thank you," she said, and meant it. "You're very fly in your tuxedo."

I gave her a little bow. "Thank you."

Stacey's mother said, "Well it's time to go. We have to make another stop to take pictures in front of my house before we go to the prom." She walked to our door on the limo and opened it and closed it like a chauffeur would.

I really didn't want to be seen riding through the hood in that limo. It was that bad. We drove up in front of Stacey's house on Carroll Street. There were a lot of people taking pictures of us, including Stacey's mom. I couldn't wait to leave and go to the prom to be with my boys, Rob and By'ron.

Fifteen minutes passed. Stacey was becoming impatient. "Mom, come on, it's time to go to the prom."

"I am, Stacey. You and your date look wonderful. Just one more, Stacey."

"Ma, hurry." I thought we were famous, her mother was taking so many pictures. Plus, people from the neighborhood fish bowled us.

Ghetto Legend Graduate
Cornelius Kinchen

After the picture taking, we got in the limo and went to the prom. It was at the Brownstone. When we arrived, I saw Marv and his date and other couples taking pictures in the front. I saw By'ron with two dates, Mateasha and her cousin, Rob with Shannon, and Tanisha with little Corey.

Stacey and I got out before anybody could notice what we rode in. As we were getting out the car, Stacey's mother said, "Y'all have a good time." Stacey and I kept walking. She waved but I didn't. I was hot and glad to be at the prom.

When I got in the prom, By'ron and Rob were already there. I gave them dap. We continued to take pictures with the ladies. By'ron walked up to Rob and with two hands giving us 'Johnny Gills' on our necks from the bet we made. Rob and I thought he wasn't going to have two prom dates, but he surprised both of us. I saw Frank looking like a little Jigga with his prom date Alesha.

I partied, ate a little and had a great time. I really didn't like the DJ's style. He played a variety of music from hip-hop to Latin to reggae. I loved hip-hop only, and waited until he played hip-hop, and only then did I get up to dance.

The prom ended at ten o'clock. Everyone had enjoyed themselves. We continued to take pictures after the prom. I wanted my Uncle Gilly to pick me up. I did

Ghetto Legend Graduate
Cornelius Kinchen

not want to ride in that scary limo. Therefore, I called him and had him pick me up from the Brownstone. He came and I rode home with him. I told him the prom was great. I had fun, and the food was exclusively exotic. I was still hungry, because I didn't eat much.

"Can you take me to McDonald's?" I asked.

"Yeah. You got money?"

"Yeah, I'm rich tonight. Might as well enjoy it."

He laughed. "You have money. Oh, Lord, it's going to rain! It's a miracle! I don't have to pay! Just kidding around, son."

We went to the drive-through at McDonald's. I ordered a number two with a raspberry ice tea. He ordered the same and paid for it. I tried to pay for it and he said, "No, I have it son." Then we went home. I ate, took a shower and took it down.

Ghetto Legend Graduate
Cornelius Kinchen

June 1997. From Sandy Hook to Graduation.

    The eighth-grade class was going on a three-day, two-night field trip to Sandy Hook during the second week in June. We had to have permission slips signed by a parent or guardian. I received my permission slip on that Monday. By Wednesday, I handed the fee of seventy-five dollars, and my permission slip signed by my father. For the small fee, it included the stay, the tour and food. I couldn't wait to go and be away from home with my friends. I wanted to have fun and have a memorable moment with my class on this trip to Sandy Hook.

    I packed my things over the weekend for the trip. I received extra money from my father and Uncle Gilly to buy souvenirs. On Tuesday, my class and I boarded the big yellow school bus. The sun shined on me so bright: I couldn't wait to go to the beach. I never went to a beach in my life before this trip.

    So I got on the bus, and sat next to Neria on the bus. We talked and joked the whole time. It took about two hours to get to Sandy Hook. While riding on the bus, I looked out the window. We passed a McDonald's that delivered. I couldn't believe they had one in South Jersey and not up North. I wished for one in Paterson. We

Ghetto Legend Graduate
Cornelius Kinchen

already had turkey and cheese sandwiches on the bus during the drive, so there was no need to stop there. When we arrived, it was just after twelve-thirty. We stayed in a dorm like hotel near the beach and the basketball court. We had the dorm to ourselves. The trip seemed to promise a fun time away from home.

I shared the last room on the left across from the shower and bathroom with all nerds. It was five of us to a room. I shared a room with Joe-sef, Allen, Jay and Clark. I was surprised to be in a room with them. They were cool, too.

When I got up to the room, they were unpacking. I sat on the bed I claimed and said, "I got this bed." They were laughing and joking, happy to be away from home, too. I began unpacking and put my things away. I wanted to take a shower because I sweated my shirt out on the bus.

After I unpacked and waited, I joked in the room with Clark, Allen, Joe-sef and Jay. We walked to the end of the hall to visit the girls, and then back to our room.

Mrs. Dunelly looked in our room and said, "It's time for dinner guys. Wash your face and hands, and come to the dining room area on the first floor."

All the boys on that floor had to share the bathroom. The bathroom had approximately twelve to fifteen showerheads in a straight line. The door stayed open, too. The floor and the wall was painted gray. It also had fluorescent light bulbs over blurred mirrors. The

Ghetto Legend Graduate
Cornelius Kinchen

bathroom looked weird, like it was stolen from jail. I thought the bathroom would be like the one in my home.

I washed my face and hands. I didn't want stinky breath talking to the girls, so I brushed my teeth, too. Afterwards, all the boys walked together to the dining room to eat. We ate spaghetti and meatballs. We all ate together, and the feeling was almost like we were one big family. It was all smiles at the dinner table.

We all received notice that we were all going to tour the Cape May-Sandy Hook Lighthouse the next day. I wanted to tour more of the facility, but it was dark outside. Mrs. Dunelly and the other teachers prepared a wonderful dinner with dessert. When they cooked, I realized that they were like parents to us. I really appreciated how they put up with teaching and preparing us for high school.

After dinner, I went upstairs to get ready for bed. I wanted to hit the shower first. I didn't want anybody in my business if you know what I mean. I was the first to get in the shower at least seven minutes before the fellows came upstairs. I showered then went to the room. When I got in there, my roommates were getting prepared to shower. Before I knew it, all the boys on the floor were rushing to shower. We had to keep the noise down after curfew because the teachers were resting for the tour.

I stayed in the room and relaxed. When they got out the shower, they relaxed too. I wanted to go to the girl's room for a little while, but we weren't allowed to

Ghetto Legend Graduate
Cornelius Kinchen

go down the hall or we would get into trouble by the teachers. Therefore, I lay down in my bed, and my roommates followed suit. It was pitch black outside our window, but it was peaceful. I had my own bed in a room I could call mine. It wasn't in the basement and I didn't have to share it. I thought about the next day. Then I fell asleep in peace.

The next morning, I woke up to a brand new environment with the sun shining through the window in another place besides the ghetto. The birds were singing their praises to God, and I was grateful to him for this small piece of happiness He bestowed upon me. I got ready and got dressed, then went to eat with everyone else. I was the last to wake up for breakfast.

When I got to the dining room, my classmates and teachers were served and eating. I went to get some breakfast, too. It was a complete breakfast hot and cold selection. From cereal to grits and pancakes were prepared. I ate both.

I walked over to where Rob, By'ron, Frank and Janard were eating. "What's up fellas?" I said.

Rob said, "What's up Cornelius?"

"Enjoying this trip."

"Now, that's what's up," By'ron said, "Let me get my gill."

I said, "Nah, chill. For what By'ron?"

"For waking up late and almost missing breakfast."

Ghetto Legend Graduate
Cornelius Kinchen

I smiled and said, "It's early and you're ready to get started."

"Yeah." Rob laughed.

We sat at the table eating breakfast talking about the girls. They looked good and were happy to be on vacation, too. After they ate, they went to the library-living room. I finished eating and we followed them. They pulled books and read for a little while. We tried to kick it with them, and they were all smiles about it.

I kicked it to Stacey the whole time. She was all smiles, too. Mrs. Dunelly said, "Listen up, everyone…in an hour we will be touring the light house. You can go outside if you like; there is a basketball court and a walking strip. Be back here in an hour." After eating breakfast, everyone started getting up from the table and throwing their plates in the garbage.

I sat in the library-living room talking to and chilling with Stacey. Everybody walked outside to view the scenery outside. I asked Stacey, "Are you coming to watch me ball?"

"Yeah, I will watch you ball for a little while," she said. "Then I am going with my girls."

"That's cool with me." We held hands, walking outside toward the court. When I got outside, it was hot. I couldn't escape the sun for nothing unless I stayed inside with the central air conditioning.

The fellows had already started a twenty-one game of basketball. When I got in the game, Janard had

Ghetto Legend Graduate
Cornelius Kinchen

the highest score of nine points. It was about ten of us going for the ball when it bounced off the rim. I grabbed a rebound, shot the ball in the basket and went to the line.

"Nobody out here can stop me." The fellows laughed.

Janard smirked and said, "Yeah, right. You didn't play me yet." I shot the ball and it went in.

"Watch what I'm talking about." Everyone was looking at the basketball rim waiting for me to shoot. I shot the ball twice and made it twice. Stacey got up to leave.

"I am leaving Cornelius. I will see you on the tour."

"All right." I watched her walk off.

I checked the ball after the third shot made. Janard and Lil Mikee walked up to double team on defense. I got around both of them, shot the ball up, and missed. After that I quit. I watched Janard win the game.

The hour was up and it was time to tour the lighthouse. The tour guide who led the way was white. She was articulate throughout the tour. Mrs. Dunelly, Rollins, Rosser and Mr. Steve led the way alongside the guide. The lighthouse was beautiful and was a significant part of the history of New Jersey. I saw army trucks and tanks as statues.

After the tour, we had lunch, and then we were able to go to the beach. I brought my towel. I didn't have any slippers to walk on the hot sand. When I say it was

Ghetto Legend Graduate
Cornelius Kinchen

hot, it was hot. I called myself walking to the beach barefooted. It took me at least thirty minutes to get there. I had to rest my burning feet from the hot sand. When I sat down, my butt burned, too.

    I finally got to the beach, I noticed the girls in their bathing suits on the beach and in the water. I went to test the beach water and it was freezing. The waves were rolling in, too. I thought I was going to freeze in that water. The sun dried me out so much that the water was ice cold to me. I tried to swim in it, but it was difficult fighting against the waves rolling in.

    I got out of the ocean and laid my towel down. I sat and watched my classmates for a while in and out the water. They were laughing and playing around having fun. While I sat on my beach towel, I was drying off and catching a tan in the hot sun.

    It was too hot for me, so I walked to the beach house where my teachers were. There was a volleyball net and ball out on the sand in front of the house. The entrance to the beach house had clear windows to see through. Some girls were playing volleyball. The teachers were inside keeping an eye on us.

    I was in and out the house, then I sat on the love seat with Tanisha. I joked with her calling her, "What's up E.T. fingers?" She had no nails and all numbs from biting them too much. She laughed and said, "Shut up Cornelius." We sat there watching the game for a little while.

Ghetto Legend Graduate
Cornelius Kinchen

    I got up after the game, and walked toward the beach front to watch the waves roll in. It was a therapy session and intervention for me. My mind was far removed from the ghetto. I worried for nothing.

    The waves continued to roll in, as I walked on the sand with shoes on so as not to burn my feet. I felt the cool breeze rolling off the water. I was truly enjoying myself. Sometimes a person has to be removed from what he or she normally knows and put somewhere else to appreciate the things they have in life.

    We all stayed on the beach to watch the sunset until it was almost time for dinner. Before I came down here, I had never taken the time to watch something as beautiful as the sun going down over the horizon. Also, four or five miles behind us was the lighthouse. I enjoyed myself. It felt like God had taken me to heaven on earth.

    After the sunset, we were called inside of the beach house for dinner. The teaching staff prepared steak, corn, and mashed potatoes. It was delicious. After I finished eating, I went back outside to watch the horizon again. Being down here was like a whole other world. The sky was pitch black, with only Fourth of July fireworks lighting traveling across it.. It was gorgeous.

    We were ready to go in after a while; because it was getting late. The teaching staff and the students walked to the dorm-hotel lodge. The path and road were dark, and the street lights were dim. We had to walk at least two miles to the dorm-hotel.

Ghetto Legend Graduate
Cornelius Kinchen

When we got there, I walked to my room and prepared to take a shower. The water was cold, so I had to wait until it warmed up. Five minutes later, I was able to take a quick shower, and then I went to bed to prepare for the next day. I had to pack my things for my trip back home tomorrow.

The next day, we packed up and left to go back to North Jersey. I did not want to face reality again. There was so much to worry about, like which high school would accept me. I applied to Passaic County Technical and Vocational High School, but they were full. I didn't want to attend Eastside, because my friends and a prescription for trouble were up there. Reluctantly, I applied to Rosa Park's High School for an education in creative writing I took their creative writing entrance exam, but was not accepted. During eighth grade, Uncle Gilly pulled me out of class to take an entrance exam at Paterson Catholic Regional High School, but I haven't received an acceptance letter from them. Therefore, I had no high school to attend.

Ghetto Legend Graduate
Cornelius Kinchen

Graduation

On the day of graduation, I felt of no importance to Ilene at this point. I didn't even know if she would make it to my graduation. I really longed for her presence. I felt my father wasn't able to attend an important event in my life either. I knew Grandma couldn't make it; however she wanted to. But I knew she was proud of me the whole year, and was surprised at my courage and strength to make it through elementary school. This was an accomplishment that my father never fulfilled. He really had no choice but to work at such a young age, because he had to help Grandma.

I walked to the graduation at School 6 with By'ron and Rob. They were happy. I felt emotionally stressed over who would attend and support me. At the same time, I was happy to finally graduate grammar school.

It was eight thirty when the three of us arrived. We had to meet in our respective classes with our teachers, to line up in preparation for walking down the aisle. By this time, the teachers had students lined up in the hallway in alphabetical order, ready to fill the auditorium.

Parents had arrived early to support their children. Mothers, fathers, grandparents, aunts and uncles were all there. My self-esteem was low, even though I had my graduation cap and gown on. In spite of this wonderful

Ghetto Legend Graduate
Cornelius Kinchen

and memorable day, I wanted to walk out that building with a negative attitude, but God strengthened me again to remain calm.

I tried my best not to cry. My emotions were trying to get the best of me. One or two tears snuck out of my eyes. I wiped them quickly.

It was 9:10 a.m., and some of the parents were seated in the auditorium and some were packed in the hallway witnessing the ghetto graduates. Mrs. Nelson played the graduation music and theme as our cue to begin walking.

As the ceremony began, I walked down the aisle in shame and embarrassment because I thought no one had cared to come and celebrate this day with me. As I continued to walk, I heard my name called to my left near the back of the auditorium entrance. I looked to my left…

My mother was there!

God showed me the person that affected me the most, the one who birthed me, was in the aisle, crying out of joy, showing her happiness, and most of all, being proud of me. The tears flowed easily after that; this time without shame. Next to her was my father, Aunt Branda, and Uncle Gilly; they were all there to support me.

My self-esteem went from negative-one to plus a million and one. It felt great to see and feel their love and support on such an important day of my life. I saw a smile on my mother's face, as if God was smiling through her.

Ghetto Legend Graduate
Cornelius Kinchen

I continued to walk toward the stage and when I got there, I noticed my family clapping proudly and waving proudly at me. My face and heart lit up like fireworks on the Fourth of July. I felt alive and transparent at the same time.

When they were calling names, and my name was finally called, at that moment I knew I had my family's love and support. This meant everything in the world to me. As I walked to obtain my diploma, my family cheered. My mind, body, and soul experienced the most beautiful feeling in the world. I felt loved.

I will always believe that it is a parent's responsibility to take part in every major event in their child's life. For a child to be constantly disappointed and neglected by their parents is harmful to a child's development. But in spite of this, some parents are selfish enough to not think of anyone other than themselves.

After the graduation, I walked into the hallway and then into my class. My teachers, friends, and I, hugged everyone goodbye. My cap and gown were wet with tears, from my teachers, my friends and me. With this milestone behind me, I was ready; I could not wait to experience high school.

My parents, my aunt and my uncle followed me to my class smiling and saying how proud of me they were. I appreciated every second and minute of it. I felt like I could touch the sky. I was emotionally uplifted by their support and attention alone.

Ghetto Legend Graduate
Cornelius Kinchen

Mrs. Rizzo handed out the real diplomas once we got back to the classroom. The diplomas presented on stage were merely blank papers that appeared to look like the real thing. I waited until the letter K was called.

While hugging my mother and aunt, my name was called I walked over to Mrs. Rizzo. She hugged me and smiled as she handed me my diploma.

"Cornelius, it was great having you as a student, and I wish you the best in high school and college. Come back and visit us some times."

"I will," I said, "and thank you for your wishes." I took my diploma and left with my parents. We went to eat at a Chinese buffet afterwards. While sitting at the buffet table about to eat, my Uncle Gilly said, "Neal, you passed the entrance test to get in Paterson Catholic High School. You were accepted."

I let out a, "Word! Now, that's what's up! Thank you, Uncle Gilly!"

He said, "Yes, son you did it, and I am proud of you." My mother sat and cried because she was so proud of me. Aunt Branda passed my mother a napkin.

"Ilene you don't have to worry about Neal's education. I will make sure he does the right thing in high school and attends college."

Uncle Gilly agreed saying, "He will make it through high school and college Ilene."

My mother wiped her nose and sniffed. "Thank you so much Gilly and Branda. Please don't let the streets

Ghetto Legend Graduate
Cornelius Kinchen

trap my oldest son or any of my children. I want them to be better than me. Keep them in church. If they get out of line do what you have to do to get them back in line."

Aunt Branda said in calm a voice, "I will, Ilene; don't worry about anything. Everything will be all right." The tears kept rolling down her face. I really loved my mother at this point. I still did not understand how serious her addiction was.

We ate and went home. My mother hugged me and said, "I love you." She went her separate way to hell in the streets, I guess to do her business. I needed her to stay here with me, but she made her choice

She left and I dreamed of her again. I wanted to know her more. The feeling was not neutral; then again, maybe it was. All I knew was the neglect that I experienced so that she could get her high. I wished that she was addicted to loving me; but she wasn't.

Once I was accepted to Paterson Catholic, one of the most prestigious private high schools in Paterson, my life scale balanced somewhat. The school was well known for its academic standards and graduation percentage rating of ninety-nine. In addition, over ninety percent of its graduates were accepted to colleges and universities. An imbalance still was that Ilene did not visit as often. She often called to let me know that she was all right, and she was thinking about me. I appreciated that, too.

Ghetto Legend Graduate
Cornelius Kinchen

That summer, I received a letter in the mail stating that I had to read a book entitled 'Mouse and Giant' and we would be tested on the material when school started in September. It was for English class. My Uncle Gilly and I went to a bookstore to purchase the book. I was excited and ready to read.

As soon as I received the book, I began reading in my spare time during the summer months. I read four pages a day for two months. It motivated and challenged me to think and figure out the moral of the story.

On the weekends, Tiana and I spent as much time as possible together. We were getting it on as much as we could.

July went by and I hadn't seen Ilene. I wondered if she was all right. Tiana assured me that she was in God's hand. Also, that she wanted to meet her. Tiana and I were dating for two years and she never met Ilene. My mother was in no condition to meet anyone. I was embarrassed and did not want Tiana to meet her.

A few days after Red's birthday, Ilene visited Grandma's house. It was hot that evening. Tiana and I had just walked down the street, when I recognized my mother from the back.

While she talked to Grandma, I walked up to her with Tiana. She said, "Hey, Boy."

In a timid voice, I said, "Hi, Ma. This is my friend, Tiana."

My mother said, "Hello, how are you?"

Ghetto Legend Graduate
Cornelius Kinchen

Tiana smiled politely and said, "Hello."

"Are you treating my son right?"

Tiana said, "Yes, ma'am, I am." My mother said, "Continue." Tiana said, "I will."

All I could think about is how my mother looked. She looked like an official crack head from the streets. From her hair falling out, to her clothes, that looked like she had found them. I was embarrassed. I still appreciated her time and I still loved her, Thinking back, I was surprised she didn't smack fire out of my face for having another girlfriend.

After the loves of my life were introduced to each other, Tiana and I waited together next to my mother facing her direction and listening to her speak to Grandma.

Ten minutes later, Ilene said, "I have to catch the bus: Neal, behave. It was nice meeting you Tiana."

Tiana said, "It was nice meeting you, too."

I said, "I will Ma." Then she left to catch the bus to Hackensack.

Tiana and I hung out a little while longer in front of my house. I wanted to cry for Ilene's addiction situation. She had a beautiful heart but a horrible addiction. The addiction affected her body; it was physically destroying her from the inside out.

At this point, I wondered whether or not Tiana still was in love with me after meeting my mother. My face showed it.

Ghetto Legend Graduate
Cornelius Kinchen

"Neal what's the matter?" she asked.

"Are you still in love with me after meeting my mother?"

"I am deeply in love with you, even after meeting your mother. Why wouldn't I be?"

I did my best to smile, even though I wanted to cry. She hugged me and held me tight, which made me feel much better.

Afterwards, the sun slowly went down and the evening was here. Tiana and I walked up the street to spend time together before she went to Friday night service. We sat in front of Deanna's house, just enjoying each other's company. It was almost seven o'clock.

Red walked up the street thirty minutes before church started and said, "Yo, Uncle Gilly wants us to help him load and set up the sound system at the church. He would like us to come to church at seven."

"I don't feel like going," I said.

"I'm about to go help." he said. I sighed, and then walked off the porch to go with Red.

I said, "Tiana, I will see you after church."

"All right." Then we kissed goodbye. Red and I walked down the street to Grandma's house to help out Uncle Gilly.

When we got there, my uncle, Bobby, Pooka and Malcolm were taking the sound system equipment to the car to take to Redwood Ave. There were chairs that had

Ghetto Legend Graduate
Cornelius Kinchen

to be set up at church. I helped set up the chairs and bought some sound system equipment to the church, too.

Once all the sound equipment was set up at church, Uncle Gilly began playing music on the piano and began singing hymns. Red sat and played the drums. My family was in church to support my Aunt Branda and her husband Gilly's religious cause for the community, too.

While sitting in church service, I felt ghetto because we went from a little garage to a remodeled garage church that looked amazing. The music flowed. The church was still beautiful. The chairs were set up on the side to create an aisle in the middle of the church; the podium and microphone were in the front of the chapel, forming the pulpit. My uncle and Red played on the right side of the church next to one another, facing the side of the preacher and audience members. It was just family involved in the church. It wasn't that crowded.

We were the only family church on the block that stuck together spiritually. The music and the microphone echoed throughout the neighborhood. Also, we had church fans to cool off. It was still humid in the evening, especially in that garage, and we weren't getting any air from the garage door being open either.

While in church, I sat in the back so I could be in and out, and closer to the air when it did blow. The church fans were on, but it still was a little humid. I was in and out until Uncle Gilly embarrassed Kevin and me

Ghetto Legend Graduate
Cornelius Kinchen

by calling us out over the microphone for us to come sit down. From a distance, while sneaking out of church, we heard his voice on the microphone. We did obey. We came back to service and sat down until church dismissed; it was almost time. Kevin and I wanted to go to the village to visit Che-Che and Kim for a little while.

Twenty minutes later, church let out. We were the first to get dropped off to Grandma's house. Kevin said, "Let's go to the village for a little while."

"Yeah, come on then." We walked to the village. When we arrived at Kim's house, they were in front of the house.

Che-Che said, "Hiiii, Neal and Kevin."

"What's up?" I said.

"Nothing, just hanging out. Kevin, Kim just went to see what her mother wanted."

Two minutes later, Kim came back outside, grumbling. "She always wants me to go to the store," she complained. "She really needs to get up and go herself."

Che-Che said, "You have to go to the store again?"

"Yeah! Hi, Neal and Kevin." Kevin laughed at Kim's angry face and minor complaint.

Kim said with a smile, "Kevin, be quiet. It's not funny."

"I will walk with you Kim," Che-Che said. "Don't worry about it. Are y'all walking with us Neal and Kevin?" We agreed to walk to the store.

Ghetto Legend Graduate
Cornelius Kinchen

After going to the store, Kevin walked back with Kim. I went to meet Tiana. I didn't want to walk back to the village. While walking to Tiana's church, I noticed they were being dismissed. I waited in the front for Tiana. When she walked out of church, she was surprised to see me. Her older sister and mother walked out and toward the car. We greeted each other with hugs.

Tiana and I walked around the corner to Netta's house. She had to get dressed. I waited for her in the kitchen until she changed her clothes. Netta's cousin Nicole waited in the kitchen with me. Chris and Nicole had a love Jones for each other. She wanted to see Chris, even though he was going out with Beonnca. I thought that was cool and slick of Chris. I wanted to follow in such footsteps one day.

Minutes later Tiana was dressed, and we spent time together until it was time for me go in the house. I knew once I got in the house, I was going to hear it from Pastor Gilly. I had all my fun before I went in the house late, moreover, hoping the Pastor would open the door for me after dissing him earlier, by leaving church early.

I knew Grandma and Uncle Gilly were looking for Kevin and me to help straighten and clean the church. I wanted to disappear tonight before church service. I had no plans to go to church, but I was forced to go. When I was forced I felt like I was not in America. I love the free will God gave me and when someone takes it away from me, I feel I have to rebel to get it back.

Ghetto Legend Graduate
Cornelius Kinchen

    After hanging out with Tiana late that night, my Uncle Gilly did open the door for me while asking, "Where were you this time of night? Cheating on me with Tiana?" I didn't know what to say and did not want to be disrespectful, so I just went to the basement. However, it bothered me a lot that he asked such a gay question. I wasn't with that gay sh*t.

    The next day I thanked God for waking me up. I did my personal hygiene and continued to read my assigned book from Paterson Catholic. I read several pages, and then went outside to the back porch. I called Tiana on the phone and woke her at 10 in the morning.

    She answered the phone and said, "Good morning Neal, I will call you back after I brush my teeth and take a shower."

    "Are you coming to visit me?" I asked.

    "Yeah, I will call you as soon as I'm finish."

    After we hung up the phone, I thought to myself that I wanted a job. I couldn't work for PIC until I was fifteen years old, and I wanted my own money. Red and I went to my Uncle T.D.'s room and stole some work from him to sell. The customers showed up looking for my Uncle T.D., and Red and I knew what they wanted. We went upstairs to my uncle's room and looked in a soda can. The stash was there. We took some out and served those customers back to back. While doing that, we had the girls come down the street to watch our back from the cops. This was the only thing we knew about the game:

Ghetto Legend Graduate
Cornelius Kinchen

watch the cops. The girls stayed for at least an hour, and then they said they would meet us up the street.

I was young and dumb to sell. I didn't think about what would happen if I got caught. I knew the consequences were jail. I wasn't ready for that either. We continued, until Uncle T.D. came back home. He arrived later that evening. Red and I went to his room and his cat was out of control jumping from wall to wall.

Uncle T.D. was about to cut up some more work. Red and I thought we were cool by selling while he was gone. We thought we were doing him a favor by doing such a horrible thing. When we told him that we served his clients he didn't really care because it kept his money coming around. However, he tricked us when he left again. He put a pad lock on the outside of his door so we wouldn't go into his room again.

We sat in my Uncle T.D.'s room later that evening while he bagged up. We watched him and the television at the same time, while the cat continued to play around in the room chasing an imaginary mouse.

It was getting late, so I called Tiana. She came to visit me. It was cool outside. Tiana and I sat in the kitchen. Red, Kevin, Bobby and I were in the kitchen having another paper football tournament. This time I had my personal cheerleader. Minutes later, Deanna walked in the kitchen cheering for Red to win against me.

We played for a little while until Grandma said, "It is getting late." I knew what that meant for company.

Ghetto Legend Graduate
Cornelius Kinchen

They had to leave soon. After the game, we walked them up the street and hung out with them on Deanna's porch for a little while.

Ghetto Legend Graduate
Cornelius Kinchen

Florida

    My aunt and uncle had planned a trip to Disney World and invited me to come along. I had never been there before and couldn't wait to get there. I was so excited; I could hardly sleep the night before. My things were packed and ready to go. My self-esteem boosted from the invite. I felt love from Aunt Branda and Uncle Gilly, knowing that it cost a lot of money and that they were spending it on me.

    The next day, my aunt and uncle woke up the entire third floor at five a.m. The sun had not even risen. Still sleepy, I carried my bag to the white van and loaded it. Everyone else who was going on the trip did the same. I was sleepy and excited to go to Florida, another place I had never been.

    By five thirty, we were all packed and on I-95 South to Disney World. Man, the van was crowded. I had the opportunity to sleep on the floor of the van seventy-five percent of the trip. The other twenty-five percent was used by my cousins.

    Days later, we arrived in Georgia and it was raining outside. I couldn't even see the road. However, my Uncle Gilly was able to drive carefully behind a truck with flashing lights. We were going to Nana's house for a couple of days to rest.

    The rained stopped, and the sun came out. We stopped at a gas station on a dirt road. It seemed like I was acting a scene in an old western movie in Texas during 1900. The gas pumps were old, and the gas was cheap, so we filled up the tank and went to Nana's house.

When we arrived at Nana's house, I wanted to rest. My body was exhausted from days of riding. Nana and her husband were walking outside to greet us with a warm welcome.

We pulled up on the dirt pavement driveway, then we all got out of the van and stretched. I noticed that Nana owned chickens and roosters and they were running around in her gated yard. I was introduced to Nana for the first time and given a warm, loving hug. While food was cooking, Nana gave us a tour of the house. The house was a clean, lovely, and seemed like a warm place to stay. It was peaceful and quiet in this southern environment. There was enough room for us; the boys were to sleep in the front in the den where we walked inside.

After the tour, Nana said, "Y'all boys can go down the road and play basketball until dinner is ready."

She didn't have to tell me twice. "Come on," I said, "let's go play ball."

I led the way out the house and down the dusty road. I had no idea where I was going, but I was determined to find the basketball court. My cousins were right behind me, as we passed a couple of houses blocked by trees.

Ghetto Legend Graduate
Cornelius Kinchen

When we passed the third house, there were two boys playing basketball in the dirt. Bobby and I introduced ourselves and asked if we could play. They didn't mind, so Bobby and I joined in on the fun. I won three games. After I was done winning, the boys respected my game. One was from Georgia and one was from New York.

After the game, I felt mixed emotion from winning and being dusty, because I had on a nice shirt. While Bobby and I rested, Mick and Pooka started shooting the ball. They shot and made several baskets. Soon, it was time to go eat dinner. I looked at my cousins, who were all covered with dirt, and said, "Are y'all ready?"

Bobby said, "Yeah, come on. I'm hungry." It was hot and humid in the dirty backyard. I was thirsty and ready to wash up and eat dinner.

Aunt Branda and Uncle Gilly were talking and laughing with Nana when we got back. We took turns freshening up, and then we sat down to eat dinner. Nanny served us fresh food from her garden. It tasted like Grandma's food, but the only difference was that the food was fresher. I ate until I was full.

After we ate, we took showers to get the dust off us. It was pitch black and humid outside, and time for us to go to bed. Nana's southern hospitality was great. She set up the foldout couch for us, and gave us clean sheets

Ghetto Legend Graduate
Cornelius Kinchen

to sleep on. There was a television set in the den, so we watched TV for a while until we fell asleep.

The next day, I woke up to the smell of breakfast being prepared. Everyone got cleaned up, and ate, and then spent the entire day relaxing, talking and laughing. I wanted to play basketball again, but I didn't want to get dirty like the day before. With the long ride ahead, we went to sleep early because we had to get up at five in the morning.

When we woke up, it was pitch black outside, but it was peaceful. Nana and her husband were up to see us off. We hugged Nana and her husband goodbye, then loaded up the van and drove down the blackest road in Georgia. Uncle Gilly was familiar with the roads, so he didn't see a problem.

Hours later, we finally made it to Florida. I was happier than happy to be with my aunt and uncle. I needed this therapy. There were palm trees all over the place. In Kissimmee, the roads were so hot we caught a flat doing seventy-five miles per hour. When the tire blew, I thought somebody had put a bullet in it.

My Uncle Gilly pulled over on the shoulder of the highway, and we got out to fix the flat. The wind from the cars riding by was hot, blasting us while we were putting on the spare. While I helped my uncle fix the flat, a huge truck passed by shaking the ground and our van. It felt like an earthquake mixed with a big heat wave.

Ghetto Legend Graduate
Cornelius Kinchen

After the flat was fixed, we went to Star Island Resort. This place was great. Palm trees lined the streets, fountains shot water in the air, cars with transparent rooftops were parked on the side of the road, and most of all, the weather was not like it was in New Jersey. The resort was five stars to me.

When I walked into Star Island Resort, it was like a dream. This was a vacation spot where rich people would have come to take their vacations. There were big bedrooms for us, and the master bedroom was even bigger. It had a Jacuzzi.

After we toured the beautiful rooms, we got dressed and headed for the pool area. We settled in, and began to enjoy our stay there. The next day we traveled to Walt Disney World, Epcot, and Water World. I was so happy and stress free. The Mickey Mouse, Minnie Mouse, Tweety Bird, Sylvester, Goofy, Daffy, and Bugs Bunny characters really brought my imagination to life; and I took pictures with all of them.

For the rest of the week, we had activities and events planned. I saw Jaws, King Kong, The Indian Jones Show, The Terminator Show and the Little Mermaid Show. I really appreciated Aunt Branda and Uncle Gilly for taking me to another part of heaven. I enjoyed this experience in Florida it was like a dream come true.

We came back from Florida in late August. It was back to the real world.

Ghetto Legend Graduate
Cornelius Kinchen

"Neal, we have to get you measured for your uniform today," said Uncle Gilly.

"I'm ready," I said.

"We have to go soon. Don't get lost."

"What time are we leaving?"

"Nine thirty."

"I'm going to Ali's house real quick to buy an icee."

"Hurry up back." I ran out the door.

I walked to Ali's house. He was outside with his grandmother, who said, "*Hola, como tu esta?*"

I said, "*Hola*, how are you?"

"*Muy bien.*" She smiled.

I said, "Ali, what did she say?"

"She said exactly what you said to her in Spanish," he replied.

"Ohhh, okay.... I want a coconut icee." Ali went inside to get the icee. I waited on the porch and watched his grandmother walk the dog up the street toward my house. Minutes later Ali walked outside with the icee and I gave him a quarter.

Ali asked, "Neal what are you going to do today?"

"I'm about to go get measured for my uniform with my uncle."

"What high school are you going to?"

I said, "Paterson Catholic. What about you?"

Ghetto Legend Graduate
Cornelius Kinchen

He said, "I'm going to Passaic County Technical Institute in Wayne. I'm going for baseball. They recruited me this summer."

I was almost jealous, but didn't show it. "I'm going to try out for the basketball team or football."

He said, "Yeah you should play both sports."

I sighed. "Yeah, I will see what happens when I try out. But I have to go now." He said, "All right, I will see you when you get back."

"All right." I went back up the street.

Uncle Gilly and I went to the Co-Ed Uniform Store on Route 4. It wasn't crowded, which was a good thing. He said, "This is exactly why I like to go to places early, to be first in line to be served." I looked around, and saw that there were older people working there as tailors. I was the first to get measured. Gilly bought me the shirts with the school's name on them, a burgundy shirt, a white shirt, button ups, ties and two pair of pants. Then we went to Value City and he bought me shoes.

We had shopped for everything I needed for school. While riding home, I was happy that I was going to a prestigious high school. When I got home, I went to try my uniform on so Grandma could see how it fit. After trying everything on, she approved of the size. My Uncle Gilly folded the clothes nicely and neatly and put them up for school.

Ghetto Legend Graduate
Cornelius Kinchen

I went to read my book again for a little while. The book was getting good, too and I was almost done with it.

Uncle Gilly said, "Neal, are you almost done reading the book?"

"Almost. I have fourteen more pages to go."

"All right. You know you have a test the first week of school on the events that happened in the book, and a summary of the book is due, too." I said, "Yeah, I'm working on it now."

Roger had moved out to live with his girlfriend. I wanted my own room, so I took advantage of the opportunity to get the room.

"Grandma, can I have Roger's old room?" I asked.

"You will have to clean it out," she said. "You will also have to keep it clean. That will be your responsibility along with the garbage on the second floor, too."

"No problem," I said.

I put my book down and went upstairs to see what I needed to clean the room up. I opened the door and it was dark in there. I turned on the lamp, and saw that the room needed to be vacuumed and mopped on certain areas of the wood. It had a bed, a TV, a nightstand, dressers and a huge mirror. I had everything I needed, thanks to Roger. I started cleaning up thoroughly. The room was also very dusty.

Ghetto Legend Graduate
Cornelius Kinchen

Bobby came to the door and asked, "You're moving in here?"

I said, "Yup, we are going to have real fun, too." He smiled, pointed to the roof and said, "You know you can open the roof right."

"How?" I asked. He went and got the broom, and used the broomstick to open a door in the roof. He pushed it up and to the side.

"How did you know that, Bobby?"

He laughed and said, "I live in the next room, and Roger showed me."

"Oh. I do need the air. It is real dusty in here."

"Do you want me to help you?"

"Yeah, come on." He helped me bag some of the garbage and old clothing. We took them down to the garbage together.

An hour later, we were done. I moved my things in, and Uncle Gilly came up to check on us. He commented on the good job we did.

I said, "Uncle Gilly, I need some new sheets to go on the bed."

"I have some downstairs," he said. "Your bed is the same size as mine. I will be right back." He left to get the sheets. While he did that, I continued reading the last nine pages of the book.

After a few minutes, he interrupted my reading and said, "Here you go, son."

Ghetto Legend Graduate
Cornelius Kinchen

I thanked him and threw the old sheets away, putting the new ones on the bed. I was excited to have my own room. Bobby hung out with me for a little while. Once he went downstairs, I continued to read.

After I finished reading, I started writing the three page summary and opinion of the book, which was John Steinbeck's *Of Mice and Men*. Bobby came back into the room and set up the Sega Genesis and began playing Madden. I just continued working on my paper. Uncle Gilly checked on us again, and was impressed with my work ethic.

"Son, you have your own room, take care of it. Keep it clean and neat, too." Then he went back downstairs.

After he left, I had two pages done and I was working on the third page. As soon as I finished my paper, I re-read it and made corrections. Then I wrote it over with the corrections made. Then I played Bobby. Bobby bought one of his fans in the room so we could be cool. I noticed bird shadows as they flew over the roof. I continued to play the game, and said, "Bobby I hope the birds don't fly in here."

He laughed and said, "I hope not. Neal, you can have this fan because you don't have one."

"Thank you, Bobby. I'm still going to beat you in Madden."

My cousins and I loved to play Madden, and I loved to win. They loved competition, too. We played for

Ghetto Legend Graduate
Cornelius Kinchen

at least an hour. I could not wait for Red and Kevin to come over and visit, and see my new room. They had their privacy, and I finally moved up to having my own privacy. I was satisfied with my room.

After playing Madden, Bobby and I went outside for a little while. The sun was going down and began to cool off outside. Kevin was on his way down the street to Grandma's house for rehearsal.

Uncle Gilly was preparing for choir rehearsal. My cousins and I sang in the church choir. We were giving God the glory through song. But Uncle Gilly worked us hard. Sometimes we would be in choir rehearsal for hours. It would be late, and dark, on a school night, but he was only concerned with perfect praises through our songs.

Bobby and I sat on the front porch waiting to go to choir rehearsal. Kevin crossed the street and joined us. Kevin said, "What's up? Where is everybody?"

"We're waiting for Uncle Gilly now to come back with the van," I explained. He went to pick up Maurice, Robert and the Passaic crew for choir rehearsal."

"Oh," said Kevin.

Minutes later, the van arrived in front of the house. Uncle Gilly said, "Let's go-oh!" We got up and got into the van. Uncle Gilly beeped the van horn for Mick, Fanny and Pooka to come outside. The van was packed with youth. Once everyone loaded the van, we pulled off.

Ghetto Legend Graduate
Cornelius Kinchen

We arrived at the church on Redwood Avenue at quarter after seven. Uncle Gilly opened the church, and we went to the front to sit in the choir section. We rehearsed new songs every week to perfection, for hours.

Ghetto Legend Graduate
Cornelius Kinchen

Back to school

By the end of the rehearsal, I was tired of singing and my throat was hurting. It was back to school weekend, and I wanted to have fun However, I had to be in choir rehearsal according to my uncle, especially since I knew he was going to pay for me to attend Paterson Catholic. I went along with that deal, until I could prove myself academically.

Rehearsal was over and we stopped at Grandma's house for a while to hang out with each other. Maurice was two years older and taller than me. He looked like Babyface, but from the hood. I wanted to box him, to test his gangster. It was natural for me to do so.

"Maurice, we have to box. Come on let's go in the basement. I have boxing gloves we can use." He agreed. My cousins and I went to the basement. They watched us put on boxing gloves, put our hands up and square off to box. I punched Maurice with a fast rushed five-piece combo to the face Uncle T.D taught me. Then he punched me twice back to back in the jaw, causing me to be dazed a little. I continued with the combos until my father said, "Stop, before somebody gets hurt now." We immediately stopped and gave each other dap. From then on, we were cool cousins.

Mick laughed at the site Maurice getting punched in the face like twenty times to two on the score cards. As

Ghetto Legend Graduate
Cornelius Kinchen

we went to my room, Maurice said, "Yo, I have NBA JAM for Sega Genesis. Do y'all want to play?"

"I got first on the controller," I said. "Come on, let's go upstairs." They argued over who had next after the loser." When I got upstairs, I changed my mind.

"Matter of fact I don't want first, I want the winner from the first game."

Kevin said, "You have your own room?"

"Yeah. We are going to have fun, because I'm nice in NBA Jam."

He laughed and said, "Yeah, right. I will play first then."

"All right. Maurice is going to beat you. Then I'll play him." Maurice was quiet with an eager look on his face.

When we got upstairs, Bobby had to turn on his light, for me to see well enough to unlock my bedroom door. When I got the door open, I felt for the lamp twice and found the switch. I turned the light on, and Maurice began hooking the game up. He put the game into the console, and it was game on.

Kevin and Maurice were on the controllers deep into competition. I noticed the game between Hawks and Boston were tied in the first quarter. Kevin had broken the rim and the glass backboard.

I couldn't wait until my chance to shine on the game, moreover, in front of all my boy cousins on my father side of the family. I anticipated my skills on the

Ghetto Legend Graduate
Cornelius Kinchen

controller. Minutes later, fourth quarter and the game tied. Suddenly, Maurice lit up a three, stole the ball from Kevin and broke the rim and the glass. The room went crazy. Kevin was down five points with 10 seconds on the NBA Jam clock.

    Kevin gave the controller up, and it was my turn to compete. I picked the Bulls and Maurice picked the Hawks again. We started the game. He got out the gate with a ten-point lead on me. Before the first quarter ended, we were tied going into the second quarter, and throughout the game into fourth quarter. Toward the end of the game, with three seconds left on the clock, we were tied. Maurice inbounded the ball and I stole it, causing us to go into overtime.

    Eventually, at the end of over time, he hit a buzzer beater from the three-point line, winning the game. Maurice looked at Kevin and me and laughed aloud. I wanted my rematch. Uncle Gilly yelled from down stair, "All right y'all let's go! Y'all better be in the van when by time *I* get to the van!"

    My cousins dapped up and went downstairs to get in the van. I cleaned my room again and got ready for bed; this was my first night in my new room.

    I finally had my own space after years of sharing a bed with someone else. I controlled the rules in my room. I prayed and read the book of Proverbs Grandma told me to read for wisdom, knowledge and understanding. I appreciated that advice. Proverbs gave

Ghetto Legend Graduate
Cornelius Kinchen

me silent and sound wisdom, knowledge and understanding, which I benefited from in many life situations as I was maturing.

    Minutes flew by, and I was getting sleepy. I prayed again for God to add a blessing to my life through the reading of his word, and to forgive me of my sins. Also, I asked God to bless and protect my family, the sick, the poor, and the sinners. Then I turned my lamp off and fell asleep.

Coming Soon:

GHETTO LEGEND GRADUATE II

Ghetto Legend Graduate
Cornelius Kinchen

CORNELIUS KINCHEN

Ghetto Legend Graduate
Cornelius Kinchen

First Day of High School

The summer was over and it was time for my Paterson Catholic debut. I woke up and went to the bathroom on the second floor. It was seven in the morning and Grandma was sitting in her room reading her Bible and listening to Benny Hinn on the church channel. She said, "Good morning."

Good morning Grandma," I said.

I went in the bathroom to wash my face and brush my teeth. Then I used some of Aunt Branda's face cream to clear my face from acne. I wanted to impress the ladies on my first day of school.

I went into Grandma's room and my Uncle Gilly was ironing his shirt and pants, along with mine. I waited until he was finished ironing. I had never worn a uniform before, and I thought it was cool.

I didn't have to worry about what I was going to wear. Now I didn't have to worry about people throwing jokes and put-downs on my clothes. I had a number of uniforms to wear for school.

My Uncle Gilly finished ironing and said, "Here, son. Get dressed so you can go to school. We have to go in a little while. You have to be school at seven-fifty. Anything after that is considered late." I grabbed my shirt and pants and went upstairs to get dressed in my new room. I put my uniform on, but I couldn't tie a necktie. I put my shoes on, went downstairs, and borrowed a tie

Ghetto Legend Graduate
Cornelius Kinchen

from my Uncle Gilly. I watched him tie a tie, and learned from him. This was extremely important to me at the time.

Pretty soon, it was time to leave. I grabbed my book bag and went to the car. It was cool outside, and my cousins were also getting in the car. I sat in the front with my Uncle, because my little cousins Bobby, Fanny, Pooka and Mick, were getting dropped off at School 21 first.

Uncle Gilly dropped us off at our respective locations. When I got out of the car, I read my schedule. I had to go to homeroom for attendance and my lunch card. Everywhere I looked, I saw uniforms.

There were a lot of girls with dresses on rolled up to look short. I kept a straight face. I went to my locker to get familiar with the locker system before I went to homeroom. The freshmen had their own hallway with lockers. Where I came from, this was unheard of. There were almost two hundred freshmen in our class, out of five hundred and fifty students in the entire school.

I did see some familiar faces from my old school, which made things seem to go a little more smoothly. However, I did have to get used to a new set of rules, including rules that were in regard to the wearing of the school uniform.

We had to have on the full uniform at all times. It was like being in the military. If anyone was caught out of uniform, they were sentenced to detention. I followed

Ghetto Legend Graduate
Cornelius Kinchen

the rules, because I realized that it was necessary. It felt like I was on "Saved by the Bell" but in a Catholic school environment. This was totally new to me.

I was use to the ghetto environment in school; playing in the playground, play fighting with other students, and full of chaos. This was the total opposite of School 6, and somewhat like Martin Luther King Jr. School; it was more organized.

I went to homeroom, and when my name was called, I raised my hand and was marked present. After morning prayer, the flag salute and announcements from Sister Gloria, my homeroom teacher turned on the TV for the morning news. We had minutes in homeroom before the bell ring for first period class. The bell rang and I was off to my first period class.

While walking in the hallway, a dude came up to me. He was about five-foot nine, one-ninety, and had dark skin. He looked like a linebacker.

"Is your last name Kinchen?"

"Yeah. Why?"

"I am your cousin, Reggie Brown," he said. Your uncle has known my father from years of church activities. You should come try out for the football team."

I said, "When and what time?"

"Today after school."

"All right, let me think about it. I have to ask my uncle. I have to maintain good grades first. I don't want to waste my Uncle's hard-earned tuition money."

Ghetto Legend Graduate
Cornelius Kinchen

He gave me dap and said, "I hear that. Just let me know by tomorrow." I embraced him along with the handshake and said, "Yeah-yeah no doubt." With that in mind, we went to our first period classes.

When I walked in, I went to the front of class to sit. I took my books and writing utensils out, and placed them on my desk. I sat with good posture and my hands folded. The bell rang and soon the room was filled with kids wearing uniforms. The teacher began her introduction and read the lesson's objective from her Microsoft Word document.

I learned and practice typing in this class. I met Shanequa and Kytia, who were from the projects. They were cool girls that loved to do their work and joke around from time to time. I told them that I was from the Fourth Ward. I loved working and joking with them. From that point, the three of us became close friends. Both girls were the same height and weight. The only difference was that Shanequa looked better than Kytia. Kytia's personality became more popular in our freshman class. Kytia was cool with everybody, especially Tisha from Martin Luther King Jr. School.

Tisha wore so much ice on her wrists, fingers, and her ears, I thought she was hood rich. Come to think of it; she *was* hood rich. Her hair was always done in a doobee or down. But she was to cool, and had mad jokes, too.

Forty-five minutes later the bell rang. It was time for my next class, which was religion taught by Sister

Ghetto Legend Graduate
Cornelius Kinchen

Virginia. When I got to class, I saw Neria from School 6. I smiled knowing the history we shared. We were in seven grades together.

Neria smiled back and said, "Hi, Cornelius. I didn't know you were coming here. Who else is here?"

Before I could say anything, the bell rang for class to start. I sat, and prepared to learn something new. Sister Virginia was tall and slender. She looked like she just stepped out of the book of Psalms. Ironically, she meant business. She taught religion with a passion. She was also a very organized person.

I met Harold, Marcus, and Kerwin in that very same class. We became friends quickly. Forty-five minutes later, Harold and I walked to gym class. I met my basketball partner after I got dressed for gym, and his name was Jason. He was burnt like toast, and about my height and weight. We were like Jordan and Pippen in gym class. We even challenged the upper classman to gain their respect. We drew even closer during our basketball relationship, playing one on one to make each other better. We always stayed on each other about our grades, basketball and scoping the girls out.

All too soon, it was time to get dressed. This was the only part of the day I hated. I had to run downstairs, remember my new combination to my gym locker, wash off real quick, dry off, then share space with my classmates getting dressed in a hotter uniform. I felt good from the adrenalin rushing through my body from getting

Ghetto Legend Graduate
Cornelius Kinchen

dressed and staying cool on my way to my next class, which was business. I actually had a business course. My interest was caught.

Across sat a girl name Ann Marie and her cousin Mandy. Ann Marie had a huge crush on me. During class, Mandy wrote and passed a note saying, "Dear, Cornelius, my cousin has a crush on you. Talk to you after class, ended with a circle smiling face.

The bell rang, every student was seated. I placed my books on my desk and paid attention throughout class. While I enjoyed my Business class by doing my work correctly and neat, I looked up at the clock it and there were only five minutes left. So I completed and handed my work in. I had time to prepare to go to lunch, and relax until the bell sounded.

A minute later, the bell rang. I went to my locker, put my books inside; and went to lunch. The line was long, and I was beginning to wonder if I would get a chance to sit down and eat my food.

My boy Harold was in the middle of the line. He let me cut in front of him when the line monitor wasn't looking. I laughed, gave him dap and said, "Good looking son."

He said, "Yeah, right, you're my son, son-son."

"Duck Tails got jokes." Everyone on that line laughed aloud.

Minutes passed, it was time to go in through the café to get our lunch. At the register, you have to have

Ghetto Legend Graduate
Cornelius Kinchen

your meal ticket for the month. The colors of the tickets changed every month. By the end of the month, my ticket looked like the end of notebook paper with the shredded parts at the wire. The following month it was laminated.

Harold and I got lunch and picked a table. Before we could pick a table, Jason yelled out waving his hand like the American Flag, "Yo, Neal and Harold, Over here!"

Harold and I walked over to the table, sat and ate lunch. The food was gone in five minutes. For the remaining of lunch, we drew a crowd of students. We were entertainment to the student-fans. When they were out of their seats, the lunch monitors would come over and seat them.

While Kerwin dropped lyrics, I continued mixing beats on the tables with my hands at our table. I felt like I was at an amusement park performing on stage with Bad Boy Entertainment. Then the lunch monitor came over and warned us to keep the volume down.

Toward the last five minutes of lunch, the student-fans came over to our stage and fish-bowled our concert, raw and uncensored, until the bell rang. We went back to our freshman hallway-lockers feeling like rock stars.

After a live lunch, and the good news of knowing I had science As I arrived to science class, Mr. Ed was in class making seat arrangements. He sent some football players to get more desks to seat thirty-nine freshmen. It took us at least ten minutes of the period to get settled.

Ghetto Legend Graduate
Cornelius Kinchen

  After class was settled, my friend Eddie farted so loud. It sounded like a Harley Davidson starting up. The entire class laughed so hard, we had tears in our eyes. Mr. Ed just smiled naively and said, "Keep natural gases controlled, class." The class laughed even harder. While the class laughed, my stomach and rear released the similar "Natural Gas" Mr. Ed said to control. My body couldn't help it. The class fell to the floor because my fart was so loud.

  Time went by and we weren't able to get into our lesson. This meant more homework for the whole class. I couldn't wait to go home and tell my family about my first day of high school, and do my homework at my Grandma's kitchen table.

  My Last period, a free period for study, or relax. There were students in the lounge that I didn't even know. Everyone was lounging on comfortable sofas, listening to the radio, and playing checkers. Brother Paul, a teacher, baked ziti for us. I ate my baked ziti, and then I played checkers with Matthew. He was also one of the students in my business class. We played with the checker kings until submission. Minutes later, we agreed to call the game a tie.

  After the game, I sat at a table. While I listened to the hip-hop radio station, I did all my homework. Forty minutes later, it was time to go to homeroom to be dismissed. The only thing I thought about was my boys

Ghetto Legend Graduate
Cornelius Kinchen

from Auburn having beef with East Nineteenth, was where I was headed after I left school.

I wanted to go to football practice, but I had to call home so my Grandma wouldn't worry. It was nice outside too, the sun was shining bright and it was warm. I walked to School 21 first to fight a kid name Keno

When I got to the school, Keno had just been dismissed, as their principal was outside monitoring the students' behavior. I approached Keno with my hands up, throwing punches in his direction. I landed at least three and ducked a left hook from him; however, the security and principal broke up the fight.

After the fight, I went to Aunt Beverly's house on the same block where Keno lived. He lived next door to my aunt. After the fight, Keno was nowhere to be found. While I waited, I double checked my home work until my uncle picked up my cousins and me.

Hours later, he showed up to get us. When I got home, I ate my dinner. Then I went to my room to get comfortable. As soon as I put my street clothes on, Grandma called me.

"Neal, your friend is here to see you." I walked downstairs, and saw that it was my boy Frank.

"Frank you could come up," I said.

When we got to my room, we dapped, and he said, "Yo, your room is cool."

I said, "Yeah, what's good? You're in Eastside?"

Ghetto Legend Graduate
Cornelius Kinchen

"Yeah. Some of our classmates from School 6 go there. It was a fight today."

I said, "Who was beefing?"

"The Fourth Ward vs. the Alabama Projects,"

"Who won?"

"The Fourth." I looked down at his boots and they weren't cool. I looked in the corner at my own boots.

"Frank, what are you doing out this late? Shouldn't you be home getting ready for school tomorrow?"

He took a deep breath, and then exhaled forcefully. "I'm thinking about hustling drugs on the block. My mother can't afford to pay bills and get me nice clothes, and everybody in Eastside is fresh except me. Not to mention, my father isn't around to help either."

I understood exactly what he was saying, because I had been there. I decided to do something nice for him. "Frank, you can have my brand new Tims. I only wore them three times. I don't need them; I wear black uniform shoes to school every day.

"Word up!" Frank said with a big smile on his face. He gave me dap and said, "Thanks Cornelius." His tone changed to a low humble tone saying, "Are you sure?"

I smiled. "Yeah, I am sure Frank." He put the Tims on with a smile: and said, "Good looking out for me. That's real."

Ghetto Legend Graduate
Cornelius Kinchen

"No doubt. But yo, I have to get ready for school tomorrow. Come holla at me sometimes." We dapped and I walked him outside.

After he left, I felt a peace within my spirit for giving from the heart. I hoped Frank would reconsider what he said about selling drugs, after getting the boots. That was my boy and I didn't want to see him locked up. Afterwards, I got ready for bed.

As the school days continued, I loved my school. I was happy to be at PC. My stunted growth was at full speed in school, and I had pride about my academic career.

After a week, I decided to try out for the football team. There were so many freshmen on the football team. We even helped the Varsity Team. The coaches thought we were something special, and we were. I made the team; however, I had to earn my equipment by being on time and working out with the team each practice.

They worked harder than little league, to win. I wasn't use to the intense workout drills for defensive-corner backs. I definitely knew I wasn't playing offense, because there were so many players in each position competing to shine for playing time in five games.

A month passed, I was still on the team surviving the intense play and workouts. One day after practice, Freshmen "Big Devon" was recruited to play offensive and defensive line for varsity. He was like a giant. He was from another hood called Brook Slope projects. I had no clue where that was, and I didn't care.

Somehow, he thought I was a pretty boy punk. I proved him differently. We were in the football freshmen locker room getting dressed. Somehow, my boys from class, Marcus, J.P., Flea, and my cousin Reggie instigated us to play fight.

Big Devon and I squared off to slap box and wrestle. I was too fast for him with the hands. He tried to grab, I slapped him up and slammed him to the locker room floor. The entire locker room heard it. All the boys laughed at Big Devon. After I helped him up, we dapped afterwards and became cool dudes. My rep was up in PC.

By time I left practice, it was completely dark and cold outside. I couldn't wait to get warmed in the car. I walked to my uncle's car and slammed the door. He said, "How was practice?"

I sighed wearily. "My body is tired from all that running and those football drills."

He understood. "As long as your grades ain't tired."

"Oh, yeah… I know that; I'm working hard in class. I got a B+ on my business and English tests that we took. I can't wait until the first marking period report card comes out so you can witness the greatness."

He laughed "Yeah, right. We will see."

Ghetto Legend Graduate
Cornelius Kinchen

I was serious. I didn't play when it came to my schoolwork. "It would be a good surprise for you." We arrived home. I ate and got ready for school the next day.

In the beginning of November, I quit the football team to try out for the basketball team. I thought football practice was hard, but it was nothing compared to this. We worked and ran harder in basketball practice. There were a lot of freshmen boys trying out for the team. Todd from the South and Schoharie from the Underground Funk, were recruited.

I didn't make the team. My self-esteem was low. Then later in the week, my Uncle Randy suggested I read Michael Jordan's autobiography. After I read it, I found out he was cut from freshmen tryouts, too.

Now, after leading his Chicago Bulls to winning six NBA championships, Michael Jordan is considered the best player in history. I felt hope, and believed that the same thing could happen to me.

Every day after school for two weeks, I hung out with Schoharie playing one-on-one in order to make each other better. He wanted to beat Todd in one-on-one. He continued practicing with me to benefit the basketball team.

Back to school night was here, and I had done what I had to do academically throughout the first marking period. I worked hard and consistently. I didn't want to make my uncle and aunt feel like they were wasting money on me.

Ghetto Legend Graduate
Cornelius Kinchen

During the first marking period and beyond, I valued my education and privilege to be at Paterson Catholic. Uncle Gilly and I arrived at the Paterson Catholic to pick up my report card. We immediately went to my homeroom. My uncle talked with my teacher for several minutes about my potential; but I couldn't wait to see the first and second honor roll list.

After my Uncle finished talking, he and I walked toward the honor roll list. I searched for my name carefully. As I went through the first honors list, I noticed my name. We both were smiling. I was so happy. This meant, I was academically prepared on a high school level, thanks to the public school education I received, and especially thanks to the Almighty God for giving me the strength and the will to keep pressing on. It felt like I received an acceptance letter from a division one college. I wanted to jump for joy.

My Uncle was so proud that he couldn't wait to tell my Aunt Branda, Grandma and my father the great news. When we got home, Grandma said, "Your mother called to check on you."

I said, "Grandma, I made the honor roll." She smiled and gave me a hug. She said, "I am proud of you. You have to keep up the good work."

"I will, Grandma," I promised her. I went upstairs to get the phone to call Tiana. I took the phone into my room and called her. I told her the great news about my

Ghetto Legend Graduate
Cornelius Kinchen

academic achievement, and then I told her I would talk to her later.

After I hung up, I took my shower and waited for my mother to call back. I waited for two hours, and she didn't call. I figured she would call me tomorrow. I read the book of Proverbs, prayed then I fell asleep.

Ghetto Legend Graduate
Cornelius Kinchen

Thanksgiving

Pretty soon, the week of Thanksgiving had come. I woke up ready for school two days in a row, forgetting that there was no school. Then I thought about Tiana, I couldn't wait to have fun with her. She was going to stay over in Paterson to be with me, until Monday. A whole week, we were planning to spend quality (puppy love) time together. I had already asked her to have a son with me, and she agreed.

Thanksgiving Day----Tiana came over from Hackensack, Red and I was up the street until Thanksgiving dinner was ready. Deanna's mother was out of town, and we had so much privacy that nothing stopped us from making our baby. I don't know what I was thinking, because neither of us had a pot to pee in, nor a window to throw it out of. If I could do it all over again, I probably would have waited until I got married, then had a child. Being a teenage parent is not easy, because the child's needs have to be taken care of. This is a life-altering event.

After our lovemaking, I got dressed and invited Tiana to dinner. She declined.

"I am going to eat with Netta. But I will walk with you."

"Come on."

We walked down the street together. When I got to the house, everyone was in the dining room, my little

Ghetto Legend Graduate
Cornelius Kinchen

cousins were in the kitchen and Grandma said, "Everyone join hands," she began praying and thanking God for our Thanksgiving dinner.

Minutes later, prayer ended in an 'Amen', and dinner was served. We ate soul food and there were plenty of desserts

    I asked Aunt Kate, "Can you fix Tiana a plate and wrap it up for?" She looked at Tiana, and hugged her with a smile.

    "Sure, she is family."

    Tiana said, "Thank you, Aunt Kate."

    "Any time," Kate said, and fixed her plate. I continued eating my turkey, fried chicken, macaroni and cheese, corn bread, yams, collard greens and rice. Tiana tasted my food. She couldn't wait until she got her food. She wanted to change her mind after tasting my grandma's food. I smiled.

    Aunt Kate passed me Tiana's plate, wrapped in aluminum foil.. After I gave her the plate, she stayed for ten more minutes until I finish eating. When I was done, I walked Tiana up the street to Netta's' house.

    I then walked back down the street to be with my family until Tiana had finished spending time with Netta and her brother. When I got back to Grandma's house, everyone was there still grubbing on the best soul food in Paterson.

    After all the boys ate, we went upstairs to play video games. Everyone got a turn to play in the

Ghetto Legend Graduate
Cornelius Kinchen

competition. We had fun until about midnight. Then everyone was packing up food, sweet potato pies and cake, and preparing to go home.

When everyone had left, I called Tiana to see what she was doing. She was helping Netta clean up the kitchen and said that she would come get me in the morning to lay with her. I told her I had to stay to clean up my room, and I would see her the next day.

I cleaned up, took a shower, and relaxed thinking about my love. I felt good about myself. At the same time, I thought of my mother. I wondered if she enjoyed her dinner. I wished I could have seen her, to thank God for her, during the grace at dinnertime.

"Neal, telephone," Grandma called out, interrupting my thoughts. I grabbed the phone from near the steps, brought it to my room, and said, "Hello."

"Hey, boy." It was my mother. My heart swelled with all the love I had for her.

I was so happy to hear her voice, that my words came out in a rush. "Hi Ma. I thought you up. I thought of a prayer for you Ma. How was your Thanksgiving Ma?"

"It was fine, son. How is everything including school, son?"

"I made the honor roll at Paterson Catholic."

She began to cry on the phone. She said, "I am so proud of you." I cried openly and without shame. I cried for the time lost between us. I cried for the love I wanted for so long, and was just now receiving. I cried for the

Ghetto Legend Graduate
Cornelius Kinchen

anguish we were both feeling, because of the gulf that separated us. But the main reason I cried was because God revealed just how good, kind, and merciful He was because he answered my heartfelt prayer, and at that moment God gave me the one thing I longed for, and that was to hear my mother's voice on a day of Thanksgiving.

I cried so much, I needed tissue for both my eyes and my nose. We talked for a while longer, with me pouring my heart out, and both of us crying. We ended the conversation, telling each other, "I love you," then we hung up.

I brought the phone back downstairs to Grandma's room. I knocked on the bathroom door. Grandma said, "Come in." The shower had steamed up the bathroom mirror. I wiped my face, and went back up to my room, and fell asleep in peace.

The upcoming holidays were not events I was looking forward to. Money was tight, so I wasn't expecting anything for Christmas. Mom was not around when the New Year came in, and I definitely did not expect anything for my birthday, because too many had gone by that were filled with disappointments. Nevertheless, what I will say is that I did not let anything keep me from striving towards excellence. The rest of my life was headed in the direction *I* wanted it to go.

Ghetto Legend Graduate
Cornelius Kinchen

Final words from the author...

Stay positive and express positively"...

Author Cornelius Kinchen

www.ingramcontent.com/pod-product-compliance
Lightning Source LLC
Chambersburg PA
CBHW060107170426
43198CB00010B/796